Demystifying the Out-of-Body Experience

About the Author

Born in 1972, Luis Minero graduated with honors in chemistry from Florida International University. He has been studying and developing paranormal phenomena since his adolescence. He became a volunteer in conscientiology in 1995 in Miami, Florida. He has been giving classes on OBEs, paranormal phenomena, and spiritual growth since 1996, including at the college level (Miami-Dade College) from 1997 to 2002.

Since he speaks English, Spanish, Portuguese, and German, Minero has lectured on various topics related to the out-of-body experience in Europe, North America, and South America, and has helped thousands of individuals to develop their own skills.

Because of his experience, Minero has been invited to speak at several international conferences in the United States, Portugal, and Brazil. He has also been featured on a number of television and radio programs around the world, as well as being the subject of interviews by magazines, newspapers, and periodicals of global distribution.

As a researcher, Minero has published several papers and has developed research lines in the sciences of projectiology and conscientiology. Several of his works have been published in the scientific *Journal of Conscientiology*. Also, he is responsible for the translation and revision of over half a dozen conscientiological books from Portuguese into English and Spanish.

Minero has developed courses on assistance, universalism, experience, intuition, and evolutionary intelligence. He was the director of the Florida International Academy of Consciousness (IAC) from 1999 to 2001, and has been the executive director of the IAC California center since 2003. From 2006 to 2012, he was the administrative director of the IAC globally, and since 2012 has been the education director of IAC global. Visit him at LearnOBEs.com.

LUIS MINERO

Foreword by Wagner Alegretti

Demystifying the Out-of-Body Experience

A Practical Manual for Exploration and Personal Evolution

Llewellyn Publications
Woodbury, Minnesota

FIRST EDITION
Third Printing, 2015

Cover art: Earth and sun: iStockphoto.com/Paul Paladin
Abstract circle background: iStockphoto.com/Roman Okopny
Cover design by Ellen Lawson
Edited by Andrea Neff
Interior illustrations by Mary Ann Zapalac (pp. 5, 7, 32, 69, 70, 77, 97, 124, 127, 129, 152, 189, 190, 195, 221) and the Llewellyn Art Department

The author has graciously transferred the author's rights to this edition to the International Academy of Consciousness (IAC).
Revisions by Martin Azambuya, Rodrigo Medeiros, Tatyana Ovcharova, Veronica Serrano, Patricia Sousa, Analaura Trivellato, and Eduardo Vicenzi.

Llewellyn Publications is a registered trademark of Llewellyn Worldwide Ltd.

Library of Congress Cataloging-in-Publication Data
Minero, Luis, 1972–
  Demystifying the out-of-body experience : a practical manual for exploration and personal evolution / by Luis Minero. — 1st ed.
       p.   cm.
Includes bibliographical references and index.
  ISBN 978-0-7387-3079-0
1. Bioenergy — Out and about — How-to — Extraphysical consciousnesses — Consciential maturity — Planning a life. 2. Astral projection. I. Title.
  BF1389.A7 M54 2012
  133.9/5'1210—dc23
                              2012016054

Llewellyn Worldwide Ltd. does not participate in, endorse, or have any authority or responsibility concerning private business transactions between our authors and the public.
  All mail addressed to the author is forwarded but the publisher cannot, unless specifically instructed by the author, give out an address or phone number.
  Any Internet references contained in this work are current at publication time, but the publisher cannot guarantee that a specific location will continue to be maintained. Please refer to the publisher's website for links to authors' websites and other sources.

Llewellyn Publications
A Division of Llewellyn Worldwide Ltd.
2143 Wooddale Drive
Woodbury, MN 55125-2989
www.llewellyn.com

Printed in the United States of America

Other Works by Luis Minero

"Universalism and Health," *Journal of Conscientiology*, October 2010

"Originality in Conscientiology," *Journal of Conscientiology*, October 2008

"Evolutionary Intelligence," Intensive Course,
International Academy of Consciousness (IAC), 2006

"Globalization and Conscientiological Expansion through Languages,"
Revista Conscientia, 2006

"Qualitative Experience and Quantitative Experience,"
Journal of Conscientiology, October 2003

"Intuition: The Basic Sense of Perception," Intensive Course, IAC, 2002

"Correspondence," *Journal of Conscientiology*, July 2002

"Lucidocracy," *Journal of Conscientiology*, May 2002

"Universalism: Evolution without Limits," Intensive Course, IAC, 1999

"You and Your Level of Assistantiality," Intensive Course, IAC, 1997

*To all well-intentioned individuals
who are seriously considering
the evolution of their consciousness.*

Contents

Figures

Foreword: A Multidimensional World
by Wagner Alegretti

It is indeed an honor and a pleasure to write the foreword for Luis Minero's first book, and I think that contextualizing this meritorious contribution to conscientiology and consciousness studies in general can help readers to grasp the depth and possible benefits of this work.

Conscientiology was formally proposed with the publication of the book *700 Conscientiology Experiments* in 1994 in Brazil by the medical doctor Waldo Vieira. This work followed the publication a few years earlier of the treatise *Projectiology: A Panorama of Experiences of the Consciousness Outside the Human Body*, wherein Vieira disseminated his structuring of studies on out-of-body experiences.

Due to his personal experiences with psychic and paranormal phenomena starting at the age of nine, Vieira strived to include non-ordinary human manifestations within the scope of science under a new paradigm: the consciential paradigm. By the time *Projectiology* was published, he and many other collaborators, myself included, founded the International Institute of Projectiology and Conscientiology (IIPC) to promote research and education of these new sciences.

In 1994, when conditions were mature for a more international exposure of conscientiology, a new phase started during which some of the researchers-instructors left Brazil to establish the conscientiological and projectiological work abroad. This led to individuals going to Lisbon, Portugal, and to New York and Miami in the United States.

Motivated by the certainty my wife and I have about the reality of all these phenomena, since we'd had our own out-of-body experiences since childhood, we moved to Miami, where we worked as hard as the human body can bear in order to continue in our goal: educating anyone interested on the multidimensional nature of life and the universe.

Operating internationally under the name of the International Academy of Consciousness (IAC), our first challenge was to adapt the Brazilian curriculum and the dynamics of the courses to an American audience, focusing more on practical, direct experiences. This allowed for a wider and more pragmatic use with great benefits including studies and techniques. Based on our experience and the help of other colleagues, we devised the Consciousness Development Program (CDP), aiming to deliver it in the right proportion of theory and practice, for consciousness evolution and personal growth, with philosophical content and practical tools for everyday life.

It was during this initial phase of our work that Luis Minero showed up in our classes in 1995, still a university student, interested in gaining a better understanding of his out-of-body experiences and enthusiastic about producing them at will. A few weeks later he became our first seriously dedicated volunteer, a commitment he highly honors to this day. In no time he showed interest in becoming an instructor.

After only four months (a standing record to this date) he was ready to offer conscientiology classes, having learned enough Portuguese to read the entire 1,517-page book *Projectiology* and other required literature. During the process of coaching and preparing Luis to become an instructor, we understood why he was an honor student at the university. We recognized that we had an invaluable colleague, manifesting a rare combination of strong traits such as neophilia, a very good memory, multimodal intelligence, polyglotism, quick learning, a high level of adaptability, and charisma. But the rarest of all of Luis's strong traits was (and still is) his willingness to adjust his life to be able to maximize his availability to teach something that he and we believe is essential to one's life: the tools that may allow others to reach their own confirmation that we are more than a physical body. Our dedication to disseminating the knowledge associated with self-awareness of the nonphysical world lies in the conviction, which is confirmed regularly in our classes, that awareness and understanding of the mysteries of life and death can alleviate one's insecurities or fears and encourage maturity. In this broader context, our studies, as you will find in this book, consider the ethical and practical consequences of such knowledge.

Indeed, the openness to clarify the nonphysical reality and the wish to empower readers to have their own firsthand experiences are the motivations of this work. Through all these years, regardless of his life's circumstances, Luis has always put the endeavors of assisting people and accomplishing this task ahead of his personal interests.

This book fills a very important niche. Since the beginning of our work in Miami, students have been asking for a more accessible book, one that could complement the Consciousness Development Program as a textbook. Dr. Vieira's books can be daunting to some people, in part because of their sheer size and in part because of their particular style and terminology. Luis decided to embrace this project and wrote this book based on Dr. Vieira's material, his training with us, and his experience as a long-time conscientiology instructor.

This book achieves what is the most difficult challenge of all in any area of science: it makes the material digestible without losing its essence and depth. This can be done only by those who really understand the issue being discussed. As Einstein once stated, you do not really understand something unless you can explain it to your grandmother.

Whether you browse this book by jumping pages to follow a particular sequence of ideas or read it from cover to cover, you will find enough material to get an introduction to the consciential paradigm; the study of consciousness as a principle independent from the physical body; the multidimensional nature of consciousness; the techniques and practical applications of out-of-body experiences (OBEs); as well as the ethical consequences of this knowledge. Even if you don't want to leave your body, you will learn about bioenergy (chi, prana, orgone, vital energy) in a way that will empower you to transcend the normal capabilities of the physical body. In addition, the discussions about consciential maturity and consciousness evolution are a breath of fresh air in a time when a considerable number of existing studies tend to be more superficial and repetitive.

You will also see that we have not—so far—found a way to prove the objective reality of OBEs beyond any reasonable doubt; i.e., in a way that can be replicated by independent researchers. But while we work on that, people can be taught to produce their own experiences and repeat them to the point of having their own personal certainty of this reality. If a significant percentage of human beings were able to leave their bodies with enough lucidity and recollection, the need for a formal proof would be transcended; just as nobody, so far, has seen the need to prove the existence of dreams. But how much would a significant percentage of humankind be? Perhaps 10 percent would be enough to warm up the arena. Luis Minero is contributing to the achievement of this goal.

Knowledge is the best vaccine against fear, which is still the most common and important factor working against the direct experience of multidimensionality. More than folkloric fears of being attacked or getting lost outside of the body, the real fear most people have without realizing it is the fear of change. People want to grow and evolve without changing, which is impossible.

We are responsible for the cosmoethical use of the knowledge we have, or for not using it. I hope you dare to evolve.

I personally look forward to Luis Minero's next book.

Wagner Alegretti
Electrical engineer
Author of the book Retrocognitions: An Investigation into Memories of Past Lives and the Periods between Lives
President of the International Academy of Consciousness (IAC)

Preface

As the world keeps developing and information continues to accumulate, fields of knowledge start to uncover areas that previously were obscure. Leaving the body, paranormal phenomena, vital energies, evolution, and reincarnation, among others, are ideas that most people have heard of at some point in their lives. Many people do not pay too much attention to this information and discard it as irrelevant or as fantasy. Others find the information interesting but, like many other intriguing ideas, simply do not give it the necessary attention. Still others not only find this information interesting but are also willing to give it the necessary attention because they understand that many benefits can come from it. Some individuals might be scared or concerned to read the information on these pages, others might be indifferent, and yet others might be delighted. However, as evolution continues, this information—and the number of reports, cases, and accounts of phenomena and experiences that expand one's consciousness—can no longer be cast aside.

The topics discussed in this book have historically caused much confusion and have generally been rejected by the masses, much like science was rejected during the Middle Ages. Back then, people were burned, stoned, and killed because they were "different" or had paranormal abilities. They could not hide, deny, or ignore these capacities, even though not even they knew how or why they had them. My main intention with this book is to bring all of this information to the forefront and to share it in a clear, logical, and systematic manner. I also seek to help interested individuals to develop their capacity to leave the body and to extract all the possible benefits from these experiences.

This book covers a vast amount of material ranging from the fundamentals of out-of-body experiences to advanced conclusions based on extraphysical (beyond the physical, or out-of-body) observations. My highest aspiration is for it to be an introductory textbook. It is based on the sciences of projectiology and conscientiology, which were first proposed by Dr. Waldo Vieira in his books *Projectiology* (2002) and *700 Conscientiology Experiments* (1994). Thus, this volume seeks to introduce and present the main ideas of these two new scientific fields. Another reason I wrote this book was to create a work that would allow individuals living in cities far away from centers where conscientiology and projectiology classes are given (see the "IAC" section at the end of this book) to access this information. Students who have already taken these classes also have asked throughout the years for a book that presents the ideas in a more direct way.

An important source of information for this work is the experience I have shared with many researchers and instructors of conscientiology. Certainly it must be noted that I'm standing on the shoulders of giants. This book is permeated with influences from colleagues' lectures, examples, and heuristic devices; informal and formal discussions with colleagues; other books on the subject; and, naturally, my own experience, both inside the body (years of giving classes on OBEs) and outside the body (lucid projections). Thus, many examples used to clarify certain aspects in the book were originally used by some of my colleagues. Therefore, much is owed to the conscientiological research community in this regard.

In a 1994 speech, Caltech professor David Goodstein noted that estimates indicate that 90 percent of all scientists who have ever lived are alive today. This percentage is even higher with regard to projectiology and conscientiology, which are relatively new sciences. Direct experiences (OBEs) should be the first step toward the understanding and study of OBEs. While a picture is worth a thousand words, an experience is made up of and is worth a thousand pictures. Consensus among researchers should be the second step in the development of the study of OBEs. Thus, this volume presents much of the consensus that has been reached thus far by these academics.

This book is not only a very instructive volume but is also a how-to manual. It provides many exercises and techniques for leaving the body. The techniques in chapter 4, many of them new, will enable you to progressively develop your capacities. For the best results, *the reader should refer to the entire book and not only to the practical exercises.* It is the understanding of where ideas come from, and where they will lead us, that allows us to extract more benefit from the practical techniques.

Readers who consider themselves to already have a fair amount of knowledge in this area would also do well to read the entire book. All chapters have new and relevant information as well as new concepts that help explain many old phenomena in the best and clearest possible fashion. Readers have likely never read some of this information anywhere else, and it will help to organize the sea of material in this area.

Throughout the chapters you will find answers and explanations for many aspects of experiences that you probably have already encountered. After reading the book methodically, you will be able to clearly understand how certain conclusions were reached once you get to the practical exercises and later discussions. Otherwise, it could be relatively easy to get lost within the wealth of information and areas that the volume draws from. It is of the utmost importance for you to practice the exercises with energy in order to get good results. In this current world of fast, easy solutions and short-term fixes, there are still no long-term substitutes for personal effort, will, perseverance, and patience.

Likewise, the book has the intention of demystifying the out-of-body experience. Throughout time and in countless cultures, many folkloric aspects have been associated with the OBE. Several of them have very little bearing on the actual development and/or understanding of this natural capacity. Thus, at various moments in the book, these aspects will be clarified.

Great effort has gone into trying to make this book accessible for everybody. As a result, the book is not philosophical in tone but rather is written in common, everyday language. In the later chapters and in discussions that are totally new to readers, the simple explanations will be much appreciated. Most individuals have never experienced a big part of what is written, especially in those pages, and therefore a more straightforward approach will help readers more easily understand the information.

The Plan of the Book

The layout of the book is as follows.

The "Introduction" presents the approach to this entire study on OBEs and their effects.

"Chapter 1: Fundamental Concepts" introduces out-of-body experiences and various other basic concepts. It also presents the sciences of projectiology and conscientiology. This chapter sets the tone for the entire book by explaining the consciential model and introducing the bodies we use for manifesting ourselves both inside and outside the body.

"Chapter 2: Bioenergy" explains the concept of bioenergy as a central factor for developing control. Discussions are presented on the types of energy, the concept of energetic information, and the characteristics of the energetic body. The basic exercises with energy are likewise examined.

"Chapter 3: Out and About" addresses how the extraphysical (beyond the physical) reality works. This chapter focuses on dimensions, characteristics of the nonphysical body, types of projections, the scale of extraphysical lucidity, what forms these dimensions, projections with other bodies, and other topics.

"Chapter 4: How-To" explores the stages a projector goes through while having an OBE. Optimization tips, sensations, OBE techniques, and strategies for a better recall are included.

"Chapter 5: Extraphysical Consciousnesses" analyzes the interactions that projectors have with other individuals outside the body. This chapter covers the range of personalities that may be possibly encountered, what affects the interactions with them, and the means of communication employed extraphysically.

"Chapter 6: Consciential Maturity" explores the many attributes of the consciousness (soul, spirit, essence) and how to reach a more mature, evolved condition. Several key concepts of evolution are expanded on here, such as assistance to others, a higher level of ethics, and universalism.

"Chapter 7: Planning a Life" explains, using the OBE perspective, the death-rebirth cycle of the consciousness and its many tasks throughout, as well as those concepts associated with this condition: karma, where we go when we die, what we do, how we prepare for the upcoming life, who helps us in this, and how we plan our next life task.

Boxes with accounts of out-of-body experiences will be found at key moments of the discussions to illustrate certain conditions of the extraphysical reality. Priority has been given to the ideas about OBEs and their effects rather than to OBE accounts themselves. Even though this is not a book solely with OBE experiences, every chapter has at least one OBE account; furthermore, I have included some of my own personal experiences as well, especially in the later chapters. With the intention of being as instructive as possible, I selected OBE accounts that would better fit the information being explained. Thus, I also drew on accounts from several other colleagues to reach this end.

At the end of each chapter you will find a summary of key points to help you focus on the main concepts. Likewise, the book is sprinkled with text boxes with icons that include definitions of terms, examples, and further clarifications, some of which will help you to reflect more deeply on certain points. For an understanding of these icons, refer to page xxvii.

Throughout the text you will see endnotes for bibliographical references and additional explanations that can help you find more information on any of the topics presented. At the end of each chapter you will find the notes for that particular chapter. So as not to repeat long bibliographical references many times over in different chapters, the notes at the end of the chapter make reference to the main sources listed at the end of the book in the standard abbreviated fashion: author, year published, page number. For example:

[22]Arakaki, 2005, 169–70.

In certain instances, there are authors who published two works in the same year. In such cases, the format of the notes is: author, abbreviation of work-title (in italics), year published, page number. Here is an example:

[22]Vieira, *700*, 1994, 609.

With this information you can look up the exact source in the bibliography at the end of the book. Great care has been placed on the bibliographical notes and references, mainly to demonstrate consensus; to present the broad amount of information available about the topic, for obvious ethical reasons; and to enable interested readers to find further information.

In this book you will find clear and concise information that will lead you to greater understanding; however, this is only the beginning. For further documentation the reader is encouraged to refer specifically to the two books from Dr. Waldo Vieira already mentioned, *Projectiology* and *700 Conscientiology Experiments*.

Other invaluable sources of knowledge are conscientiology courses, such as those offered through the Consciousness Development Program (CDP) at the International Academy of Consciousness (IAC). This book does not in any way replace the value of these courses, mainly because of the richness of direct experience itself that can be gained through the energetic exercises and practices of even more techniques for producing OBEs than are contained in this volume. This book does not cover all the material presented in the CDP.

Likewise, though you will find much information in this book, there is no way to duplicate the energetic environment of the classes and their very real effect on the development of the participants. Furthermore, during the classes you enjoy the benefit of discussing issues directly with instructors, not only about the mechanics of some phenomena but about your own personal energetic development as well.

I invite you to go to LearnOBEs.com to download the full glossary of conscientiological terms, as well as to receive a free bulletin with information about the next CDP classes in the city closest to you. On this site you can even download a coupon to receive a discount on the CDP courses.

Introduction

**Don't believe in anything.
Not even in what is written in this book.
Experiment!
Have your own experiences.**

More than just a few phrases, this is a philosophy, a style of approaching all the endeavors contained in this volume. It is interesting and important to discuss the ideas contained and implied in the above sentences. First of all, "Don't believe in anything." The intention is not to appear as knowing the absolute truth about these or any other matters. As is well known, there are certain groups, cultures, religions, philosophies, and organizations that deal with what are called *absolute truths*, meaning they already have a certain body of ideas that are untouchable or not up for discussion. Individuals either accept these ideas (believe) or not, but there is no debating them. For them, these ideas are already absolute realities. However, this is not seen as the best method for acquiring knowledge.

It is best to work with *leading-edge relative truths*—the best information we can gather right now, at this moment in time. It is more effective if there are discussions of ideas, research, experimentation, consensus, and especially *renewal* of information. Therefore, if new experiments are developed, and they start taking the current information in a different direction, then by all means there has to be a renewal of ideas. Keeping this concept in mind, it is implied that the information contained in this book is a collection of leading-edge relative truths.

Consider a simple example of the relevance of information renewal. If we needed to undergo surgery, for any reason, how confident would we be if it were to be performed by doctors from the Middle Ages, using only the equipment and level of knowledge of that period? More than likely we would not feel too confident. Obviously the renewal of ideas in medicine is very positive and has brought many benefits. Life expectancy today is over eighty years of age in developed countries, while during the Middle Ages it was around thirty-five. This is direct, positive evidence of the constant mechanism of renewal of ideas. The same can be said about all sciences that have developed throughout the centuries, and this is why the renewal of ideas is so valuable.

It is especially relevant to consider this point with regard to out-of-body experiences (OBE), paranormal phenomena, nonphysical dimensions, and so forth, since many of the ideas related to these subjects are in need of renewal because they are quite old. Since humanity began having a written history, there have been accounts of people leaving the body in virtually all cultures throughout the centuries. However, this information, especially in the Western Hemisphere, belonged historically to closed (hermetic, esoteric, occult, secret) groups, and most of them were (and still are) *absolutistic* groups—as religions are. So in most of these groups the ideas that form the basis of the groups are held as absolute truths and are non-negotiable. Granted, that may have been the best information that existed at the time, and was perhaps even the leading-edge information of the time. But now, through the gathering and accumulation of data, and the very relevant association of ideas with other sciences that did not exist earlier, there is much more information to draw from and thus the ideas are much improved.

As noted at the beginning of this introduction, it is important to emphasize the idea of experience. It is one thing to *theoretically* know or understand a particular concept or technique, and quite another to have experienced it. One good example of this comes from studying people's reactions toward death. The vast majority of people understand or at least accept that they (their essence) will not die with physical death, yet they still behave as if they do not know this, as if this will be their only life. At the most basic level, this means that individuals continue to behave differently from what they *theoretically* understand.

Another of the main goals of this book is to offer as much information as possible so individuals develop their own capacities, or learn to have their own experiences, independent of any type of dogma, indoctrination, attachment, or dependency (such as requiring them to come back periodically for a specific session or treatment). It is important to point out that this book, the sciences of projectiology and conscientiology, and even the many institutions that study conscientiology have no connections to any form of politics, mystical ideas, religions, or traditions or to any other organizations or countries. The intention has always been to study the information in an open-minded, direct, realistic fashion, without any preconceived or biased ideas or any type of dogmatic, commercial, secretive, or manipulative agenda.

The ability to leave the body and master the bioenergies, when developed, becomes an inherent capacity of the individual, similar to the capacity to read, ride a bicycle, swim, and so forth. When you know how to read, you can go to any bookstore or library and simply choose from all the books available the one you want to read. This selection is done with complete freedom, since you can access any of them.

It is known that conventional science asks for objective, physical proof of phenomena, something that can be measured by the physical instruments of the researcher. Even though certain OBEs can be objective phenomena—in the sense that they can be verified—the best way to confirm this reality is to leave the body and experience it directly. Certain OBEs can be physically verified, yet certain realities go well beyond the physical dimension and are not provable in the restrictive, physical sense or with current technology. Thus, taking a truly scientific approach means that it is best to keep an open and discerning mind when dealing with these realities.

One of the key elements of this book that is implied, but is very important to mention explicitly, is that it is a *descriptive* work as opposed to it being a *prescriptive* work. Descriptive works describe the phenomena, while prescriptive works discuss what individuals "ought" to do. A prescriptive approach could be considered "preaching" in many instances. This book has dozens of instructions on several different topics, especially when discussing practical techniques. These instructions are based on hundreds if not thousands of experiences, and the intention is to help and inform the reader. The efficiency of all the techniques has been observed time and time again, and that is why they are described in this book, as a guide.

Nonetheless, when analyzing the information that is perceived outside the body, the discussion may seem to turn more subjective and appear more prescriptive. Some of the findings outside the body could be considered by many individuals as having moral implications. Far from shying away from these discussions (which would be easier, safer, more comfortable and more politically correct), effort is made to dive into them and clarify them (which is more challenging and controversial). In these instances, instructions are given regarding the best information available to achieve specific results. Especially in the second half of the book, many such *moral* topics naturally arise, simply because they do form a part of reality, including here the extra-physical, or beyond-the-physical, reality.

One cannot strive to integrally study the nonphysical realities by limiting the research. Therefore, such moral discussions are contained herein. Far from being inculcations, however, the indications given are a description of the attitude, technique, posture, and/or perspective that have been observed to be the most efficient, especially with relation to consciential evolution. The main objective of this work is to inform, not to convince anybody of anything. The aware and scrutinizing reader should put everything to the test and then use all the information that is considered valuable.

Notice as well that having lucid projections (OBEs) implies having the opportunity to experience different realities. Upon observing different patterns, individuals will naturally tend to interpret them. These interpretations will become part of the life experience and part of the reference system against which all subsequent life experiences will be analyzed (whether inside or outside the body). Thus, these observations will challenge our values in the same fashion that learning about a very different culture would. Therefore, be ready to be challenged and to grow.

Emphasis is again placed on the importance of the renewal of information—in this case, at an individual level. Not everything that you will find outside the body will match the ideas we already have about the universe. Far from it—in many instances, very little will be in agreement. Naturally, as we are able to have different perspectives and in many instances observe more of reality (both physical and nonphysical), and as we incorporate these observations, there is a need to refine our concepts (in essence, this is evolution). Therefore, an initial recommendation becomes pertinent here: If you are more conservative and traditional in your values and do not wish for them to be challenged, this book or, more importantly, the practice of this phenomenon will probably not be your cup of tea. Challenges arise due to the need to make sense of the reality encountered while outside the body, and in many instances they will most definitely go against traditional values, and even against newer liberal, semi-established values.

It is therefore important to keep all of this in mind. The questioning, analyzing, and critiquing of everything is encouraged. In this sense, it would be greatly appreciated if any information or reference that is incorrect is brought to my attention. The words at the beginning of this introduction are the *anti-brainwashing* phrases used in all conscientiology courses everywhere in the world. It is important to mention that all the information contained herein is based on the sound experiences of thousands of people and on consensus, debate, and much research. Yet, do not believe it. By all means, please go ahead and experiment! Have your own experiences.

Icons

Throughout this book, you will find text boxes with icons. They will give you additional information about the material at hand.

 More information. These boxes will show you where to get more information about the topic being discussed.

 Definition. These boxes contain definitions of new concepts and words as they are introduced.

 Indications. In these boxes you will find recommendations and key points to pay attention to when doing the exercises and putting the ideas in this book into practice.

 Example. In these boxes you will find examples illustrating the concepts under discussion.

Renewal of information. In these boxes you will find further clarifications and ideas, as well as information that will help you become aware of old information and how it has been renewed by new data.

 OBE experience. These boxes contain firsthand OBE experiences demonstrating the practical application of the ideas being presented.

 Self-research. Challenging questions and information are found in these boxes to help us understand where we stand with regard to a specific topic, and to show us the consequences and implications of these concepts.

Acknowledgments

To my *family*, or groupkarma, for their support, especially during my formative years. Through our good humor and healthy coexistence, we were able to keep ourselves sane during the rough times. I would not mind having you all again in the next life.

To all my *evolutionary friends, colleagues, and volunteers* at IAC and all conscientiological institutions, for all of the lessons we have helped each other to learn, and for all past and upcoming struggles that keep catalyzing our evolution.

To *Waldo Vieira* for formalizing and sharing his experiences and knowledge, and for his opportune personal advice.

To *Nanci Trivellato* and *Wagner Alegretti* for their living examples, patience, and endless conversations—the positive and the difficult ones—and for being important reference points in my existential program.

To the *extraphysical helpers* for their constant assistance and trust in me, and for making it a challenge for me to keep up with all the evolutionary opportunities they put in front of me.

Fundamental Concepts

Leaving the body! This idea certainly provokes different reactions in people: curiosity, anxiety, indifference, enthusiasm, excitement, or inspiration. However, once we start to consider this possibility seriously, the next logical step is to start investing in the development of this phenomenon so as to produce it with greater frequency and control. My colleagues and I, together with findings from an international survey,[1] corroborate that the vast majority of people who have lucid out-of-body experiences (OBEs) are of the opinion that these experiences are priceless and the benefits immeasurable. As we shall see throughout this book, this phenomenon, for most people, is positive and safe—contrary to some folkloric notions of paranormal phenomena.

The relevance of the out-of-body phenomenon rests on a simple and relevant idea: at this moment, there seems to be no other human experience that provides us with the comprehensive knowledge and experiential background about the nature of the consciousness *beyond physical reality*. As such, the out-of-body experience is not considered an end in itself, but is rather an *invaluable and irreplaceable tool to explore our multidimensional reality*. In this first chapter we will explore the fundamentals of out-of-body experiences, as well as concepts regarding the nature and study of the consciousness—who we are—and its ramifications. This will set the groundwork for the chapters to come.

The Out-of-Body Experience (OBE)

Let us introduce and define some basic characteristics of OBEs.

The *out-of-body experience* is the phenomenon whereby individuals project (separate) themselves from their physical body, manifesting in dimensions beyond the physical one using other subtler bodies, or vehicles of manifestation.

During an OBE, our physical body remains at rest, usually in the sleep state, while we—the soul, spirit, or consciousness—distance ourselves from our physical body, exploring and experiencing other realities. We travel with a vehicle or body subtler than the physical one and with quite different and unique abilities from those of the physical body. We can venture far away from the body and gain access to realms and planes that are not necessarily similar to physical reality.

The out-of-body experience is also known as *projection of the consciousness, astral travel, extracorporeal experience, conscious* or *lucid projection, unfolding, mystic voyage,* and several other names. Throughout the book, we will use these terms interchangeably.

The reasons people become interested in practicing the OBE are manifold. Among the most relevant and common *benefits* of OBEs are the following:

- Enjoying leisure OBEs (i.e., visiting new places)
- Promoting increased happiness and general well-being
- Improving interpersonal relationships
- Losing the fear of death
- Promoting greater overall health
- Contacting relatives or friends who have passed away
- Understanding our physical life more profoundly and why it is the way it is
- Looking for and receiving assistance of the most varied kinds
- Identifying our life's purpose or life task
- Helping or assisting other individuals while projected
- Replacing beliefs about the nature of life and death with direct personal experience and observation
- Contacting more evolved beings or consciousnesses (spirit guides, masters, helpers, and others)
- Achieving greater levels of ethics and understanding
- Achieving greater maturity (spiritual growth)

Extraphysical[2] (beyond-the-physical), or nonphysical, reality can be quite different from physical reality. In extraphysical reality, perceptions are much more refined and not limited to the basic senses that we are accustomed to inside the body. We can enjoy an expanded level of awareness, accessing information and memories that are beyond the physical brain. Communication can take place without the barriers of language. As a result, we undergo new and meaningful experiences and acquire greater knowledge, which in turn leads to a deeper appreciation of the nature of our existence.

OBE Generalities

Contrary to what is sometimes believed about paranormal phenomena, including the out-of-body experience, the production of these phenomena can be learned.[3] We do not need to either be born with the ability to leave the body or simply wait for it to occur spontaneously. Like any other human capacity, such as learning how to read, swim, or ride a bicycle, we can all develop our capacity to project outside the body (projectability). It is just a matter of acquiring some information and dedicating time and effort to the training required, and the capacity will develop accordingly.

There are people who have a greater predisposition to leave their body, and it may seem at first glance that these people are "gifted" or special in some way. However, if we take into account the multi-existential cycle or the process of multiple physical existences, we can easily understand why some individuals seem to be born with certain skills and predispositions; the reason being that they have previously invested time and effort in that skill in one or more past lives and they readily recover this ability in their current existence. We will explore this more in later chapters.

Disconnection

To leave the physical body is part of our human, or better yet, consciential,[4] nature. Because of this, we can affirm that *"everybody disconnects from their physical body every night."*[5] A *natural and spontaneous* separation takes place whenever we go to sleep and we basically stay floating above the body (figure 1.1). Yet the great majority of people are unaware of this condition, because they remain unconscious throughout this process.[6]

The fact that we all undergo this natural separation has been reported by many conscious projectors who have seen, for instance, a relative, neighbor, or friend floating a few inches above their body while sleeping. This observation has likewise been reported by projectors throughout the centuries and from all over the world. You too can attempt to see someone else "asleep" outside their body and verify this for yourself. This can be an interesting "projective target." What you see is a shape identical to the sleeping person's physical body. This "other" body is called the *psychosoma* or *astral body*.

It can be pointed out that not all of us disconnect from the body at the same distance. While some people may disconnect a couple of feet or more away, some individuals disconnect just a couple of inches from their body. This actually varies from

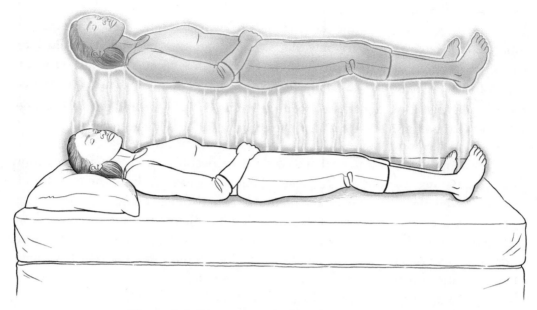

Figure 1.1: Disconnection during Normal Sleep

person to person and also from night to night. We will explore this idea in more detail later on.

An obvious benefit from having *lucid* projections is that we start recuperating time lost during sleep. In general terms, the average person sleeps eight hours a day,[7] which is a third of the day. At sixty years of age, that would mean that we spent about twenty years of our life sleeping! This is an unnecessarily huge amount of time spent unconscious. Clearly, the physical body needs to sleep, yet we—our essence, the consciousness—do not. We can use this time when the physical body is asleep in a more productive fashion to explore, learn, and help ourselves and others through our out-of-body experiences.

One of the reasons that lucid projections are not as common as we would expect has to do with intention. Think about what it is that most people want when they go to bed at night. What is their primary motivation? Certainly they want to rest and sleep. Some people just want to have a quiet, eventless night and wake up in the morning rested. Others prefer to not even dream, but to be "out like a light" the entire night. These intentions, then, not surprisingly, result in the person sleeping without much awareness the entire night.

We tend to identify with the physical body to such an extent that we become conditioned to behave as if we are only this. Even though most individuals would agree that they are more than their physical body and even theoretically understand and accept that they will continue existing in some fashion after biological death, in practice—in their day-to-day life—they behave as if their physical body is their *only* reality. As a result of this conditioning, when the physical body sleeps, the consciousness becomes inactive, dormant.

Quite simply, we can deduce that an essential aspect that can help us to have more lucid projections is intention. To project lucidly, we need to have the intention of wanting to remain aware during the night. Most individuals do not have this intention. In most instances this is not due to any fault of their own, but because of conditioning and not having enough information on the subject. So it is important to understand that one thing is the body—the "biological machine," the vehicle of manifestation—and another thing is us—the consciousness.

A powerful and basic way of trying to produce lucid projections is then this:

 Every night when you go to bed, affirm to yourself, "I will let my body sleep, but I want to remain aware." Say this with intention, really mean it. *Make sure that this is what you really, deeply, sincerely want!*

Having this strong intention is already a 180-degree change in behavior from our usual nights. It will increase the probability of remaining lucid during our projections. Accomplishing anything starts with intention.

Types of Projections

There are three basic types of lucid projections:[8]

- Spontaneous
- Forced
- Provoked at will

The *spontaneous projection* is the most common of all. These are called spontaneous projections because there does not seem to be an obvious reason for why we recovered our awareness outside the body. A classic spontaneous projection normally has several specific characteristics. In most cases it tends to happen when we are sleeping in a place other than our bedroom, such as at a friend's house or in a hotel room; in other words, places we are not regularly used to or are unfamiliar with altogether. In these instances, we wake up and regain consciousness outside of our body, many times floating close to a wall or to the ceiling; i.e., still relatively close to the physical body—where we have been most nights of our life. This time, however, we became aware of the experience.

Most spontaneous experiences tend to last only a few seconds. One reason for their shortness is that we normally become surprised when we realize we are outside of the body, which causes us to quickly return. In some cases we even have the opportunity to look at the physical body, a phenomenon called *self-bilocation* (figure 1.2).

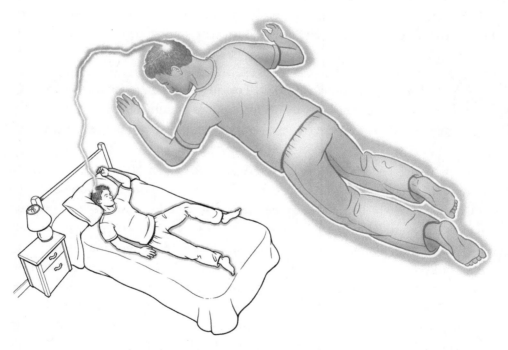

Figure 1.2: Self-Bilocation

In order to understand why the return to the body tends to be quick in spontaneous projections, it is important to understand the difference between having extraphysical awareness and holding or maintaining it. To appreciate this difference, let us use the analogy of a child learning to ride a bicycle. To begin, a child on a bike with no training wheels is usually held steady by an adult. Once the adult gives a little push to the bike and releases it, for a brief moment the child is in equilibrium. But since the child does not know how to maintain their balance yet, they fall over after a short distance. From this practical example, we can appreciate the difference between briefly having a specific condition (equilibrium, balance, awareness) and being able to maintain it longer.

Thus, outside the body we have to know how to become lucid and stay lucid; otherwise our experiences will tend to be unnecessarily short. Teaching this skill is one of the major objectives of this work.

Forced experiences are the second type of lucid projection. Near-death experiences (NDEs) are the most common type of forced projection. Individuals undergoing NDEs are literally *forced* outside of their body as the result of an accident, surgery, anesthesia, drowning, ailment, heart attack,[9] or other circumstance.

 A *near-death experience (NDE)* occurs when an individual is forced outside his or her body by critical human circumstances.

Though there are specific differences between OBEs and NDEs, it is worthy to note the similar patterns that NDEs have. Usually while outside their body during a NDE, individuals describe being able to see their body, whether while leaving or upon returning to their body. They are able to see whoever is physically there trying to help them (doctors, nurses, lifeguards, and/or others). Most of them describe seeing a tunnel of light and seeing more light at the end of the tunnel. After passing through the tunnel, they sometimes report encountering a group of individuals, among whom they commonly recognize family members who have already passed through the physical death. Within this group, there generally seems to be an individual who is directing the group and who normally in a few or many words tells the person experiencing the

NDE to return to their physical life. In other cases, the situation is more symbolic and there is nobody there to greet them.

Upon returning, many of these individuals are able to describe physical details with great accuracy that would have been impossible for them to have observed from where their physical body was during the NDE—especially considering the fact that their body (heart and brain) was dead during those moments. A point noteworthy of attention is the fact that people tend to describe the same basic pattern of experiences even though the individuals come from different religions and social systems and have different value systems, levels of education, and traditions. This speaks to the *universality* of the phenomena.[10] A conclusion that can be drawn from this is that independently of how we understand life now or of the experiences or education we may have had in this life, there is a certain reality outside the body, waiting for us.

It is interesting to note that people who undergo a near-death experience commonly report that their physical life is more meaningful after the experience. Some of the reasons for this, among others,[11] are the following:

Most people, as a result of having a near-death experience, lose their fear of death. Due to this, other phobias, insecurities, and fears they have manifested in their life also disappear. This results in their existence becoming more balanced and less stressful, and they feel more secure, grounded, and open.

- In general, people who have had a NDE become more assistantial—they try to help others more.

- They come back with a sense of a "life task" (existential program) and go about trying to execute it with more energy and motivation. They convey the idea that they understand life better.

- Many of them express that they are better people now, and this is what is referred to as "inner development."

A relevant question that can be derived from the experience of individuals who have had a NDE is: if they receive all of the above important and deep benefits with *only one* NDE—many times traumatic, certainly unplanned, and risky—what can we expect in terms of evolution (inner growth) from years of out-of-body experiences; for example, five years of *lucid* out-of-body experiences?

Beyond the NDE, a projection is also considered forced when it is produced by drugs. However, *provoking OBEs through the use of drugs is not recommended at all.*[12] Drugs that produce out-of-body projections are normally heavy chemicals, psychoactive, and can have negative side effects on the physical body, especially on brain cells. It is commonly known today that people who use (abuse) drugs regularly lose mental acuity, reliability, and effectiveness.[13] Sometimes, after a single use of a heavy drug, the person is never the same again.

It is important to note that the brain does not produce our mental faculties. These functions are, to a certain extent, independent of the brain.[14] Yet the brain has to process these commands—so as for the body to obey—and these functions are affected. This is similar to what happens when we have a computer whose software is impeccable but the processor is damaged. The level of the processor's impairment will determine its decline in efficiency.

Another shortcoming associated with the use of drugs is their effect during the projection itself. Many times the perceptions of the projector become "clouded" and distorted due to the drug's influence. For this reason, the accounts in these situations are rarely reliable. When the person comes back into the body and tries to bring this information into the brain, due to the unnatural chemicals (or unnatural levels of chemicals) in the brain, memories in many instances are not easily fixed in our gray matter.[15] So not only does the drug distort the perception, but the memory is also distorted upon reaching the brain and the end result is a very low-quality experience.

Drugs also can have the negative side effect of creating dependency. In general, what occurs is that people who use drugs *weaken their will*—since the drug is the agent causing the effect in the person. Once outside the body, it is through our will that we control everything we do and everywhere we go. We develop and carry the strength of our will from life to life, and thus we want to nurture it. When meeting people outside the body who use drugs, we notice that they are usually in a stupor and much less sharp. In most instances individuals resort to drugs because of a weak will, in some cases because of peer pressure (weak will), to escape reality (weak will), or because they are unable to produce the capacity on their own (weak will).[16] Inner development means becoming a stronger individual, not a weaker one.

Lastly, the most logical aspect with regard to drugs is that they are simply not needed. We do not need to expose ourselves to these chemicals and have undesirable experiences when we can learn to provoke OBEs in a healthy and natural fashion. As a rule of thumb, the fewer the objects or external elements used to produce something, the greater our capacity is and the more self-sufficient we become.

The third type of lucid projection is the one *provoked at will*. There are many techniques for this, as we will see later on in chapter 4. In order to understand what is needed to provoke lucid projections at will, we must first recognize two facts. The first is that everybody leaves the body every night, as mentioned previously. We spontaneously and unconsciously leave the body every time we fall asleep. The second is that coming back to the body is likewise easy, since we do this every time we wake up in the morning. In fact, there are biological and energetic factors (which we will explore later on) that do not allow us to stay projected forever—or even for very long periods of time. Coming back to the body is no problem; our challenge is to remain outside of it with awareness.

If leaving the body and coming back to it are relatively easy to do, then what is it, in essence, that we want to learn? To fully enjoy all the benefits of a lucid projection, we need to develop two attributes:[17]

- We need to have *lucidity*,[18] or awareness, while outside the body. This can be learned through not only a more complete understanding of how the entire process works but also the practical application of projective techniques and energetic exercises.

- We need to *recall* the experience, since a projection is not necessarily automatically recalled. The reason for this is that everything we perceive and experience outside the body is not automatically recorded in the brain and is not automatically accessible. On the contrary, this information accumulates in the nonphysical bodies, which are the ones that are active at the moment of the experience. In order to have this information accessible while intraphysically[19] awake, we need to recall the information while inside the body. Using a computer analogy, it is like downloading information into the physical brain. We will also study how to improve our extraphysical memory and the "downloading" process.

It is interesting to note that lucid projections provoked at will are the least common compared to the spontaneous and the forced ones. The reason for this is that up until now, especially in the Western Hemisphere, this information belonged to secluded, esoteric, or occult groups. This phenomenon can be and is now being studied in a more direct, realistic fashion.

Statistics

According to international surveys,[20] individuals reported the following levels of lucidity at night while sleeping:

Unconscious experiences
    (normal sleeping without much awareness):   89%

Semiconscious experiences
    (the level of lucid dreams):   9.8%

Conscious experiences
    (lucid projections, OBEs):   1.2%

It is interesting to pay attention to the last category. Though this is a small percentage, the number is bigger than what is popularly thought. About 1 percent of the population means that in a city with two million people, 20,000 individuals have had lucid projections!

Dreams and Lucid Projections

What is the difference between dreams and lucid projections? The main difference is the level of lucidity, or awareness, that we manifest when projected consciously outside the body. Furthermore, lucidity is an attribute that does not depend on the physical body. To put things into perspective, while outside the physical body we can find ourselves with the same level of awareness and control that we have when we are awake in ordinary daily life; and just as we do not confuse the condition of ordinary waking life with dreams, experientially, when projected with a good level of awareness, there is no confusing lucid projections with dreams.

In certain cases we can become confused because we may be outside the body but only partially aware.[21] In other instances we can have experiences during the night in which we enjoy a level of semiconsciousness. Such is the case with lucid dreams. The condition of lucid dreams occurs when in the middle of the dream we realize we are dreaming.[22] The reasons for this realization can be many, such as fears, incongruence, unusual activities in the person's dream, and others. In most cases of spontaneous lucid dreaming, the period of awareness tends to be short, similar to the spontaneous lucid projection that was previously discussed.

Lucid dreams are a step between normal (non-lucid) dreams and lucid projections, and they can also be nurtured and developed. We can learn to maintain our awareness for a longer period of time and also to control the elements in our dreams. Even though we have control over our dream, it is important to stress that it is still a dream. The lucid dream can be, however, a training path toward having lucid projections.[23]

In the same fashion that we are able to will ourselves to dream with other places or conditions, we can also will ourselves to stop the dream and see the extraphysical reality.

When you realize that you are in a lucid dream, give the command to stop the dream and see the extraphysical reality. For example, you could say the following: "I want to be aware and see my actual room now!"

With some practice, after giving this command, the dream will dissipate and we will find ourselves, in most instances, floating above the physical body in our bedroom. In some cases we might be far from our physical body. When aware and lucid extraphysically, we are first of all able to recognize the fact that we are outside the body. We have all of our mental faculties working, meaning, unlike while dreaming, we have access to our memory: address, phone number, what we did during the day, and so forth. In other words, we are able to recall our physical life in detail.

Outside the body, we have full capacity to make decisions. We can decide to go to a relative's house, to a physical place that might be very far away, or to other dimensions, or we can simply stay and contemplate our own house from the extraphysical perspective. Our logic is naturally and spontaneously active. We are able to reason outside the body without problems. In other words, we may find ourselves with the same level of lucidity, awareness, and sharpness that we enjoy while in the physical waking state. In some instances this level of awareness can be even greater than the one we enjoy in ordinary waking life.

With this increased level of awareness, and since the experience is real and actually happening, we can *confirm*[24] it—something that dreams do not allow. This verification can occur even in a simple fashion with physical details that we may happen to see. For example, while we are away on a trip, a relative of ours decides to reorganize our living room, moving the furniture to different positions. We can observe this at night while projected and confirm it once we return home.

Assisted Projection
Silvana Meira (2006)[25]

Saturday, January 28, 2006, Corte Madera, California

After waking up to go to the bathroom, I returned to bed and lay down, placing a pillow underneath my knees and comfortably extending my arms alongside my body, hands resting on my thighs. I immediately felt relaxed and externalized energy for about twenty minutes or so, shifting to the closed circuit of energy technique. I felt the energies flowing from my head to my feet and back. I concentrated on leaving the physical body and repeated to myself: "I'm going to leave my body. My physical body needs to sleep, but I don't."

In a state of feeling half-awake and half-asleep, a dreamlike scene appeared and I saw myself in a room with three Brazilian friends whom I hadn't seen in over five years. I was happy to see them, and they seemed surprised and happy to see me as well. As I heard my physical body snoring, the scene disappeared and I recovered lucidity. I could still feel the energy running from head to feet, and feet to head, so I knew I had to hold my intent to leave the physical body and to avoid distractions.

I heard a gentle and very calm female voice asking me in my native language, "Voce quer sair?" ("Do you want to take off?") I did not have time to answer because I felt I was being grabbed by my para-arms and pulled up, bringing me to a seated position, with the upper part of my psychosoma (astral body) separating from my physical body. I could see my para-arms stretched toward the ceiling whilst the para-legs remained with my physical legs. Aware of my situation, I could not see the helper, but I knew she was there. Looking to the ceiling I tried to take off, telling myself to go up, but my position did not change. Instead, what happened was the elongation of my para-arms. As I noticed that my effort was not sufficient to lift off, my psychosoma was brought back to the horizontal position, where I was then lying on my physical body, listening to its heavy breath, sometimes feeling it and sometimes not, as if my extraphysical head was bouncing in and out of my physical head.

I firmly intended to go up again, and in slow motion my psychosoma went up, stopping only two inches from the ceiling. I looked at the details of the surface of the ceiling, which I had never before seen so closely. I was getting distracted and losing lucidity when a clear message directed me to get away from my physical body so I would not return to it. I started to move, first looking at the ceiling then turning my head and seeing the chandelier. I noticed that my extraphysical bedroom was bigger than it is physically.

"I need a target!" As soon as this thought occurred to me, I knew what I wanted to do. I wanted to see "L.", one of the friends in the dreamlike scene perceived earlier. Adopting a vertical position, I went out in the open, flying for what felt like a minute. Stopping at what seemed to be my destination, I saw my friend "L.", and a woman was with him. I could not identify her, but they were seated at a table facing each other. From where I was I could see her back, and her hair caught my attention. My friend was wearing a light blue shirt and he did not have his beard, which he'd had the last time I saw him.

Something pulled me back, and shortly I was back in my physical body. I did not recall my flight back. It did not feel like I woke up because I never lost consciousness during the process. The memory of what happened was vivid in my mind. I did not move for a couple minutes, going through the details of my experience. I moved to the side to check the time; the clock marked 6:50 AM. I took note of it and wrote 12:50 PM next to it, the time in Brazil.

It was still dark. I turned on the lights, got my notebook from the nightstand, and sat in bed to write down my experience. After getting my friend's new contact information that weekend, I wrote to him, telling him I'd had him as my target and what I'd seen when I got to him. He confirmed that at that time he was at home with his partner. He was wearing a light blue shirt and did not have a beard any longer. He also mentioned that by my description of the scene he could tell my angle of perception and that everything about my experience could be validated.

I thank the extraphysical helper for this opportunity.

Furthermore, manifesting this mental state while projected—with access to all of our mental capacities—can also help us to verify, with one single experience, that the mental faculties that conventional science attributes to the physical brain are not actually of the brain. This is an interesting conclusion, because though the brain is an important object of study, it is still part of the hardware, and it is not responsible for our capacity to be aware, conscious. Thus, our consciousness is not a product of the hardware (or of biochemical interactions); on the contrary, the physical hardware is the receiver of consciousness, a tool we can control.

There are other very effective energy techniques that we will discuss in the following chapters that can help us to accomplish this extraphysical awakening with greater ease. The levels of lucidity will also be explained in greater detail.

A Word about Words...

Certain technical terms and expressions (neologisms) used in conscientiology (and in this book) are different because they refer to concepts that are new. These concepts describe realities that have not been identified or formalized before, like *cosmoethics*, *thosene*, and *existential moratorium*.[26]

However, other technical terms in conscientiology are used to describe realities that are already known. This is the case with expressions like *extraphysical consciousnesses* (beings who have passed away), *existential program* (life task), *lucid projection* (astral travel), and others. The reason for having different terms in this second case is due to understanding the energies and the connotations that these expressions bring with them.

As an example, think about what you feel inside when you hear words like *disembodied*, *apparition*, or *disincarnate*. These words are old and in some cases emotionally loaded, and are associated more with something negative or dense or something that we should fear. The state of being in between lives, however, is a neutral state, in the same sense that the state of "human being" is neutral. There are more ethical and less ethical human beings, yet the state of being human, in and of itself, is a neutral one.

When we use a term like *disembodied*, the term already brings with it an energy that is not neutral, and conveys for many an idea of something to be feared or at least something we would want to stay away from. Thus the term is inaccurate with regard to the actual state it is describing—since the state is neutral. Furthermore, it evokes energy that is not positive, but mystical, and carries meaning that is unnecessary and/or not helpful. On the other hand, the term *extraphysical consciousness* is uncontaminated and neutral, thus being more accurate to describe the actual state of being between lives.

As was mentioned previously, in an OBE, or when you feel energy well, you are able to feel the difference in the quality of the energy in a very clear fashion. Sometimes the difference between using one term versus the other can be the difference between connecting and evoking energies of less developed dimensions or of a more evolved one—and you can experience this reality while outside the body on your own.

In conscientiology, there is a committee that advises on the creation of new terms, called the International Council on Neologistics.[27]

In this book, we'll try to use the traditional terms and introduce the new and more correct terminology. Astute and observant readers will do well in starting to use the new terminology as they develop.

Projectiology

Projectiology is the science that studies the projections of the consciousness (OBEs, astral travel), bioenergy, and related phenomena.

The following are some of the main topics within projectiology's scope of investigation:

- Various degrees of projection of the consciousness (nonalignment, or discoincidence, of the bodies)
- Techniques to produce projections

- Mechanisms of takeoff
- Composition and properties of the vehicles of manifestation (holosoma)
- Perceptions and observations outside the body
- Identification and characteristics of the varied extraphysical dimensions
- Relationships among consciousnesses from the same or different dimensions
- Interaction and communication between and within dimensions
- Study of bioenergy (vital energies, chi, prana)
- Techniques to control bioenergies and psychic experiences
- Examination and categorization of the various paranormal phenomena and altered states of consciousness

Projectiology was proposed and initially structured by Dr. Waldo Vieira, a Brazilian medical doctor and dentist. One of the greatest merits of his work is the compilation of vast amounts of information from the four corners of the world on the out-of-body subject, resulting in the treatise *Projectiology: A Panorama of the Experiences of the Consciousness outside the Human Body*. Based on his extensive research, we can see that the projection of the consciousness seems to be a universal phenomenon, an integral part of human nature and culture. Countless cases of OBEs and related phenomena have been described by most civilizations, including the ancient Chinese, Japanese, Greeks, Egyptians, Hindus, and cultures of Mesopotamia, Europe, and others. For more complete information on the history of projectiology and the sociological implications of the out-of-body state, please refer to the above-mentioned book by Dr. Vieira.[28]

One of the best-known historical figures to report an extraphysical experience is the Greek philosopher Plato. In his book *The Republic*, he describes the case of a soldier (Er, the Armenian) who had a forced OBE.[29]

One of projectiology's objectives is to amass as much information as possible regarding out-of-body phenomena from conscious projectors all over the world. In doing so, the material is analyzed and evaluated and comparisons are made so as to rationally understand and reach a greater consensus on what is taking place during this phenomenon. By connecting pieces of the puzzle from the direct personal experience of researcher-projectors from different cultures, we can arrive at more logical and valid conclusions.

When applying logic and coherence to projectiological studies (as opposed to simply following traditions and superstitions), we observe that some of the information and techniques applied by some schools of thought (philosophies, religions, and others) are confirmed by serious investigations. On the other hand, we verify as well that many of these schools of thought still incorporate into their practices mystic and folkloric elements that are unnecessary for the development and understanding of extraphysical phenomena. For instance, when comparing some practices from different cultures, we verify that some are basically identical, except for one element, like the positioning of candles in strategic places in a closed room. If by using a second similar practice we are able to reach the same results as with the first one but without any candles, we can conclude that the candle element was part of the mysticism and folklore of the first group. Furthermore, such an element is unnecessary to the attainment of positive results. The biggest problem with these secondary items is that in many cases they are overvalued. Candles, dress codes, objects, altars, colors, and what they all represent for that specific philosophy (their symbolism) are not as powerful and effective as the willpower and dedication of the consciousness. We also must notice that while outside the body, we manifest ourselves without any physical objects.

Consensus

The methodology applied by projectiology, besides being based on scientific research and the researcher's own personal experience, also takes into account consensus, which is considered to be essential to a better understanding of extraphysical reality. With regard to the study of consciousness and its multidimensional nature, the number of variables is so great and the modes of perception so varied that a single point of view is not enough.

> **EXAMPLE**
>
> Here is an example that illustrates the importance of consensus when working with individual accounts. Imagine a group of people who go to see a movie, such as a science fiction movie. Afterward, one person might think the movie was the best ever, another might have fallen asleep, others might be angry because they actually spent money on the movie, another might be extremely scared and might even have nightmares, and yet another might have laughed the entire time. Are any of them absolutely right in their appreciation of the movie? The answer is no, even though they all watched the same objective physical reality (the movie). They also cannot assume that everybody else will experience or understand the movie like they did. They cannot even assume that others will have the same feelings and reactions when watching certain scenes. Therefore, there cannot be a generalization of any one person's experiences.

Unfortunately, certain authors (in various fields of knowledge for that matter) make the mistake of explaining everybody else's experiences based on their own. Books with accounts of original out-of-body experiences and observations are certainly very valuable for these studies. However, as important as they may be, we cannot forget the fact that these accounts, when they lack consensus, are based solely on the author's point of view and way of thinking, including their biases, preconceived ideas, and inclinations. Therefore, consensus among experiences and researchers must exist, especially when accounts are so inconsistent or even contradictory.

We can then state that in studying the field of OBEs the first step is to have our own experience and the second is to try to arrive at a consensus on how things work, even by understanding other individuals' accounts as well. Otherwise, we may end up with too narrow a vision of extraphysical reality. In certain cases, joint projections can be very helpful. A joint projection is when two projectors meet outside the body and share a common extraphysical experience, then compare their perceptions afterward (see chapter 3 for an example of a joint projection).

Conscientiology

> *Conscientiology* is the science that studies *the consciousness* and all of its manifestations inside and outside the body.[30]

Consciousness is another name for our essence, soul, or spirit. In this sense, conscientiology is the study of the soul, our essence. To understand the consciousness is no easy endeavor. As previously discussed, while projected, the consciousness uses different bodies and manifests in different states, which already gives us some idea of its nature. However, the manifestation of the consciousness reaches the entire universe with all of its dimensions, attesting to the complexity of conscientiology studies.

Conscientiology studies, among others,[31] the following:

- Attributes of the consciousness
- Evolution of the consciousness
- Strategies for evolution (recycling and inversion)
- Conscientiometry, or the measure of the consciousness
- Existential programs (life tasks)
- Degrees of assistantiality (helping others)
- Evolved beings (such as the serenissimus)
- Cosmoethics
- Universalism
- Mentalsomatics

Though some of these terms are probably new to most readers, many of them will be better explained as we move ahead. One of the basic premises of conscientiology is the use of the OBE as a tool in order to better understand the consciousness, meaning to be able to bring information from the extraphysical reality to the intraphysical reality in order to better understand ourselves, others, life, and our reality in general.

Because all human beings are living in the intraphysical reality, they have a physical point of view, a certain understanding of life, and of what we are that comes from the observations made in this intraphysical dimension. The intention of conscientiology is to add the extraphysical observations to this intraphysical perspective so as to have a more complete picture of ourselves, consciousnesses. This not only allows us to arrive at better conclusions based on more information but also leads to very profound consequences.

Let us consider some examples of these statements in practice. It is a fact that all living beings *only have a physical life for a limited period of time.* Specifically, we are born, spend some time in the physical dimension, grow, live, and then pass away. This observation is also applicable to animals and plants. It is easy, natural, and simple to make this physical observation and arrive at this conclusion.

As we start to have lucid projections and begin spending time in the extraphysical dimension, we are going to observe and realize that as individuals die, they spend a certain amount of time extraphysically (as an extraphysical consciousness) and then they are physically born again. This is, of course, the idea that in most circles is called reincarnation. Yet this extraphysical observation outside the body is just as natural and simple as the intraphysical realization. All that it is needed is for us to start spending time outside the body, be lucid and observe, and we will start to see how some things work. It is therefore seen that the two perspectives—the intraphysical and the extraphysical—complement each other and can be joined in order to have a more inclusive understanding. These ideas or concepts stop being a theory and become *serenely* accepted facts once we have had the experience.

This realization can have profound consequences for many individuals. For example, people who live their lives without this concept in mind, or even in opposition to it, upon realizing this will have to do some thinking. Attention must be also drawn to the fact that nobody convinced or is trying to convince the projector who observes this; projectors through their own means realize this reality and arrive at such a conclusion. Conscientiology therefore has this effect, as the researcher-projector discovers information about the reality of the consciousness, and the person changes, renews, and improves the understanding of how things work.[32]

It is safer and more comfortable for us to change our understanding regarding the properties of an atom than to renew our fundamental understanding of life. One of the reasons that many more materialistic, conventional, or traditionally based researchers do not want to study projectiology, conscientiology, and other paranormal phenomena is also because of this effect—it is safer not to.

Yet on our own we start realizing through our personal experiences that we are not just the product of the experiences of this one intraphysical life, but that our history is much larger. The combination of the study of ourselves as multidimensional beings, conscientiology, and OBEs (projectiology) will lead us to ask deeper questions pertaining to our nature.

To start to understand all the implications of this study, let us assume the following. Imagine that you have an out-of-body experience tonight—without going too far. To simplify things, let us assume you stay projected only inside your bedroom. We realize that what we are—whether we want to call it the consciousness, soul, spirit, or any other name—is independent of the physical body and existed before the creation of the physical body, meaning the consciousness, our soul, existed before we were physically born.

Thus, upon realizing this, questions can arise, such as: Where was I a year, or even two years, before I was born? What was I doing, and what was I concerned with? Obviously, we were not inside this current body. We were somewhere in extraphysical reality, or an out-of-body condition. We can then, during a projection, look for the place where we were before we were born. In a more general sense, a person can gain information to answer the age-old philosophical question: Where do I come from?

We will also observe that since we (a consciousness) are an independent reality from the physical body, when it dies (the organic, biological robot deactivates), we (the consciousness) will continue to exist. We can verify our own immortality through an OBE.

We may also wonder: Where will I go after passing away? Obviously, we will not be in the same condition we are in right now, intraphysical, but we will be extraphysical. Thus, projected we can also set out to find the place where we will be after this physical life.

Another very practical conclusion regarding the life of a person is the following. We realize that we are not the physical body. Yet in practice during the day, we remain inside the body, doing many things. So why, if we are a consciousness, do we need to use a physical body? Is this body really needed? Is there a reason for it? We can find information to answer these questions outside the body. Many times people popularly like to call this reason for having a physical existence a *life mission* or *life task*. In conscientiology, this idea is called one's *existential program;* it is the program, the plan, for this existence, for this life. We may ask ourselves, what would be the effect on us if we found out that we actually had a task for this life? This is a question that will be addressed several times during the book and in greater detail in chapter 7.

Upon understanding that we do not stop existing with the deactivation of the physical body, and understanding how the process of dying and rebirth works, we lose the fear of death.[33] This realization has many practical implications for our manifestation in the physical life. These individuals now become more confident and grounded in their endeavors and tend to live a less stressful life.

We can see from all of these examples that the consequences of conscientiological studies can be very deep. We also have to keep in mind that all of these realizations were arrived at with what was called a very *simple* projection. *We have not even left the bedroom yet!* So, we can think about the potential for gathering information that the OBE has to offer. Conscientiology tries to understand the consciousness in its most comprehensive fashion, in all of its manifestations.

To use an analogy, it is seen that individuals are similar to an iceberg. A small fraction of the iceberg's volume (about one-tenth) is above the surface of the water, while the greatest volume is underneath the water. Like the iceberg, we present only a fraction of what we are in the physical dimension. Most of what we are is "underneath the surface," not readily accessible. Yet, like the iceberg, it is this volume underneath the surface that supports what is visible and that in many instances dictates what we exhibit.

To summarize and understand the relationship of the sciences of projectiology and conscientiology, we can compare them to reading and literature. One thing is the capacity to read or the phenomenon of reading, and the other is its application and use and all the information we will read and take advantage of in our life. Projectiology is the capacity, the phenomenon. Conscientiology is the analysis, the relations and comparisons of the information. Thousands of conclusions can be derived from studying extraphysical reality both for personal reasons and for a more general understanding.

The Consciousness[34]

Following the previous example, let's explore different consequences more specific to who we are. Let's assume that you have a completely aware out-of-body experience and you look back and see your physical body peacefully asleep. This sudden realization catches you by surprise (a common reaction), causing you to become over-emotional and sending you back into your body. This common experience is a fairly simple projection of the consciousness.

First of all, *you* will notice that *you* are much more than the physical body. Each one of us has a physical name; numbers that identify us, such as a driver's license number and a social security number; and documents like a birth certificate, passport, and others. Furthermore, we also identify ourselves based on our relationships with others; for example, "I'm the brother of___" or "I'm the daughter of___." Naturally, we grow accustomed to *identifying* ourselves with all of these human labels and documentations.

However, during this simple OBE example, you realize that your physical body represents merely a fraction of what you really are and that physical reality is not the only or ultimate one. From that moment forward, your identification numbers and certificates have a much different meaning. Through your own direct experience, you come to the conclusion that existence is much more than what the physical perceptions have led you to believe during your whole life. All your mental faculties, emotions, intentions, desires, and personality—in short, everything that you associate as being *you*—goes with you in your out-of-body experiences.

So the question becomes, *What are we exactly?*

In a nutshell, each one of us is a consciousness in evolution.

The *consciousness*—the soul, spirit, ego, atman, and others—is then the essence or intelligent principle behind all beings, beyond matter and energy. It is also important to notice the difference between *the consciousness* and the state of *consciousness*. *The consciousness*, as proposed by conscientiology, is a separate and unique entity. Each human being is a consciousness. And the *state of consciousness* is a person's faculty of being aware or lucid. It is the consciousness (one's self) that animates and controls the physical body and all the other "bodies," or vehicles of manifestation, as we will soon see.

Attributes of the Consciousness

In order to better understand who we are, let us begin by discussing the main attributes of the consciousness; namely, its multivehicular, multidimensional, multi-existential, evolutionary, self-aware, and bioenergetic nature.

When we leave the physical body during an OBE, we find ourselves manifesting in another type of body, or vehicle. In the case of our previous example, you may simultaneously see two of your bodies: your physical body lying in bed and another, subtler body floating in midair. This second body is lighter and brighter and has unique abilities. Thus, we can say that for us to manifest in any dimension, we need an appropriate "vehicle" suitable for that specific dimension. This is known as our *multivehicular* nature. We possess four vehicles of manifestation. Their details and characteristics will be explained later in this chapter.

As we have seen in our OBE example, we, as consciousnesses, are able to manifest in different planes of reality, being in essence *multidimensional.* In other words, we all have the inherent ability to temporarily leave the physical body and verify this fact for ourselves. As far as it is known, there is a great number of extraphysical dimensions all waiting to be explored. However, we do not necessarily have to be projected outside the body to access other dimensions. We can learn to perceive them during the waking state. Psychic individuals are able to interact with the subtler dimensions through a series of paranormal phenomena. Through clairvoyance, for instance, they are capable of seeing energies and nonphysical beings while remaining inside the physical body. The OBE simply allows for a much richer multidimensional interaction than is possible through other paranormal phenomena.

The consciousness is also *multi-existential,* which implies that we *encompass* many existences or many *lives.* As a consciousness we have had many lives in the past. We came back once again with the current physical body and we will come back many more times in the future, occupying a different physical body each time.

 Understanding that we have had many lives, we can ask ourselves: In what other countries have I lived during other lives? How many other religions have I already followed? How many languages have I already spoken? How many lives have I had as a male and as a female? In how many races have I been born already?

We all go through these series of existences, because as consciousnesses we are in a process of *evolution.* In other words, in life after life, we become progressively more refined, complex, and mature. Notice that in order to examine this evolutionary process, we must consider how broad our scale of observation is. If individuals are observed over a period of one week, we may conclude that they did not evolve at all.

However, over a period of many lives we can verify that they have indeed matured. Furthermore, we all have our own evolutionary pace; some of us evolve faster, and others more slowly. The rate of evolution (more efficiency and less time) depends on how much priority is placed on inner personal growth.

> It is important to clarify two common misconceptions regarding our evolutionary process, the first one being that there is a fixed number of lives, and the second that the number of lives is but a few. Studies on retrocognitions, or recollection of past lives, show us that the evolutionary process involves an unknown number of lives—perhaps hundreds of thousands—and that the number of lives depends mainly on how much effort and dedication we apply to our personal growth.[35]

Consciousnesses at our level have *self-awareness*. We are able to discern the fact that we are an individual who exists independently of others. Animals are also consciousnesses (souls), yet they do not have the same level of self-awareness as we do. Animals seem to be simpler, less developed or evolved consciousnesses, occupying more rudimentary bodies.[36] While outside the body, we can observe that our dog or cat is also projected. Our pet might be simply *sleeping* outside the body or it may be *awake,* repeating the same behaviors as if it were inside the body. The pet's extraphysical awareness is then basically the same as its physical awareness—simpler than ours (humans).

Additionally, the consciousness manifests itself through *energy* and *matter*. The bodies the consciousness uses are matter, and matter is a derivative of energy. Furthermore, the "fuel" that vitalizes these bodies is also energy. Likewise, the interaction among consciousnesses occurs through bioenergies—a concept that will be further explored in chapter 2.

This initial overview helps to get a foot in the door regarding the main attributes of the consciousness. Bear in mind that as you continue with your reading, you will uncover the characteristics of the consciousness and its evolution step by step.

The Consciential Paradigm

A paradigm, according to the Merriam-Webster dictionary, is "a philosophical and theoretical framework of a scientific school or discipline within which theories, laws, and generalizations and the experiments performed in support of them are formulated." We can think of a paradigm as a model or a set of ideas on which researchers base themselves when performing their studies. It is a set of assumptions or a specific point of view from which the problem in question is approached.

The ruling paradigm in science nowadays is the Newtonian-Cartesian paradigm, or simply the *materialistic paradigm*. Its underlying assumption is that the only elements that exist in the universe are matter and energy. Matter can be transformed into energy and vice versa. It can, therefore, be said that matter and energy are two different expressions of the same substance.

According to this paradigm, the consciousness (soul, spirit) does not exist. This is an axiom of the materialistic paradigm and, at the same time, an erroneous assumption. Even though there is an enormous amount of evidence throughout the world showing that there is "something" beyond the physical dimension, conventional science has not taken it into consideration.

There are several reasons that conventional science does not accept any views of an extraphysical nature. First, many of these ideas have been historically linked to religious and/or mystical groups. Science, in its efforts to distance itself from religious connotations, simply disregards and denies some phenomena that are very much real and valid. The understanding of the *spirit* has been traditionally within the domains of religion and mysticism, while the study of *matter* falls within the domain of science. Through the consciential paradigm and the lucid projection, we can study the consciousness (spirit) through a more rigorous and experiential methodology, completely free from any mystical or religious approach.

Another reason for the reluctance of science to study realities beyond matter has to do with the dogma of *instrumentalism*. In essence, conventional science works under the following perspective: "If my instrument (supposedly objective and unbiased) can measure *something*, then this *something* exists; if on the other hand my instrument cannot detect it, then it does not exist." The problem with this type of thinking is the undue dependency and reliance on technology and instruments.

It stands to reason that if an instrument is not currently able to detect something, that does not necessarily mean it does not exist. What it does simply mean is that at this moment, the instrument is neither sensitive enough nor the technology developed enough to detect it. It is conceivable that, in a few decades with further technological advances, the instrument may then become sensitive enough to measure what appears to be nonexistent today.[37] Because of this extreme dependency on instrumentation, conventional, natural science chooses to deny our extraphysical reality.

However, when we start having lucid projections, we realize that there is another, greater reality—namely, the consciousness. Therefore, a paradigm that incorporates this reality is warranted.

> The *consciential paradigm* is founded on the principle of the existence of the consciousness, as well as matter and energy.[38]

To explain the consciential paradigm, we may as well take a more direct approach. Conventional science supports the idea that any influence on matter or energy can come only from matter or energy, since these are the only two realities that exist. Yet the consciential paradigm adds a third reality—the consciousness. Thus, the effects that the consciousness has on matter and energy and vice versa (such as paranormal phenomena) need to be studied as well.

There is no doubt that this third variable adds much complexity to the whole equation. Yet at the same time, it not only enriches our perspective on life but also offers better explanations to some of the basic questions that arise with lucid projections.[39] According to the consciential paradigm, matter and energy are elements that the consciousness uses in order to achieve its objectives, whichever these may be.

The sciences of projectiology and conscientiology are based on the consciential paradigm.

Let us take a look at a practical example of the difference between these two paradigms. A patient is seen by a conventional doctor as a collection of biological and chemical components and their interactions.[40] Awareness (in this case *consciousness*) is therefore the product of these biochemical interactions in the brain. If the patient is producing an undesirable behavior, this behavior is also the product of specific chemical reactions. Therefore, if a chemical is found to treat this condition (balance a specific chemical reaction), it is then prescribed by the doctor. This procedure may work; the patient may effectively stop producing the undesirable behavior. However, the problem with this approach is when the cause or root of the problem is not in the physical body and/or in an unbalanced biochemical reaction, but in a trauma from a previous life, for example.

The consciential paradigm takes into account a much broader perspective, which includes issues such as this one. There are numerous reports of people who, upon becoming aware of a problem originating in a previous life, are effectively and definitively able to cure it. No chemical, in this case, will be able to affect the traumas of a past life, because chemicals work only at the present physical level—and because the memories of previous existences are not in the physical brain.[41]

Because of its physical limits in trying to understand the individual, the adopted materialistic paradigm is ill-equipped to deal with some of the most fundamental issues of human nature. According to our previous example, since the problem has not been solved (since in many instances conventional science treats only the symptoms), it may reappear later on in this or in a future life of the consciousness. Upon understanding the breadth and complexity of the consciousness, we observe that the materialistic paradigm is therefore very restrictive in its reach. A long-term solution is needed, and the consciential paradigm's approach is timely.

Another key aspect of the consciential paradigm is that it inevitably requires participative research.[42] Due to the current lack of instruments to examine our extraphysical nature, scientists who adopt the consciential paradigm as the foundation for their investigation are consequently required to be both the researcher and the subject under study. The consciousness, being a nonphysical substance, cannot be placed inside a physical laboratory for study, because its manifestations reach the entire universe. Thus, instead of shying away from subjective, participative research, it is fully and necessarily embraced.

In simple terms, if we want to know more about the nonphysical aspects of our reality as consciousnesses, we must invest in the development of our paranormal and projective abilities. We can learn to leave the body so we can directly verify extraphysical reality for ourselves. That is the reason that a lucid projection is a self-persuasive experience, in the sense that once we have one, we are certain of its veracity, in the same manner that we are certain of the veracity of our waking-state experiences during the day.

Thus, the ideas expressed in this book are based on these two new sciences: projectiology and conscientiology, which have the consciential paradigm as their philosophical foundation.

Holosoma: The Vehicles of the Consciousness

Holosoma is a compound word comprising two Greek terms. The first term is the prefix *holo,*[43] which means "whole," "total," "complete," or "the collection of." The second term, *soma*, means "body." So holosoma is the complete set of bodies of the consciousness (figure 1.3).[44]

A *body* is a vehicle of manifestation of the consciousness.

A body is a tool that we use to manifest in a specific dimension. For instance, the physical body is a tool for manifesting in and interacting with the physical dimension. Likewise, the consciousness has other bodies to manifest in dimensions other than the physical. The other subtler bodies of the consciousness are appropriately used to manifest in their native dimensions. Each vehicle has its own characteristics and functions. We can say as well that each body of the consciousness has its own anatomy, physiology, and pathologies. The detailed study of the holosoma is one of conscientiology's areas of research, called *holosomatics.*[45] Here is a list of the four bodies that constitute the holosoma:

- Soma (physical body)
- Energosoma (energetic body)
- Psychosoma (emotional body)
- Mentalsoma (intellectual body)

Soma

The *soma* (physical body) is the most rustic, dense, and fragile of all the bodies. The soma has organs and allows for an excellent interaction with the physical dimension. It is interesting to note that it is this body, and not we (the consciousness), that

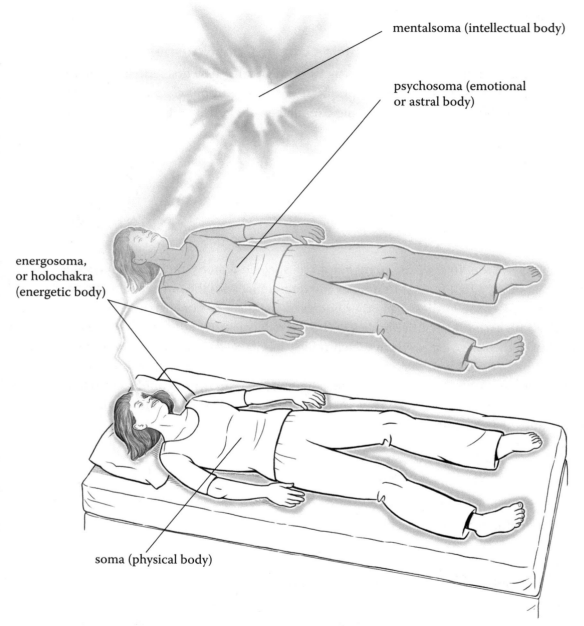

mentalsoma (intellectual body)

psychosoma (emotional or astral body)

energosoma, or holochakra (energetic body)

soma (physical body)

Figure 1.3: Holosoma: The Vehicles of Manifestation of the Consciousness

directly interacts with matter. Strictly speaking, it can be said that we, as consciousnesses, *never touch physical reality.*

The body is a biological robot with mechanisms based on mechanics, heat, chemistry, and others. It has the equivalent of two television screens or cameras (eyes) through which life is visually experienced. The soma has flexible clenching apparatuses (hands) at the end of the upper extremities that allow it to grab and hold many different kinds of objects in many positions. Two other extremities, the lower ones, are used for locomotion. They utilize a synchronized alternating motion that causes the bottom of them to push off the ground for advancing, taking advantage of traction. Following the same logic, it is observed that the soma has many other features that enhance its effectiveness in the physical dimension.

Energosoma

The *energosoma* is the energy body. In many instances, the term *holochakra*, which means "the set or collection of chakras," is used. The energosoma is also known as the energetic or etheric body. *Chakra* is a Sanskrit word that literally means "wheel." A chakra is a vortex, a center for processing energy (or bioenergy). The energosoma is a body that surrounds the physical body entirely and extends an inch or two outward beyond the skin. It is not so difficult to see the energosoma with the naked eye,[46] although most people are unable to do so. However, we can all develop our capacity to see the energosoma through bioenergetic exercises, which will be discussed in later chapters.

The energosoma has two main functions. The first is to vitalize the physical body. The energosoma is responsible for physical activity and vigor.[47] For instance, the good health of the energosoma accounts for our general well-being; we feel more confident and full of life and our memory and overall mood are at their best. Of course, the contrary is also true. People who do not have a healthy energosoma due to energetic blockages and imbalances suffer from a generalized lack of motivation and are often without energy (life fuel) to do what they desire.

The second function of the energosoma is to link the soma (the physical body) with the body we use during our OBEs, the psychosoma (emotional or astral body). This linkage is obviously related to the capacity to have projections of the consciousness. If our energosoma is more flexible, free flowing, and loose, then disconnecting from the soma with lucidity is easier. On the other hand, if our energies are more rigid and stagnated, this will create an obstacle for us leaving the body. Therefore, the flexibility of our energies (or lack thereof) is *one of the most important factors* in terms of leaving the body. We may know and practice several techniques for projecting, but if we do not care for or nurture our energosoma (through multiple daily energetic exercises, for example), then leaving the body will be much more difficult, regardless of the projective technique we apply.

Since only a minority of individuals experience lucid projections, it leads us to wonder why most people's energies are so rigid. Let us use an analogy from the physical body to explain this. Imagine a person who spends four or five weeks in a cast because a bone is fractured, such as a wrist. When the cast is removed, the person is unable to move their hand because of lack of use and a certain level of muscular atrophy. Usually the arm is thinner and it takes some days, weeks, or months—depending on the severity of the case—of exercise (therapy) before the full range of movement is regained.

Let us apply this analogy to the energetic body. It is clear that every human being has an energosoma, yet only a very small percentage of the population "exercise" their energies in a conscious and deliberate fashion. The energosoma, similar to any muscle of the physical body, needs to be exercised in order to remain in good shape. Most individuals have their energies untrained, rusty, because in general they were not educated in this regard. Unfortunately, this lack of information regarding our bioenergetic nature applies to the vast majority of the population, from illiterate individuals to Nobel Prize winners.

The energosoma is the only body that does not "carry" the consciousness.[48] In other words, it does not serve as a "seat of the consciousness." We cannot have a lucid projection with the energosoma, in which we leave behind the rest of the bodies inactive. The energosoma (energetic body) works more like a link that connects the psychosoma (emotional body) to the soma (physical body). When the physical body deactivates, or dies, this connection is ruptured. The energies of the energosoma that stayed with the physical body are then liberated and dispersed. With every new physical life (rebirth), energies of a new energosoma are formed, which allows for yet another new attachment of the consciousness to the new physical body.

It seems that each cell of the physical body has an energetic connection with the respective area in the psychosoma. During a projection of the consciousness, a portion of the energosoma remains, vitalizing the physical body, while another departs with the psychosoma. Figure 1.3 depicts the condition when we are outside of our body. The many energetic connections are now grouped into one long thread, which has been historically and more commonly called the *silver cord*.

The silver cord is responsible for keeping us connected to the soma while projected. It transfers information and energy from the soma to the psychosoma and vice versa. For example, if someone wakes us up by either touching us or making a noise while we are projected, this stimulus to the physical body will cause the silver cord to retract, and we will instantaneously be back inside the physical body.

The silver cord still allows for us to project to great distances from the physical body. In practice, there does not seem to be a limit to how far we can project nor to how much the silver cord will "stretch" in these cases. Thus, we can go very far from the physical body in terms of dimensions—projecting to realities or dimensions extremely distant from the physical one—and also go very far in terms of distance— projecting into deep outer space (exoprojections)[49] to seemingly endless physical distances.

The area where the silver cord attaches to the soma has been the source of much dispute throughout time. In many cases the perception is distorted depending on the position of the physical body when separating from it. If we leave the body by floating upward, we may conclude that the silver cord attaches to the solar plexus; if we leave through our feet, we may think it attaches to the feet; if the disconnection is through the head, we may conclude that this is the area of attachment. However, all indications are that the silver cord is attached to the center of the physical head.

Beyond this, while lucid outside the body, we can actually reach back and feel our silver cord attached to the back of the psychosoma's head.[50] When seen extraphysically, it looks like a silvery, shiny connection, which gave rise to its name.

Psychosoma

When we leave the body, we realize that we are using another vehicle, or "body." In some projections we can see our immobile physical body lying in bed, while at the same time we realize that we are using a subtler body that looks identical to the physical one. This second body, in which we have the great majority of our projections, is called the *psychosoma*.

The psychosoma is the most technical name for this body, though synonyms have been used such as emotional body, astral body, double, and many more. Unlike the energosoma, the psychosoma does carry the consciousness. In this sense, we can have projections with the psychosoma, while leaving the physical body inactive.

In general, the psychosoma is very light, and as a result of this, one of the first sensations we experience as we disconnect with it from the physical body is a lack of weight, which is a very pleasant feeling. Since the psychosoma does not have organs like the physical body does, it does not necessarily feel cold or heat; it does not need to eat, drink, or have any physiological necessities. As a matter of fact, one of the most interesting sensations while projected is a lack of breathing. It is interesting to fully realize how much work is required simply to physically breathe. We become aware of this once we have a lucid projection.

The number of OBE accounts today throughout the world is enormous. Dean Shiels, in his anthropological studies, was able to determine that out of fifty-four different cultures from which he obtained information, forty-eight were aware of extraphysical reality.[51] Robert Crookall, in his books, especially in *Lucid Projections*, compiled 838 accounts of out-of-body experiences.[52] Trivellato and Alegretti, in an online OBE survey, amassed over 3,000 responses from dozens of countries.[53] These are but a few examples of the many sources available. Combining all the historical data from accounts from decades and even centuries ago[54] with so many contemporary case studies, we arrive at the conclusion that the psychosoma is a real, objective body independent from the soma, or physical body.

Note that during a projection when we encounter a friend or relative who has passed away, what we see is that individual's psychosoma. Even though that individual already lost his or her physical body, the psychosoma is able to support itself without any need for the soma.

Mentalsoma

The fourth body used by the consciousness is called the *mentalsoma*. It is the most sophisticated and complex body of the consciousness. While in the mentalsoma, we enjoy a level of lucidity and clarity that is unattainable in the psychosoma or soma. In other words, in a projection with the mentalsoma, we are able to reach our highest level of awareness.

The mentalsoma has no defined shape,[55] no limbs, no trunk, nor a head. While manifesting with the mentalsoma, we can say as an example that the consciousness is like a point of lucidity or awareness that can go anywhere. However, the fact is that the mentalsoma is not even a point and does not look like one.

Mentalsomatic projections have been widely reported, even though they are much rarer than psychosomatic projections. Several synonyms have been used to refer to this type of experience. Certain Eastern philosophies describe it as reaching the state of *nirvana*, *samadhi*, or *satori* (which are technically different experiences, yet all fall under the same umbrella of mentalsomatic expansion). Other circles use expressions, among others, like "expansion of the consciousness," "being one with the universe," "oceanic consciousness," "union-*mystica*," and "cosmoconsciousness."[56]

The connection between the psychosoma and the mentalsoma is called the golden cord. It receives the name of golden cord simply to maintain the parallelism with the silver cord—since it is neither a cord nor golden. The golden cord, much like the mentalsoma, is not seen, yet its connecting effects are felt. There is not much information available on the golden cord, which at this point makes it very difficult to understand.

It is important to clarify that certain philosophies report more than four bodies. Sometimes this is the result of classifying the bodies in a different fashion, and also because many of these "different" bodies are actually the same. Depending on the condition of the different bodies, their density, and the individual's level of awareness, these vehicles can be in quite different states, which can be mistaken sometimes for different bodies—an error in appreciation and interpretation. An analogy would be to say that the physical body, when healthy and when ill, is actually two different bodies. Though these states are certainly different, they continue being two different conditions of only *one* body. In other instances the mistake is due to confusion with different paranormal phenomena, namely extraphysical multiplicity.[57] Extraphysical multiplicity occurs in the rare case when consciousnesses create copies of their vehicles of manifestation through their energies. This process is normally unconscious.

To summarize, the holosoma is therefore composed of up to four bodies. Three of these—the soma, psychosoma, and mentalsoma—are "carriers" of the consciousness. The upcoming chapters will provide you with greater information with regard to our holosoma.

Basic States of Consciousness

Depending on the number of bodies that it is using at any single moment in time, the consciousness can be classified into three different basic states:[58]

- Intraphysical consciousness
- Extraphysical consciousness
- Projected

The *intraphysical consciousness* is the condition we are in right now within the physical dimension. Thus, we are in control of all four bodies, which are in an aligned, coinciding, or connected state—basically one "inside" the other. This is the common physical, ordinary waking state.

An *extraphysical consciousness* no longer has a physical body. Before being born, we were extraphysical consciousnesses; after biological death, we will again return to that state. Extraphysical consciousnesses are in the intermissive period, the phase between physical lives. Thus, after discarding the physical body, the extraphysical consciousness manifests with either three (energosoma, psychosoma, and mentalsoma) or two (psychosoma and mentalsoma) bodies. Spirit guides are extraphysical consciousnesses as well.

The third basic state is the *projected* state. Both intraphysical and extraphysical consciousnesses enjoy the more temporary state of being projected. An intraphysical consciousness can be projected through either the psychosoma or the mentalsoma, but will come back to its physical body. The extraphysical consciousness can be projected only through the mentalsoma, and will later return to its psychosoma.

Is It Dangerous to Have an OBE?

Let us finish this chapter by addressing the issue of risk in producing OBEs. Many individuals initially ask whether having an OBE is dangerous. This is an understandable question that should be asked any time we are dealing with anything that is new to us. The general consensus is *no*, it is *not* dangerous.[59] However, let us see why this is so.

Many things are said about the supposed dangers of leaving the body. Some of these ideas are mentioned informally and others are even written in books. In general, most of these ideas are mentioned by people with very little experience with and relatively little information about OBEs. Additionally, some of these ideas arose in the

Middle Ages among some mystical groups with the intention of using fear as a means of maintaining the hierarchy within the group. The most common unfounded reasons that are mentioned for why individuals should not leave their body are the following:

1. You may get lost.

   Answer: Even though sometimes you may not know where you are, you will *always* be able to come back to the body, simply by thinking of it.

2. You may not be able to come back.

   Answer: This fear is probably spurred in most cases by the projective catalepsy sensation—sleep paralysis—that individuals sometimes feel as they are waking up (or coming back to their body). It is a condition in which we are not able to move the physical body, and it does not obey our commands. This condition commonly produces panic in the person. This specific sensation will be discussed in chapter 3. However, the person is able to come back, and the projective catalepsy lasts normally no more than several seconds. Projectors with some experience know that the problem is not returning to the body—since we always do return, commonly and unfortunately even before we would like to. The problem is leaving the body with awareness more often.

3. Somebody might come and cut the silver cord, which would produce the biological death.

   Answer: Nobody can come and cut your cord; the silver cord is not a weak connection and cannot be cut. Though it is called the silver cord, it is not an actual cord. It it not like a wire that can be cut in two with some type of "extraphysical scissors." It is more like a magnetic-energetic connection that, just like the psychosoma, can go through all kinds of physical objects, and likewise all kinds of objects can go through it.

4. If somebody wakes you up while you are projected, the silver cord will be severed.

   Answer: The cord will not be severed by any physical or extraphysical activity that happens to bring you back into your body. Even if the physical stimulus is forceful—like a phone ringing in your ear, a large dog jumping on top of you, or a loud bang close to your bedroom—you will be back in your body, and the cord will not sever.

5. Someone might trap you outside and you might not be able to come back.

   Answer: Just as in the previous example, this is also not possible. By simply willing or wanting to come back to the body, the psychosoma will instantly snap back into it.

6. While outside the body, somebody else may come into your body, and once you return you will find your body already "in use."

   Answer: As we are outside the body, the energosoma "stretches" into two, and some of this energy stays with the physical body. Any stimulus, whether intraphysical or extraphysical, will immediately cause the psychosoma to return. While projected, the physical body is empty of consciousness, but all of its perceptions are still active and will advise accordingly. Thus, being more explicit, OBEs do not cause people to be possessed or to experience any type of intrusion.[60]

7. While projected, we may encounter individuals who can harm us.

   Answer: This point will be addressed in detail in chapter 5, and we will see then as well that these outside-the-body worries are unfounded.

8. It may be dangerous to get close to power lines or get hit by lightning, or encounter some other kind of danger.

   Answer: The psychosoma is invulnerable and cannot be destroyed, and we will discover that these situations are also not harmful.

9. After a projection, we may feel exhausted.

   Answer: We will also see that after an OBE, we are usually not tired. On the contrary, because the physical body is resting during a projection and because of the energies absorbed during the OBE, we are usually much more rested.[61]

As already mentioned, when we experience an OBE, the energosoma divides into two and alerts us of any intraphysical stimulus that may occur while we are projected. In this sense, the physical body stays empty (the consciousness is not there) but is not unguarded. The vast majority of projectors, after gaining some experience, report that most fears about OBEs and the process of disconnecting are unfounded.[62]

The OBE is similar to leaving our house to go run errands. Like any physical activity that we may perform, having an OBE is not absolutely and unequivocally safe, just as leaving our house also is not absolutely and unequivocally safe. However, to put things in perspective, we must remember that we already separate from the body every night as we sleep. Therefore, if leaving the body was dangerous, sleeping would be dangerous too. We realize in practice that sleeping is probably the safest activity we perform in our lives. Having a lucid OBE is actually *safer than sleeping*, because while we sleep we are unconscious, and during a lucid OBE we are aware.[63]

Furthermore, as will be better explained later on, whenever we produce OBEs, depending on several variable factors, there is a helper or spirit guide with us the vast majority of the time[64]—even if in many instances this is not perceived.

Thus, it can be deduced that the OBE is a very safe activity, and we will see in chapter 3 that the psychosoma is, in fact, invulnerable. Nothing can harm it, and from all the available evidence, it is also seen that we, as consciousnesses, are immortal. Projectors with a fair amount of experience know how positive and life-enriching these experiences are, and I, here and now, through this book, invite you to confirm this for yourself.

Summary of Key Chapter Points

- The out-of-body experience (OBE) is a real circumstance in which we, while our physical body sleeps, go out of our physical body and experience this physical reality or other dimensions.

- Everybody disconnects from their physical body every night—though in the great majority of cases, individuals are unaware of this.

- Projections can be classified into three types: spontaneous (the most common), forced (e.g., the near-death experience), and those naturally provoked at will.

- The two factors needed in order to take full advantage of projections are (1) to be aware while outside the body, and (2) to remember the experience once we wake up.

- Conscious projections are very different from dreams (even lucid dreams) because they are real and verifiable and we have all of our mental faculties active.

- Projectiology is the science that studies OBEs and bioenergies.

- Conscientiology is the science that studies the consciousness—and uses the OBE and bioenergies as tools for accomplishing this.

- Projectiology and conscientiology are based on the scientific methodology of experimentation, refutation, and consensus.

- The consciousness is the object of study as well as the term used for our essence, or the intelligent principle that we are, independent of the physical body.

- The consciential paradigm studies the interactions and relations between matter, energy, and the consciousness. It is the paradigm used by projectiology and conscientiology.

- The consciousness can manifest itself at any given moment (1) as an intraphysical consciousness, (2) as an extraphysical consciousness, or (3) in the more temporary condition of a projected consciousness.

- The consciousness uses four bodies for manifestation: the soma (physical body), energosoma (energetic body), psychosoma (emotional body), and mentalsoma (intellectual body).

- The OBE is a very safe activity—even safer than sleeping.

Chapter Notes

1. Trivellato and Alegretti, 1999, p. 107. For instance, in a three-year online survey on OBEs, out of over 6,000 people, 95 percent of individuals that had out-of-body experiences responded that they believed these experiences are positive. By 2009, this survey had grown to well over 10,000 respondents.
2. *Extra-* (prefix) = outside, beyond. Thus, extraphysical pertains to nonphysical, beyond the physical or outside the physical.
3. Denning and Phillips, 1992, p. 41; and Vieira, 2002, p. 427.
4. *Consciential* (adjective) = pertaining to the consciousness (essence) or soul.
5. Monroe, 1977, pp. 203–4; Vieira, 2002, pp. 426, 821.
6. Vieira, 2002, p. 212.
7. Ibid., p. 213.
8. Ibid., p. 808.
9. Kircher, 2002, p. 9.
10. Monroe, 1977, p. 8.
11. Atwater, 2000, pp. 100–108; Atwater, 2002, p. 14; and Lutfi, 2006, p. 43.
12. Vieira, *Conscientiology Themes*, 1997, p. 14; Vieira, 2002, p. 91; and Mitchell, 1990, p. 138.
13. Alegretti, 2004, pp. 49, 154; and Vieira, 2002, pp. 887–92, 893.
14. Rampa, 1995, pp. 19–21.
15. Alegretti, 2004, p. 49.
16. Vugman, 1999, p. 95.
17. Vieira, 2002, p. 810.
18. *Lucidity* and *awareness* are used as synonyms.

19. *Intra-* (prefix) = within, inside. Thus, intraphysical means inside the physical reality.
20. Vieira, 2002, pp. 214, 964.
21. Thiago, 1999, p. 73.
22. LaBerge and Rheingold, 1992, p. 11.
23. Dries, 2006, p. 57; Rogo, 1986, pp. 130–49; Krippner, 2002, p. 67; Green, 2002, p. 131; Mitchell, 1990, p. 18; and Stack, 1988, p. 93.
24. Medeiros and Sousa, 2002, pp. 111–29; Trivellato and Alegretti, 2002, pp. 153–87; and Guidini, 2000, p. 152.
25. Meira, 2006, p. 249.
26. These terms will be explained in the chapters ahead.
27. Freire, Pinheiro, and Wojslaw, 2006, pp. 27–38.
28. Vieira, 2002, pp. 57–82, 97–98.
29. Plato, 1921–25, pp. 614–21.
30. Vieira, *700*, 1994, p. 68.
31. Ibid., pp. 81–102.
32. Ibid., p. 165.
33. Fernandes, 1998, p. 143.
34. "The consciousness" (intelligent principle, essence) is asexual, meaning it does not have any sex or gender associated with it. The physical body is the only vehicle of the consciousness that has a gender. Therefore, the term "the consciousness" will be referred to grammatically as "it" and not as "he" or "she." The same principle applies to its corresponding pronouns (its). In addition, whenever there is reference to more than one consciousness, the plural form "consciousnesses" will be used. Also, note the difference in "the consciousness" as opposed to "consciousness"—without the article. When used without the article, it refers to the state of being aware (common use), and the article "the" is used to signify the being, the essence, or the individual; in other words, us.
35. Alegretti, 2004, p. 70.
36. Minero, 2003, p. 131.
37. Musskopf, 1998, p. 54.
38. Vieira, 2002, pp. 22–32.
39. Monroe, 1977, p. 8.
40. Lima, 1999, p. 231.
41. Alegretti, 2004, pp. 46–48.
42. Daou, 2005, p. 17; Ouspensky, 1980, p. 19; and Vieira, 2002, p. 33.
43. Many new words (neologisms) in conscientiology, which will be seen later, make use of the prefix *holo-*, such as holochakra, holokarma, holomemory, and others.
44. Vieira, 2002, p. 239.
45. Ibid., p. 40.
46. Every physical sense has a certain range of perception. The energies of the energosoma are fairly dense and lie just beyond the human body's range of visual perception. Therefore, by developing our capacity a little, we can start to see the energosoma. The energosoma should not be confused with what people call the aura.
47. Bruce, 1999, p. 36.

48. Vieira, 2002, p. 259.

49. Dries, 2006, pp. 101–3.

50. Felsky, 2000, p. 55.

51. Vieira 2002, pp. 96–97.

52. Vieira 2002, p. 950; Crookall, 1980; and Crookall, 1992.

53. Trivellato and Alegretti, 1999, p. 107.

54. Fox, 1962; and Swedenborg, 1971.

55. Its shape is not a cloud as is shown in figure 1.3. The cloud is just a graphical representation.

56. Vieira, 2002, pp. 133, 176, 475, 930.

57. Ibid., p. 624.

58. Ibid., p. 104.

59. Vieira, *Projections*, 2007, p. 157.

60. Muldoon and Carrington, 1992, p. 296.

61. Peterson, 1997, p. 161.

62. Buhlman, 1996, p. 228; Bruce, 1999, p. 46; Gutierrez, 1999, pp. 53–57; Monroe, 1977, p. 9; Peterson, 1997, p. 76; and Vieira, *Projections*, 2007, p. 64.

63. Vieira, 2002, p. 214.

64. Buhlman, 1996, p. 41; and Vieira, 2002, p. 688.

Bioenergy

Energy is a term that is used widely and in the most varied of fashions. Yet the question can be directly asked: What is energy? A grandmother might say, "My grandson has a lot of energy," while a government official report might read, "Changing our usual sources of energy." Certainly they are using the same word—energy—and even though they are referring to different things, there is an underlying idea that is identical to both.

Energy, to explain it in a simple manner, can be understood as *activity, functioning*. The classical definition from physics states that "energy is the capacity of a system to do work." In general terms, we can think of energy as the "fuel" that makes all systems run and be active.

Energy comes in many forms and can be applied from mechanical systems, like cars; as well as electrical systems, like a lamp; to biological systems, like our body; and several others.

Bioenergy is a central topic in projectiology and conscientiology, and is one of the main factors for controlling lucid projections.[1] *The OBE in essence can simply be classified as an energetic phenomenon.* It must be kept in mind that everything we see, perceive, touch, process, and manipulate is energy, or a derivative of it (in the physical dimension, this is mainly mass or matter). In other words, the bodies, or vehicles of manifestation, of the consciousness are made up of either energy or matter.[2] As a result, the tools we use for processing energy are also tools that are "made" of energy. The importance of understanding bioenergy is relevant not only to the process of disconnecting from the physical body but also because the mechanisms of perception and interaction outside the body are based on energy as well.

The existence of bioenergy (sometimes simply called energy), just like that of lucid projections, has been reported in many cultures throughout history. A few synonyms were already given in chapter 1. Yet, in order to demonstrate the fact that other cultures knew about this type of energy, here is a list of twenty-five common names for bioenergy, chosen from hundreds of synonyms that are and have been used:[3]

1. Akasha (Hindus)

2. *Anima mundi* (Avicenna)

3. Animal magnetism (Franz Anton Mesmer)

4. *Arquea* (Paracelsus)

5. Astral light (H. P. Blavatsky)

6. Bioflux

7. Bioplasm (V. S. Grischenko)

8. Bioplasmic energy (Soviet scientists)

9. Chi or ki (Acupuncturists)

10. Cosmic fluid

11. Ectoplasm (Charles R. Richet)

12. Gestaltung (Johann Wolfgang von Goethe)

13. Kundalini (Yogis, India)

14. Libido (Sigmund Freud)

15. Noetic energy (Charles Musès)

16. *Nous* (Plato)

17. Orgone (Wilhelm Reich)

18. Personal magnetism

19. Psychotronic energy (Robert Pavlita)

20. Prana (Yogis, India)

21. Tao

22. Third force (Robert Monroe)

23. Vital energy (Ancient Chinese)

24. Vital fluid (Allan Kardec)

25. Yesod (Kabbalists)

Bioenergy is a specific type of energy, very different from more physical types of energy that we might be more familiar with, such as electricity. Bioenergy is the energy used by the energosoma (energetic body). In order to understand all the effects of bioenergy, we must begin by studying the types of bioenergies that exist, the energetic manifestations of the consciousness, and the energetic body—the energosoma. In order for you to begin having energetic experiences, we will finish this chapter by discussing exercises for developing the control of energies and starting to produce lucid projections.

This chapter contains several examples of the interactions of the bioenergies for two reasons: to give a good idea of the implications and breadth of the concepts that will be explained, and to help readers become more aware of all the personal energetic interactions and situations in which we are already involved, whether consciously or unconsciously.

Some individuals already produce actual psychic or paranormal experiences. Yet, for most individuals, the mechanism behind these experiences is unknown. Thus, the concept of bioenergy is essential and very central to understanding lucid projections and all other psychic and paranormal experiences.

Types of Bioenergy

Bioenergy can be classified or divided into two very broad categories: immanent energy (IE) and consciential energy (CE).

Immanent energy (IE)[4] is energy that is inherent in nature.

Sources of immanent energy (IE) include earth, air, sun, water, and others. IE is energy that has not been *processed*, or does not have any information imprinted on it. It is a type of energy that can be thought of as clean, pure, and untouched. More specifically, energy that comes from the ground is called geoenergy; energy that comes from water is called hydroenergy; energy from the air is called aeroenergy; from outer space is called cosmoenergy; and from the sun (and other stars) is called helioenergy. IE seems to permeate the entire universe.

Many Hindu traditions have various breathing exercises that work with what they call *prana*. This is a specific kind of IE, namely aeroenergy, or energy that comes from the air.

Consciential energy (CE)[5] is energy that has information, and has therefore already been processed by a consciousness.

Individual consciousnesses transform immanent energy into consciential energy by adding information to it. Everything that we are, think, and feel, as well as our motivations, intentions, sensations, moods, desires, actions, and other aspects, are manifested in our consciential energies (CEs). Once we, as consciousnesses, absorb IE, we process it by adding information about us and transforming it into CE.

Every consciousness has consciential energy, and this CE, in turn, reflects everything about the consciousness. A person's energetic information (thoughts, feelings, sensations, ideas, intentions, and so forth) can be perceived by others. It is, however, easier to perceive energetic information outside the body than inside the body. Therefore, a projector's CE is readily perceivable by anybody who has some extraphysical awareness. The intention of the individual is clearly noticeable extraphysically and is relatively easy to perceive. CEs act as the projector's "business card" outside the body.[6]

Intraphysically, however, the person can also learn to perceive energy and its information with greater awareness. Most people already perceive energies without realizing it. Here are some examples of this:

1. Have you ever had an intuition? This is one result of consciential energy (CE). We can be at work in the middle of the afternoon. All of a sudden we start thinking about a relative. At that moment the phone rings and we know before picking up the handset, "It's my mother." We pick up the phone and verify that it is so.

2. Two employees are arguing in an office. Finally, they calm down and leave the room. A customer walks in and before seeing any of them thinks, "I can feel the tension in the air." This "tension" is the energetic information, or CE, that was manifested by both individuals prior to the customer walking in.

3. A woman gets a new hairdo. A friend recognizes the new style and comes to compliment her. The friend says, "I love your hairstyle." However, the woman is left with a *sensation* that her friend was not being honest, even though there was nothing in her gestures, body posture, facial expression, or words that implied she did not like it. The sensation that the friend was not honest, nonetheless, is there. When she gets home, her sister asks what that specific friend said about her hairstyle. She concludes, "My friend really did not like it." This conclusion came from the *sensation, impression,* or *something* that she got from her friend. Later on, she confirms this with somebody else who tells her that her friend gave the compliment to be polite.

(continued)

4. When buying a car, a salesperson tells the buyer, "The best price is $18,000." The buyer answers, "I can pay only $15,000." Both of them *have the impression* that the other can relax their position more. Even though both are holding their physical position firm, they are both *feeling* energy and making decisions based on it. More than likely, neither of them has ever heard of CE.

5. A man dresses in a certain shirt and pants and goes to work. He thinks he has done a good job of combining the right colors for his outfit. As he arrives at work, he starts feeling uncomfortable. No one says anything, but the man can *feel* that everybody is thinking that his clothes do not match. Initially not sure of this feeling, he later confirms it by overhearing two coworker's commenting on his color blindness.

Possible examples of energetic perception are endless. This will become even clearer as we continue our discussions, but let us try to qualify this further.

Though these perceptions are nonphysical, here are some questions that can help us intraphysically to be more aware of the energetic information that is "floating" everywhere:

- When talking to a person, have you ever felt as if they were *interested* in you?
- Have you ever felt that a person was lying to you, or that they did not mean what they were saying?
- Have you ever felt something was not right or something was going to happen when you entered a specific place?
- Have you ever developed a headache when you were near a specific person or in a specific locale or situation?
- After coming in contact with somebody or something, have you ever felt, for no apparent reason, very tired or in a bad mood, or felt a pressure or pain in the back of your neck or on your forehead, or you began yawning?
- Have you ever slept in a hotel room in which you experienced strange dreams and thoughts at night?

People describe how they sometimes feel "drained" when they come into contact with something or somebody. In some cases there is no need for this contact to be extensive. A person may talk on the phone with somebody for thirty seconds and feel afterward like they need to take a nap, or they feel sluggish, drained, or something similar. In certain cases, even sensitive physical equipment (such as computers) can be affected by energies.[7]

Thosene

Let us describe these energetic perceptions in even more detail by introducing the concept of a *thosene*. The word thosene is made up of three other words or ideas:

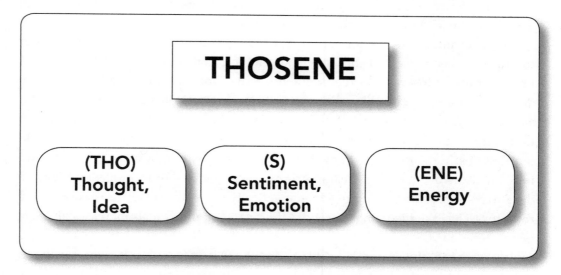

Figure 2.1: Thosene

The "THO" in thosene comes from ***tho**ughts* (or ideas), the "S" comes from ***s**entiments* (or emotions), and the "ENE" from *en**e**rgy* (figure 2.1).[8] Consciential energies (CEs) are manifested in thosenes. At our current evolutionary level, consciousnesses are always manifesting these three units together: thoughts, emotions, and energy. It is observed that we cannot produce a pure emotion without having a thought associated with it and without using energies for its production. The same reasoning applies to the other two elements.

A *thosene* is the unit of manifestation of the consciousness.[9]

Consciousnesses are producing energetic information, CEs, or thosenes, all the time. This is a nonstop, continuous process. In popular circles, laypeople or psychics may say that they are reading the aura of another person. Technically speaking, we can describe this process as the psychic being able to *feel* the thosenes of another person and to decode them. It is observed from this and from the previous examples that this information is very specific. The capacity of the person to feel energy will determine the level of detail and specificity perceived.

Let us examine further some previous examples of energy perception in order to explain other aspects of thosenes. In example 1, when our mother thinks about us, she emits a thosene. If at that moment we are more sensitive, we will be able to decode the thosene and will realize what our mother actually wants. Most individuals are unable to feel this level of detail, and many times we just feel the other person thinking about us without knowing the actual intention or reason that they are thinking about us. Yet, outside the body this mechanism is extremely clear. When the two individuals involved have a greater affinity or closeness—for example, mother and daughter—then it is easier for one to energetically access the other, and easier for the receptor to feel the incoming thosene. Affinity among individuals increases all energetic interactions.

In example 2, the customer is able to feel the prior argument. It is interesting to note that energies of a dispute, argument, or any situation involving great emotion are always easier to feel. They are closer to the physical reality, "denser," more palpable and obvious, and this is why the customer feels it.

Even though we always manifest a full thosene (all three components), the intensity of each one of the components can be increased or diminished. For example, a pattern of energies can be manifested in the following fashions:

THOsene
tho**S**ene
thos**ENE**

In the first case, the thosene manifested (or sent out) carries a greater emphasis or weight on the "THO" element. This implies an intellectual, more mental manifestation. An example of this is when we pick up a textbook on science or philosophy. As we read it, we are manifesting energy—many thosenes. Yet, because of the nature of this specific activity, the energy is not primarily emotional. The intellectual aspect of the manifestation is enhanced compared to the other two elements. So, as the graphical representation shows, the "THO" element is emphasized while the "S" and "ENE" elements are not.

In the second case, it is the sentimental, emotional[10] aspect that carries more weight. This occurs, for example, when we decide to watch a soap opera or read a romance novel. In these cases the drama is clear, meaning there is nothing too complex to be understood—it is not a heavy intellectual endeavor. The "THO" aspect is thus diminished. However, since we are emotionally involved in the story, we are manifesting a thosene with greater emphasis on "S", the emotional aspect.

In the third case, the energy, "ENE," is the element emphasized. This occurs when, for example, the person is jogging, swimming, or doing anything where they are expending a lot of energy. Notice that the person might be manifesting patterns with a lot of energy and the other two aspects are both diminished, or it can also be the case that two elements of the thosenes are emphasized while the other is not. An example of this would be being worried about something (sentiment, "S") while we jog (energy, "ENE").

Intellectual energy, with a greater emphasis on the "THO" aspect, is more balanced and subtle (more difficult to perceive). Emotional energy, with a greater emphasis on the "S" aspect, is denser (easier to perceive) and less stable. Many examples of this will be seen in the subsequent pages and chapters of this book. OBEs also confirm this condition, as becoming more emotional leads to a loss of lucidity and a prompt return to the body. This extraphysical condition is no different from physical situations—it is simply more obvious extraphysically. Intraphysically, when individuals lose their emotional control, they say and do things that they did not intend; they "lose their head" (stability) as a result of the emotional outburst.

It is interesting to point out that this occurs equally both with "negative" emotions and with "benign" emotions. Individuals lose their lucidity, control, or self-management because they have an attack of anger, rage, desperation, or other "negative" emotion. The same effect is observed when individuals become too happy or euphoric ("benign" emotions).

Holothosene

In practice, once we start leaving our body, the concept of energetic information—thosenes—will become increasingly clear. People manifest thosenes all of the time. Furthermore, they have been manifesting thosenes for an unknown, even longer time as a consciousness. The consciousness manifested thosenes before this physical life, during the previous one, and in the one before that, and so on. If all those thosenes were averaged out, they would yield what is called a *holothosene*.[11]

A consciousness manifests a thosene: a single "packet" of energy with information, a single unit of CE. Yet, a consciousness is defined by its holothosene: the collection, set, accumulation, and/or average of all these thosenes.

  A *holothosene* is the collection of thosenes, or of energetic information associated with something specific.

Other writers have come close to the idea of holothosene. Jung's idea of the collective unconscious and Robert Monroe's concept of "M-band noise" and "rote" are examples of this.[12]

In order to understand this central idea and all its implications better, let us analyze several cases. *Individual consciousnesses* have holothosenes since they manifest thosenes, which have the tendency to accumulate. Yet, holothosenes are also found in *places*, *objects*, *activities*, *institutions*, and *ideas*.

It is important to keep in mind that holothosenes in general *are clearly felt outside the body*. The manner in which individuals acquire information extraphysically is through thosenes and holothosenes. So even though most of the following examples are physical examples, the same holothosene will be felt, and with greater clarity, outside the body. Also keep in mind that it is important to discuss holothosenes because they have an *influence on* the flexibility of our energosoma and therefore *our projective ability*. Let us first discuss the different holothosenes found in places.

Places

Houses, buildings, rooms, cities, and other places have holothosenes—even though these constructions do not produce thosenes of their own. Specific holothosenes of places are the product of the thosenes that consciousnesses have manifested there. A house has a holothosene from the family that lives there. It manifests as an average of their energetic information. If this is a family in which the members get along, laugh with each other, try to help each other, and the like, then the holothosene reflects this and is more positive.

1. Let us consider an example (it is negative and extreme, but this will make the idea clear): What are the most common intentions, thoughts, sentiments, and ideas found in a prison? If the holothosene of a prison is a product of the prisoners' thosenes, what are these thosenes? Certainly many answers come to mind, such as revenge, loneliness, aggressiveness, and despair. Now, all of these thosenes accumulate in that place and stay there. Even if all the prisoners are taken out, this holothosene is still felt, meaning holothosenes tend to linger.

2. We go to drop off a present at a friend's house. We simply drop it off, greet the family, and leave. Afterward, we feel tired, start yawning, and have a strong desire to take a nap. What happened here? The holothosene in the house of the friend was not compatible with our individual holothosene. Therefore, because of the incompatibility of the energies and our lack of energetic defense, we suffer an energetic impact or draining. In this case we were not necessarily drained energetically by a person, but by the holothosene of a place.

This type of effect or consequence received from the holothosene is called *holothosenic pressure* or *influence*. Depending on the specific holothosene, its strength, and the quality of the information it contains, this influence can be stronger or weaker, positive or negative. Because of their relative lack of energetic awareness, most individuals do not realize they may be in an unhealthy holothosenic environment or condition.

On the other hand, sometimes individuals even pay to be in that condition! The previous example, of a prison, was labeled as extreme and negative. Yet Alcatraz was a prison and is now a tourist attraction.[13] Tourists go there with a very open attitude, full of energy, and feel drained afterward most of the time because of this. There are cases of individuals who even enter into the cells of inmates so as to "feel" how the prisoner felt. This leads to becoming contaminated, or *intruded*, with the thosenes that were left there.

The energosoma becomes polluted with this unhealthy energy, and this will affect the person. If the energosoma of the person becomes too polluted, the person may develop energetic problems, decompensations, or blockages, which will have repercussions on the health of the physical body and on the person's projective and psychic performance. We will discuss energetic blocks and how to remove them later on.

Let us discuss two characteristics of holothosenes: strength and feedback mechanism. The *strength* of the holothosene in a specific place comes from the amount of energy that has accumulated in that place.[14] This accumulation is, in turn, the result of the number of individuals who manifested that specific holothosene and the amount of time it was manifested (days, weeks, months, years, centuries).

> **EXAMPLE**
> Even a relatively new university, maybe just fifteen years old, in a relatively new city, with 10,000 students, has a well-established holothosene. Yet a university in Europe, maybe 200 years old, with 30,000 students, has a much stronger holothosene. The influence or desire to study, or the influences of the university culture, will be more readily felt at the European university.

Holothosenes present a *feedback mechanism* that makes them grow. As each individual consciousness comes into contact with a specific holothosene, the energy has an influence on the consciousness. This influence in turn makes the individual consciousness start to produce thosenes that are similar to the place's holothosene, and these new thosenes manifested by the individual feed the established energetic information (holothosene) and thus make it stronger. Therefore, unconsciously, individuals tend to reinforce holothosenes as they come into contact with them, since our energetic systems are constantly exchanging energies with the environment.

Here are some questions to consider that can help determine the holothosene of a place:

- What activity was performed here?
- Who lived here before?

We are walking in a nonsmoking airport. As we walk through the corridors, we see areas, sometimes small enclosed rooms, where people are allowed to smoke. We decide to go into one of them. Since we do not smoke, our lungs do not have any smoke in them. Yet with every moment we spend there and with every breath we take inside the smoking room, our lungs start to have a greater content of smoke in them—and this will have an effect on us. We are always exchanging energy with the surroundings, just like we need to exchange air with our environment. The longer we stay in that place, the stronger the influence.

- How old is the place?
- What is the history of the place?
- How many people manifested that specific energetic information?
- Regarding the individuals' activity, what were their desires in realizing such an activity (amount of energy)?
- In the thosenes manifested, what was the predominant emotional or intellectual content (intention of individuals)?
- How balanced are the energies?

Basically, every physical place has a characteristic holothosene. It is therefore important to identify the holothosenic influence of the places where we spend most of our time. Every place can be analyzed. Here are some places, among many, that can be considered:

- What is the holothosene of traffic?
- What is the holothosene of a specific city?
- What is the holothosene at my friend's house?
- What is the holothosene in my office?
- What is the holothosene of a job (as an activity)?
- What is the holothosene of a particular country?

- What is the holothosene of ancient ruins? What were the inhabitants' rituals?
- What is the holothosene of the house/apartment I am moving into?

Unfortunately, because of lack of information, most individuals have not had the opportunity to develop a clear perception of energies. As a result, they are not fully able to identify the effect that the energetic influences (in some cases energetic pollutants) have on them.

As a general tendency, women are more sensitive and open to energetic information than men. However, they also tend to have less control over it and suffer more with this condition. Men, on average, have better control over their energies, but generally they may perceive the subtle activity that is going on around them less. The ideal is to develop both: perception (or sensitivity) and control. Naturally, there are women and men who have both.

We will see at the end of this chapter how holothosenes are changed. Let us now discuss the holothosenes of objects.

Objects

Objects have the most varied kinds of holothosenes. Similar to places, objects acquire the holothosene from the energetic information that consciousnesses around them manifest. They also develop the holothosene from their intended use. A pen will have a different holothosene than a vacuum cleaner. Also, a red pen that is used only to correct students' tests will have a different holothosene than a luxury pen used only to write love letters. The concepts of holothosenic influence, strength, and feedback mechanism apply to objects as well.

Different holothosenes between two objects, or between an object and a place, will interact among themselves until they arrive at an average.[15] In order to explain this, let us imagine that there are two rivers (figure 2.2). One (X) has very clear water, and the other (Y) has muddy water. They two meet in a valley. In situation A, if river X has four times more volume than river Y, then once they mix, the resulting river will be a little muddier than what river X was, but it will not be as noticeable. In situation B, however, if river Y has four times the volume that X does, then the color of the resulting water will be a lighter brown, but not by much.

Objects and places do not have a will of their own; therefore, their interaction is a *passive* one. Neither of them has an "interest" in outweighing the other. So two passive holothosenes that come into contact will average out after some time. The holothosene

An otherwise average couple could have the following experience. A friend of the couple buys an object and gives it to them as a present. The object has negative energies, but it matches the color of the carpet perfectly. Once the object is inside the house, its holothosene starts mixing with the holothosene of the house and starts producing an influence. The husband (an average male) does not feel anything; he is, however, in a bad mood that evening, which he attributes to something else. The wife (an average female) does not know what to do to make her headache go away. She does not understand where it came from, but has had it for days. Their baby, who unfortunately is much more open energetically—more perceptive and with fewer defenses—cries more than usual for some weeks. Their dog also is very restless and will not stop barking. Part of the reason this is occurring is because we tend to choose things based only on physical criteria, like aesthetics—the color of the carpet, in this case—and we are generally unaware of the energies of an object.

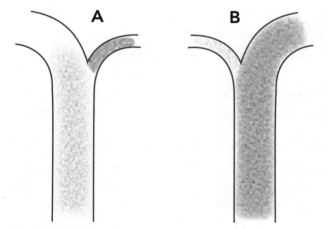

Figure 2.2: Two Rivers Depicting the Interactions of Holothosenes

that is initially the stronger of the two will be mainly responsible for the *new* holothosene of *both* objects (just like the resulting river).

People

The most complex interactions and influences are by far the ones among individuals. People's energies not only have an intention but also carry a will with them and can be focused with greater precision. Even though we can modulate our thosenes to be of a more specific nature, they already have a general characteristic holothosene. Some people have energies that are more assistantial (helping), others are more authoritarian, others more docile, or more pessimistic, and so on. Here are some examples of the effects of energies between people:

> The group at the office is on a lunch break. They are eating in the designated lunch room and some of them are telling jokes. Bill, in particular, seems to know more jokes than the others. Suddenly the boss walks into the room. The boss is concerned about a phone call that he has to make in few minutes, yet he stopped by the kitchen simply to refill his cup with water. Even though everyone knows it is lunchtime and the boss could not have paid less attention to the people who were there or what they were saying or doing, while he is in the room nobody tells any jokes, not even Bill. It is as if the volume of the room has been suddenly lowered. Once the boss leaves, somebody seems to remember another joke and decides to tell it. After that, the volume is raised again and everybody is back to laughing.

What happened to Bill? Why did nobody want to tell jokes while the boss was in the room? What is the influence of the boss's *presence* upon all of them? A typical boss has roles within a company that command action, request work, delegate responsibility, and verify that the work gets done. The thosenes of these roles accumulate and are reflected in the boss's holothosene. Individuals tend to behave in a different fashion toward bosses—even though they may be bosses from other companies. Bosses, through their activities, develop a holothosene of authority. Thus, even when they are not thinking about checking up on people, this is part of the impression that gets transmitted, because the *average*—or the more representative characteristic—of their energies already has this information.

Here is another example:

> It is the grandmother's birthday, so everybody gathers at her house and they simply talk about old events, other relatives, and the like. Most of the jokes are known and repeated, so pretty soon everybody is fairly bored. Yet here comes Uncle Don, who always has a million jokes and makes everybody laugh. He sits in the middle of everyone and then Susan, his sister, immediately tells a joke. One of Susan's daughters then tells a funny story from school. Carol, a cousin, also joins in with another joke after that. Pretty soon, the simple gathering becomes a party. Everybody is laughing and having a good time. Then there is a knock on the door. It is another one of the cousins, Mark. He always seems to be undergoing some personal problem and is having a hard time emotionally. Even before this new problem, Mark was never one to smile too much. He enters the room and congratulates his grandmother. He sits next to her, looking down. Somebody stands to get a drink. Two sisters begin talking quietly in the corner. In a few minutes, the party has diminished in intensity, and now most people are staring at the floor.

What are the effects of Uncle Don and Mark on the rest of the people? Notice that neither of them was the first one to start talking after they sat down, but they had an effect on the environment just the same. What are Don's and Mark's holothosenes? Since they both seem to have more specific and stronger-than-average holothosenes, when they came in, were they influenced by the holothosene of the party, or did their holothosene affect the others? Notice that none of the individuals present at the gathering knew anything about energy nor did they have the conscious intention of affecting anything or anyone.

Which holothosene is going to predominate in a group of people depends on who has the strongest holothosene. Have you ever noticed that in a group of friends there is one who usually decides what the group is going to do? This person has stronger energies—but not necessarily the best ideas or intentions.[16]

In the case where individuals are unaware of energies and therefore passive in their regard to them, the resulting holothosene will follow rules similar to the prior example of the two rivers. So when there is no *energetic awareness* between the parties, the dynamics of holothosenes resemble *osmosis*. Problems can arise when the person with the stronger energy has an unbalanced or less positive holothosene. In this case, that person can energetically drain and/or pollute others and the environment.

An individual in an unbalanced condition "loses" energy and in many cases remains generally devitalized. Energy, however, is everywhere. The problem is not necessarily lack of energy; rather, it is the lack of *equilibrium in the content (information) of the energy.* In other words, the content in the ideas ("THO") and emotions ("S") of the person, which are not balanced, cause this; for example, feeling sad because a relative passed away, feeling worried about being fired at work, being concerned with bills, and so forth.

Even though the problem is not a lack of energy, unbalanced individuals will unconsciously try to find energies to make them balanced. Therefore, these people may drain several people in the process. This can leave others feeling "down."

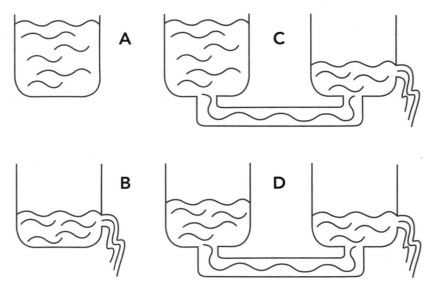

Figure 2.3: Tanks of Water Depicting Holothosenic Capacities and Exchanges

Let us analyze figure 2.3 as a graphical analogy for understanding this clearer. In this figure, individuals and their energetic capacity are represented by tanks of water. A normal, balanced person keeps their level of energies almost at the limit of their "volume," or energetic capacity—this is shown in example A. If the person has certain conflicts, this is the equivalent of having small leaks in the tank, whereby the energies "escape." If the person has more problems or greater issues, more energy will "escape," and the person will feel unmotivated, disinterested, and devitalized (without energy)—example B. Now when this person comes into contact with another, they will establish an energetic connection, which is the equivalent of placing a tube to connect the tanks—example C. Once again, *if there is no awareness* (no stopping valve, no perception of the process) *in the exchange of energies*, then the energy will clearly flow in one direction. One (the person in energetic lack) will "drain" the other person energetically. Unfortunately, the one doing the draining will not take advantage of this energy for their replenishment (example D) because this person has "leaks" through which the energy continues to escape.

This means that an unbalanced person can and will drain somebody else who comes close, and will keep doing so continuously until the person is able to overcome this condition. Typically, individuals overcome a negative condition by simply forgetting, even though this is not the best method. As time passes, they tend to become involved in other things—the routine, for example—and they start paying less attention to the "cause" issue. As they distance themselves from the event, the energetic information that was causing the unbalance is lessened and less prominent in the holothosene of the person. The person starts having fewer leaks in their energosoma.

It is important to point out several aspects of this condition. First of all, the person doing the draining normally does not have the intention of draining. What is happening is simply unknown to them. The one being drained also does not know what is occurring, but afterward may feel uncomfortable. After talking to somebody, individuals sometimes notice that they feel tired, start yawning, need to take a nap, or are in a bad mood, irritated, or have a headache and/or other symptoms. Exercises for effective protection from these occurrences will be discussed later in this chapter.

It is also important to pay attention to the fact that if individuals do not know about the mechanism of energy, then *it is just as easy for them to be drained by others as it is for them to drain somebody else*. Most of us have a difficult time coming to terms with the fact that we might have already drained others on various occasions, which is a common occurrence.

With regard to the dynamics of the holothosenic interactions between individuals, let us explore a different example. Imagine we begin a new job. We have our own personal holothosene, and we are going to start experiencing the holothosene of the new workplace every day. Let us place our holothosene and the one of the new job in a relative scale of holothosenic balance (figure 2.4). The higher the holothosene is on this line in the representation, the better and more positive it is. The lower the holothosene is on this line, the less balanced and lucid the energies are. Our holothosene is represented in situation 1 by line a, and line b represents the holothosene of the group at the new job. The length of the line represents the strength of the group. Therefore, line b is stronger because generally the twenty individuals (line b) that have already been working there are energetically stronger than the capacity of one new employee, in this case, us (line a).

Once we begin to work in this place, the holothosenes start to interact and merge. If there is no energetic knowledge and/or awareness by any of the parties involved, the resultant holothosene will be line c of situation 2. Line c will be the new average of all the energies in the workplace. Line c is also stronger (longer) than line b because it now incorporates the energies from twenty-one employees, meaning our energies are now accounted for.

If we have a better quality of energy than the group, then line c will be better in quality than line b, as shown in situation 2. In this condition, the group "gains" energetic quality with our energy and presence. Likewise, we also "lose" energetic balance in the new job—because we were assimilated by the stronger holothosene as well. All of a sudden, we find ourselves acting in agreement with the behavior of the rest of the employees on the job. For example, we are now making and laughing at jokes that we did not used to find humorous. We have assimilated expressions, phrases, and attitudes that are common to that job. We are now one of them.

In situation 3, the condition is the opposite. The group has a better quality of energy (line b) than we do (line a). The resultant, the new average, when there is no energetic awareness, will be line c. Line c is stronger but has less quality than line b. The twenty employees energetically "lose" with us, and we energetically "gain" with the new job and workplace.

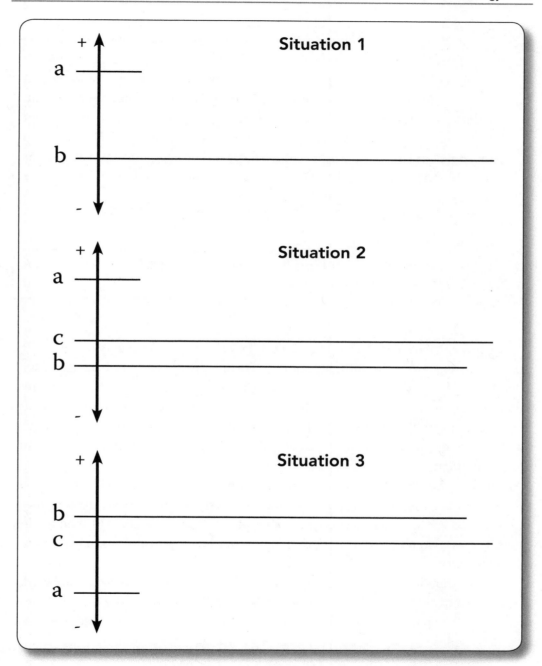

Figure 2.4: Relative Holothosenic Levels

Regarding energies, we always either gain or lose something energetically in all our relations. It is beneficial for us to evaluate from an energetic perspective the relationships we have, understanding that individuals are not always in the same condition. People have a certain holothosene that represents them more accurately, but at any given moment they might be more balanced or more unbalanced than usual. The idea is to set some limits. Relationships that are more or less energetically closer to our holothosene, whether relatively positive or negative, are fine. However, the ones that are too extreme and negative are not ideal.

Ask yourself: What is my holothosene?[17] What effects does my holothosene have on others?

Our holothosene also determines the probability of specific events happening to us or not. Events occur in our lives not because of coincidences but because of synchronicities.[18] They happen due to the convergence of many factors, including how balanced and organized our energy is. Our holothosene already makes us resonate, frequency-wise, with certain activities, people, situations, institutions, and others; it also likewise distances us from other specific activities, people, situations, institutions, and others.[19]

If the holothosenes we manifest and encounter are denser and less balanced, our energosoma is going to reflect this. When our energosoma is denser, its looseness and flexibility are diminished, and it is more difficult to produce OBEs (disconnecting from the body, stretching the energosoma) as well as have perceptions of extraphysical reality and energies.

By understanding holothosenes well, the study of how extraphysical reality works and the practical energetic exercises given later in this book will be clearer. These exercises will help us gain energetic capacity, defense, strength, and flexibility in order to leave the body much more often. The concept of holothosene will be further illustrated and applied as we move along in the book, with other examples and more discussions on the topic.

Energosoma

The *energosoma* (also many times called the *holochakra*) is made up of all the chakras and their energies. It has the functions of connecting the psychosoma to the soma and of vitalizing the physical body. The energosoma surrounds the physical body entirely and is sometimes perceived as a glow around the physical body of the person. Other synonyms have been given to the energosoma across cultures and time periods, including etheric double, bioplasmic body, bardo body, and pranamayakosha.[20]

A chakra is a vortex of energy, a center for processing energies in the energosoma. The chakras are doorways of absorption and exteriorization (sending) of energy. When discussing chakras, most philosophies study the seven main chakras. However, the latest consensus and estimates indicate that we have around 88,000 chakras throughout the body.[21] To give a rough approximation of this, we can think that we have a chakra in each pore of the skin.

Chakras look like a vortex, similar to when the kitchen sink is filled with water and then the plug is removed. As the water drains, it forms a swirl. This swirl is similar to the image of a chakra in the body. The opening of each chakra lies just outside the physical body, on the surface of the energosoma, and its "tail" extends inward, deep into the body.

According to their function, chakras are closely associated with certain energetic processes and activities. They help in processing bioenergy that the physical body (soma) uses for maintaining its physical activities. They also handle the communication between the psychosoma and soma. The following is a brief explanation of the ten most important chakras (figure 2.5), starting with the seven chakras that are better known. You'll find them here with their more proper and technical name, followed by their common name.[22]

- **Sexochakra (base chakra):** This chakra is also called the root or basic chakra. It is located between the legs, on the surface of the energosoma, and faces slightly backward. It is called the root or basic chakra because it feeds the rest of the energosoma.

- **Umbilicochakra (solar plexus chakra):** This chakra is located about half an inch above the belly button. It has a direct relation with the solar plexus and processes energies from more instinctive and organic (related to the body) activities.

- **Splenochakra (spleen chakra):** This chakra is situated in the region of the spleen. It selects and distributes vitalizing energy through the organs of the body. Its vitalizing activity can help individuals leave the body. It has a strong connection to the entire energosoma.

- **Cardiochakra (heart chakra):** This chakra is located in the center of the chest. It deals with the affective processes of the consciousness, such as emotions and romanticism. This chakra is strongly associated with the psychosoma.

- **Laryngochakra (throat chakra):** This chakra acts in the communicability of the consciousness. Singers, for example, normally have this chakra more developed. This chakra is very sensitive to holothosenic pressure. It is positioned in the region of the throat.

- **Frontochakra (third eye chakra):** This chakra is located in the center of the forehead. Also called the third eye, it is strongly related to the capacities of clairvoyance and concentration.

- **Coronochakra (crown chakra):** This chakra is strongly related to rationality, awareness, and more evolved sentiments. It is situated on the top of the head and has a close association with the mentalsoma.

- **Sole chakras (plantochakras):** These chakras are located in the soles of the feet. They absorb geoenergy from the ground, which then runs through the legs and accumulates in the sexochakra. Therefore, they are also associated with fertility and potency.

- **Palm chakras (palmochakras):** These chakras are located in the palms of the hands. The energy they absorb runs through the arms and accumulates in the cardiochakra. Therefore, they are related to sensibility as well.

- **Nuchal chakra:** This chakra lies at the back of the neck. It is associated with mediumship and with the capacity to perceive energies.

The chakras are all interconnected by channels of energy (meridians).[23] They are also more flexible in terms of their position. Sometimes we may feel a chakra as being more toward one side, or a little lower or higher than its usual position. Their more common positions can be seen in figure 2.5.

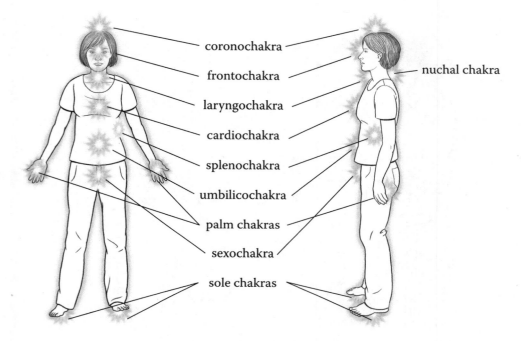

Figure 2.5: Ten Main Chakras

Aside from the chakras that process energy, the entire energetic system is also composed of another element: the aura, or, better yet, the *psychosphere*.[24] The psychosphere is a manifestation of the energosoma. It is much subtler than the energosoma, and it is here where our holothosene is contained. As we move about our day, we are manifesting energies everywhere and leaving many thosenes in the environments wherever we may pass by. In the same fashion, as we exist, there is a greater accumulation of our thosenes in our psychosphere, which in turn forms our holothosene that others are able to feel.

The psychosphere is a very dynamic system, expanding and contracting all the time. It is observed that when we think about someone else, thosenes of that intention reach the other person. In many cases it is like a tentacle of the psychosphere from the emitter that stretches to the psychosphere of the receiver. If the receiver is more energetically perceptive, they can then become aware of this activity.

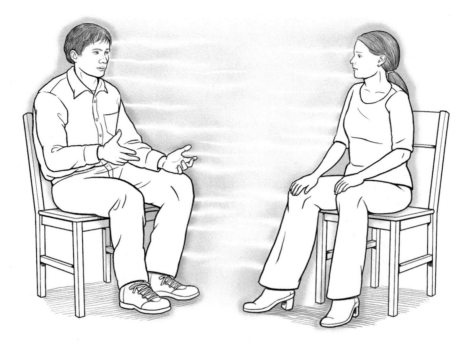

Figure 2.6: Auric Coupling

Auric Coupling and Sympathetic Assimilation

Energy is always exchanged between individuals when they enter into contact with one another, even through a simple look. However, when two individuals focus their energy on each other more, they can establish a condition called *auric coupling*. The auras, or psychospheres, of both individuals fuse together (figure 2.6).

It was previously mentioned that when a person thinks about another, an energetic connection is established with that person. If the interaction continues, the connection grows. The end result is that the energetic exchange rate between them increases. Affinity between the two parties will make this process establish itself faster. If the exchange of energies continues to increase—whether in time, interest, affinity, and other ways—then both parties can arrive at a deeper condition of energetic connection whereby the energosomas of both basically connect directly. This condition is called *sympathetic assimilation*.

> *Sympathetic assimilation* is the condition reached when the amount of energetic information being exchanged between two people is increased; it is an intensification of the auric coupling.[25]

In other words, sympathetic assimilation is a more profound and intense state than auric coupling. In this condition, we can feel what the other person is feeling. Depending on the lucidity, sensitivity, or energetic openness of the individuals, they can even have recollections of a past life with the other individual.

Two individuals who are close and share a strong affinity can be in a condition of a permanent yet dormant sympathetic assimilation, which awakens only when something involving denser energies occurs—like an accident (denser energies). For example, a child may be away at school. The moment that something happens to the child, the mother at home feels it immediately.

In some cases of twins, this may also spontaneously occur—when something happens to one, the other feels it. Sympathetic assimilations sometimes also occur in cases of couples who are expecting a baby. The woman is pregnant, and simultaneously the father is feeling all the symptoms. There are cases in which he feels the kicks of the baby or wakes up in the middle of the night to vomit; in essence, he experiences physiological repercussions from the energetic causes of sympathetic assimilation.

Basic Mobilization of Energies

Now that the manifestation of energy and the structure of the energosoma have been discussed, let us examine exercises that will help us to develop our energetic capacity. Any capacity is developed through training and effort,[26] whether it is an energetic, physical, or mental capacity. There are three basic procedures to mobilize energies:[27]

1. Absorption of energies

2. Exteriorization (externalization) of energies

3. Closed circuit (VELO) to reach the vibrational state (VS)

Let us first discuss each of these procedures in more detail. Then we will focus specifically on how to work with these energies in practice.

Absorption of Energies

Absorption is the reception of energies.[28] The entire energosoma is capable of absorbing energies. People can and do absorb energies through their feet (mainly geoenergy), through their head (upper chakras), through their hands (palm chakras), and so on. One of the applications of absorption is for revitalization purposes.

Our entire mechanism of bodies, or holosoma, already has basic, automatic systems for absorption of energies:

- *Breathing* is the more constant absorption mechanism. When a person inhales air, it is not only oxygen that the person is consuming but also bioenergies—in this case, aeroenergy.

- Another natural absorption mechanism is *sleeping*. While we sleep, all of us disconnect from the soma (body). One of the main reasons for this is that in this disconnected condition, the psychosoma is able to absorb more energy. As a general rule, the more we disconnect from our body, the more energy we absorb. If our energies are in better shape, more flexible, then we will separate more from our soma during sleep. The tendency also is that the more we separate from the body, the easier it is to regain our awareness outside the soma.

- *Eating* is also a source of bioenergies. When a person eats, it is not only the chemical and biological elements that the person is consuming but also the bioenergies in the food. One day the person feels like eating, for example, an apple—not just any other fruit, like a banana or a pear, but specifically an apple. In some cases the person spends some days with the desire to consume an apple. Once the person eats an apple, the craving finally disappears. In many instances this is due to the fact that at some underlying and subconscious level we know that the kind of bioenergy we need is found in an apple. This is also one of the reasons that it is ideal to eat a balanced diet, because then we have all types of energy in our system that we can use when needed.

- We can also learn to absorb energy at will. However, usually as we become progressively better at working with energy or as our entire energosoma gets in better condition, we start needing to absorb less energy. This is due to the good condition or efficiency of the energetic system.

Absorption is a process that is similar to the interaction between an athlete and oxygen. Just like oxygen, energy is available everywhere. In fact, there is more bioenergy than air and we are all immersed in an ocean of air and bioenergy.[29] An athlete or even a person in good physical shape does not need to inhale more air so as to "store" oxygen during normal life. Because the system is in better condition, the system itself will regulate the intake of oxygen, so whenever needed, the system will simply consume more. With time, absorption is the exercise that we do the least, and it is usually done only in specific cases.

Furthermore, it is important to point out that individuals tend to have more energetic blockages because of an excess of inactive, stagnated energy than because of a lack of energy. Similarly, the most common problem for many people nowadays is excess weight and not the opposite. Thus, the key is keeping our energetic system in good shape.

Exteriorization of Energies

Exteriorization is the transmission, externalization, or outbound broadcasting of energy.[30] As with absorption, any area of the energosoma can send out energy. Certain individuals prefer to send out energy mainly through their hands; however, this is not the only way. Exteriorization has two main uses: (1) changing holothosenes and (2) assisting or helping others.

Let us consider the first aspect by using the following situation in order to see a practical example of changing holothosenes. What is the main holothosenic intention that most people have in their bedroom when they go to bed at night? Mainly we want to just sleep, to rest, and many times we want to disconnect from the world and not think about anything at all. Sometimes individuals prefer to see pitch black the entire night and wake up in the morning well rested.

If this has normally been our intention, there is a consequence to this. Normal unconscious sleep has a holothosene that is the opposite of lucidity and counter to the intention of being aware outside the body. In other words, most individuals have already built a holothosene in their bedroom that is working against them being lucid during the night. Some of us might realize that this is the case and thus would like to change this holothosene. For our purposes, we would like to establish a holothosene of greater awareness.

To change this holothosene, we need to start exteriorizing energies in our room. The first effect of exteriorizing energies is that the flow of energies being pumped into the room is going to make the energies that are stuck and accumulated there start to flow. This will renew and refresh the energies of our bedroom.

This effect is similar to spraying water with a hose onto a puddle of stagnated water. As the new water hits the puddle, the stagnated water will start to swirl and be oxygenated. As the water level rises, the water will start to flow out of the puddle. Similarly, we can recycle the entire holothosene in our room. Just as with water, notice that the healthy condition of energy is when it flows, as opposed to remaining stagnant.[31]

The second necessary condition for changing a holothosene is to send out a different pattern of thosenes or energetic information. The way to send out a specific thosene is by generating the condition we want inside of us and then pushing it outward. In other words, if a person wants to send "positive" energies, the person needs to be and feel positive before exteriorizing. Sending energy alone, without thinking about the content, will have a limited effect. The individual determines and is solely responsible for the information within the energy. If the energetic information being sent out is the same as the established holothosene, no change will occur.

Imagination or visualization *does not* have much of an effect on changing holothosenes. Therefore, if we are sad inside but want to send out positive energies, we will not have much success using imagination to send out happiness. At the core, we will either *be* happy or not. While the person remains in a sad state, what the person sends out is sadness. Visualizing the word "positive" or "happy" in any color will have very little effect. The person needs to actually *be* in that condition (in this case feel positive) in order to send it out.

Trying then to change the holothosene of the bedroom and to establish greater awareness, the following practical question can be asked: How does an individual add information of awareness to the energies that are being sent out? The answer is by feeling and being aware, thus generating this internal condition.

You can do a simple exercise right now to test this method. As you read these lines, become aware of all the sounds that your ears perceive. Notice how, as you become aware of this, your attention on your inner condition increases. Now start paying attention to everything that your body is feeling. Can you feel your toes, your hair, elbows, legs, and so forth? Keep these two perceptions in focus and become aware now of all the colors and tones that your eyes are capturing. Again, feel how you are becoming more *aware* of your surroundings, more awake, lucid. Now, also pay attention to everything that you are thinking. Observe all the thoughts that have been coming into your mind and how you deal with them. In deepening this condition, you develop a state of greater awareness. In this state, feeling very aware and alive, you want to send out energies into your room, manifesting flows that are intense, so as to renovate the energetic information.

This method of holothosenic cleansing is extremely effective. It is more effective than any type of object the person might use to clean energy, such as crystals, pyramids, pendulums, talismans, and other psychological crutches. All of these objects have a *limited* effect. *You and your capacities are inherently stronger than any object for cleaning energies.* The energy of objects, when placed in any environment, will start to mix with the energy of the place. Within hours, days, or maybe a couple of weeks, depending on the strength of the energy, the object's energy will have already averaged out with the energy of the environment—thus, the effect of the object is a passive one.

This effect is just like that of a piece of ice that is thrown into a bucket of water. The ice will make the water somewhat colder, but after a few minutes it will melt and become part of the water. If the piece of ice is larger, its effect will last a little longer. Objects lack an element that consciousnesses have that makes all the difference. This element is called *will*. A person can decide one day to go and externalize in a room. The person can use their will to externalize a second day, and a third, a fourth, and so on. Will gives individuals the capacity to be stronger than any object in terms of energy.

The other use of exteriorization is in helping others.[32] Assistance to others is one of the paramount applications for any capacity. The development of a given capacity is one thing; how this capacity is applied is yet another aspect. Assisting others energetically is a reward in and of itself as well as an inherent evolutionary endeavor for all parties involved. The topic of assistance will be discussed in detail in later chapters.

VELO to Reach the Vibrational State (VS)

The third exercise to develop energetic capacity is the *VELO* (closed circuit) to reach the *vibrational state (VS)*.[33] VELO is the acronym for Voluntary Energetic Longitudinal Oscillation (figure 2.7).[34] This exercise entails moving the energies inside the body from head to feet, then from feet to head, back down to the feet, back up to the head, and so on. We remain in this up-and-down movement of our energies until we start to control and feel this energetic flow better. Then we start to gradually accelerate the speed of the flow inside the body, which will eventually induce a resonance condition in the energosoma called the vibrational state.

When a person reaches the vibrational state (VS), the chakras of the individual will start opening and closing very fast. This condition is the best exercise for the energosoma.[35] It will develop the capacity of the chakras and the capacity to process energy, to absorb and externalize it. There are also several other aspects of energy that will be developed and controlled with time, such as the direction of the flow; the intensity, speed, and direction of exteriorization; and others.

The VS has the following effects or benefits:

- Increases our energetic capacity
- Cleans our psychosphere
- Unblocks and balances our energosoma

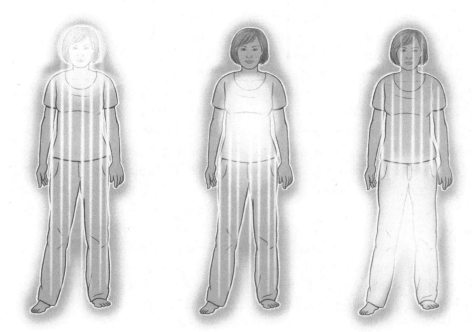

Figure 2.7: Voluntary Energetic Longitudinal Oscillation (VELO)

- Protects and defends us from polluting holothosenes[36]
- Prevents the onset of energetic blockages or problems
- Makes us physically healthier
- Produces a sympathetic dissimilation (disconnection of a sympathetic assimilation)
- Makes the energosoma (holochakra) more flexible
- *Predisposes and induces lucid projections*

Continuous Conscious Projection Provoked by Vibrational State
Bernardo Farina (2001)[37]
The experiment described here took place on January 8, 1999, and was conducted in the apartment I occupied at that time in the city of São Paulo, Brazil. The weather that day had been cold, and a light rain fell throughout the night.

OUT-OF-BODY EXPERIENCE

(continued) I began Penta[38] [a donation of energy—see chapter 7] at 1:00 in the morning, following a period of energetic exercises. The day had not been an ordinary one. I had returned to São Paulo from Rio de Janeiro, where I had been trying to find a job and a place to live, as it was my intention to relocate to Rio in order to pursue my volunteer work at the Institute's head office [International Institute of Projectiology and Conscientiology]. My trip had been successful. I had received good news relating to my efforts and the prospect seemed full of promise. That evening I would be traveling once again in order to give a class in another city.

Around 5:30 in the morning, I was enjoying a light sleep when I began to perceive an animistic-mediumistic energetic signal in my right ear; intuitively I became aware that this event was being sponsored by an extraphysical helper. The energetic signals were very clear, and I had no doubt that these signals were the means of communication used by the extraphysical helper.

I began to experience a vibrational state throughout my holosoma. The intensity of this condition increased until I felt the beginning of the departure of my psychosoma, remaining lucid throughout.

Whilst I remained aware during the takeoff period, lucidity was dimmed when compared to the conditions experienced during the initial period of the vibrational state, and my psychosoma directed itself toward the nearest wall and the ceiling of the bedroom. During this particular stage of the projection, I moved in slow motion.

My lucidity increased considerably when I left the room during the projection and found myself outside the building where I was living. This "re-increase" in lucidity is explained by the sphere of extraphysical energies surrounding the soma, with a radius of approximately three meters, diminishing lucidity and making it difficult for the psychosoma to move more freely due to gravity and the strong influence of the silver cord.

I began searching for visual references to help orient myself in space while flying with my psychosoma. As I intended to project off the planet, I chose the brightest star and increased the speed of my flight in its direction. I experienced some difficulty maintaining my direction, which caused me to change my reference points (stars) every now and then.

I am unsure how far I traveled in my psychosoma, as I was interrupted by the extraphysical repercussion caused by a physical touch in my soma. This impact caused my immediate return to my bedroom (physical base) and partial realignment of the psychosoma with the soma, without losing lucidity. My partner, sleeping by my side, had touched me involuntarily.

Once again, I had an intuition that I should take advantage of this partial realignment of the psychosoma, install the vibrational state as intensely as possible, and try to experience another continuous conscious projection. I installed the vibrational state, perceiving an increase in intensity throughout the holosoma until takeoff, with a relatively undiminished level of lucidity, until I reached the external environment and began my journey once again.

I do not know how long the second projection lasted. My inability to completely control my emotions (I felt euphoric at achieving a second projection through the installation of the vibrational state) provoked my involuntary return to the physical base and the partial realignment of the psychosoma, again maintaining the lucidity.

I tried to maintain control of the situation by containing my emotions and energies. I wanted to keep experimenting and made every possible effort to maintain my focus and balance to the best of my abilities.

I installed the vibrational state for the third time, trying to provoke misalignment. The process seemed more difficult, as my partner had touched my physical body several times and the subsequent repercussions had caused a loss of focus and difficulty in exteriorizing the psychosoma. I could feel the physical touch on my left arm and leg and at the same time the psychosoma partially out of alignment, in the vibrational state. With some effort I managed to produce a new projection of the psychosoma. This time I had more difficulty maintaining movement and control of the speed and direction of the psychosoma, as well as finding reference points in space. I returned to the physical base with almost no lucidity, completely realigned, and went through the hypnopompic state and finally returned to the ordinary physical waking state.

> *(continued)* In relation to this experience, I would like to highlight some points:
> 1. I managed to produce a projection of continuous consciousness three times in a row.
> 2. Although an extraphysical helper was the sponsor of this experiment, my will constituted an essential factor in the production of the vibrational state and in continuing the experiment for as long as possible.
> 3. My frame of mind was positive, confident, and optimistic, generating the conditions predisposing the experiment; however, my emotions made it difficult for me to maintain it.
> 4. Among the reasons that made this experiment possible, I could identify my own motivation and my trust in the extraphysical team.
> 5. Despite having experienced innumerable projections of the consciousness induced by projective techniques, including exoprojection (the projection of the consciousness outside the planet), this particular experiment was extremely rewarding for an instructor of projectiology.

While moving the energies up and down the body, the person can do a self-diagnosis of their energetic condition, even identifying what are called *energetic blocks*. These can arise for many reasons and in various areas. For example, a person who represses emotions might have a block in their heart chakra (cardiochakra); somebody who watches too much TV may have problems in their third eye (frontochakra); an individual who has bad eating habits might have a block in their solar plexus chakra (umbilicochakra); and so forth.

Blocks can also arise because of energetic contamination or pollution. The thosenes we receive (and emit) throughout our day accumulate in our energosoma. When the thosenes are negative, this is similar to dirt on the physical body. If we spend several months without taking a bath or cleaning our soma, the body will develop a film or even a crust of dirt. Likewise, energetically speaking, such a condition is not positive or healthy for the energosoma. It also hinders projections.

Upon moving the energies up and down the body, we can identify exactly where any blocks are. We will recognize them because one or more of the following symptoms may be present. There may be an area where the energy does not pass, or where a discomfort is felt, or where there is no sensation (lack of perception). There also may be an area where we lose our concentration when trying to move energies. This last symptom is the hardest one to notice.

The VELO will help to remove any blocks as well. Once we have identified an area that has a block, we will need to place more attention on that area and "force" the energy to flow through it. Wanting and making energy pass through the area has nothing to do with physical strength, physical effort, or tensing muscles. It is an activity that is happening in the energosoma. It is a matter of putting our attention on the area, setting our will and resolve, and following perceptions throughout the body. As the flow of energy starts to pass once, twice, and so on, we will feel how the block is offering less resistance. It is the equivalent of a lump of sand that dissolves as water passes over the top of it a few times.

This exercise will leave the energy of the energosoma flowing more freely. This is analogous to the blood flow within the physical body. The ideal condition for blood is when it is flowing; any stoppage or any action that threatens this flow is not healthy.[39] Eastern medicine is based on the healthy flow of energy through the body. It is well known in acupuncture that energetic blocks cause physical problems. Therefore, we become physically healthier with the free flow of the energy. Once the block is gone, we still have to treat the root cause for the block; otherwise, the block might form again.

The vibrational state can have a great effect on our physical health, because it can leave the energosoma extremely healthy, in good shape. Because of the lack of knowledge about energy, unfortunately in many cases individuals are carrying holothosenes that are very old and that consequently decrease the performance of their energosoma. Reaching the condition of the vibrational state (VS) is the equivalent of giving the energosoma an energetic bath and also of exercising it. The energosoma is more easily polluted than is the physical body, so it is of the utmost importance to maintain its health.

The VS is also used for energetic self-defense. We can defend ourselves from holothosenes in the environment, objects, or individuals. By doing a VS, we balance our energies and our entire system. This expels any external intruding energy from our energosoma.

> **RENEWAL** ♻ **RENEWAL**
>
> Using the vibrational state (VS) as a protection mechanism is far more effective than "imagining" the creation of a shield of energies through which nothing comes in and nothing goes out. Creating an imaginary energetic shield does not work well because energosomas are open systems. We are not able to stop the flow of energy, and furthermore this would be undesirable. The healthy condition of energies is when they are able to flow freely.
>
> In this context, imagining the creation of a shield is also not a very mature technique. When children are scared, they hide under the bed or put a pillow over their head—this is the equivalent of "thinking" about putting up such a shield. One of the main problems with the "pillow over the head" reaction is that we are sacrificing our external perceptions for a false sense of security. While this might be better in our mind, upon doing this, we lose our ability to act accordingly because we do not actually know what is happening.
>
> A VS will leave *us* in control and in balance. We will also know and continue to perceive what is happening. This gives us a greater capacity for action and for development, because we can better understand what is occurring, and at the same time we are stable enough to do something about it—including helping others.

The VS will disconnect any residual energetic tentacles or auric couplings in our psychosphere. Thus, part of becoming energetically clean is doing sympathetic *dissimilations.*

This kind of energetic cleansing will leave the energosoma of the individual much more flexible, which in turn will help the person produce lucid projections. If a person goes to bed with dense emotional energies in their system, the energosoma will be more rigid and the probability of a projection will be reduced. The quality of sleep will also be lower, due to the person disconnecting at a closer distance to the body and therefore absorbing less energy in the process.

It is important to highlight the impact that the quality of our thoughts (thosenes) makes on the quality of our holothosene, which in turn is reflected in the flexibility of our energosoma. If the person has their energosoma "block-free" and more flexible, not only will the person be more predisposed toward leaving the body, but the quality of sleep will also be better.

Finally, besides the fact that a flexible energosoma is helpful in order to leave the body, the VS in itself is also a *technique for leaving the body*. If the person produces a strong enough VS, the psychosoma will become nonaligned and will separate from the physical body. Because of this resonance condition, the psychosoma will basically "pop" out of the body. Several contemporary and historical projectors[40] used the VS as their main technique for leaving the body throughout their lives.

Working with Energy

The mobilization of bioenergy in any direction is executed through our will, whether we are moving it outward (exteriorization), inward (absorption), or up and down within our body (VELO). This is similar to how the will is the only thing needed to open and close our hand. The motion of opening and closing our hand is very easy for us to do now because we have ample experience with it. Yet the first several times we tried it as an infant, it did not work as it does today. It was just a matter of practice.

In the beginning, you should do these exercises while undisturbed and isolated—maybe in your bedroom with the door closed, while calm and focused. You can be either sitting in a comfortable chair or lying down. Relax your body well for a few minutes and then, using your will and determination, *think* about exteriorizing (or absorbing) energy to (or from) your surroundings. Think about doing this in a very direct and straightforward fashion, without imagining. It is as though you are blowing energy through all of your chakras or from all of your body when exteriorizing, and bringing energy in throughout your entire body when absorbing.

As you send out or absorb energy, you want to feel this flow moving outward or inward all over your *skin*. Likewise, when doing the VELO inside your body to reach the VS, you want to attentively follow the flow of energy as it moves through your body. You want to place your awareness on the different areas of your body and guide the energies with your attention. You begin by trying to feel the energies, for example, first in your head, then moving downward through your face, entering your neck, arriving at your shoulders, flowing down your chest, and so on until they reach your toes. Then reverse the direction and send the flow back up, guiding it again through your body with the greatest possible concentration.[41]

In order to develop energetically in the long run, you should practice these exercises several times a day. Make sure, at first, to really take the time to concentrate on the different areas of your body and on the possible sensations of energy as they arise. With each exercise, you want to try to identify, discover, uncover, recognize, and/or understand your own physical and energetic sensations. Also, you will notice that there are certain areas of your body that are more sensitive and on which you feel the sensations first. With time, you will feel the sensations clearer and on all areas of your body.

For the first couple weeks at least, you should reserve about twenty minutes for each energetic practice session. While lying down or sitting, and concentrating, take two to three minutes to relax your body, and repeat the three exercises (absorption, exteriorization, and VELO to reach the vibrational state) for about five minutes each. The sequence of the exercises can vary. The first week, you should try to repeat these exercises at least twice a day. As you develop further, you will need less time to work with energy and the results will begin to come faster.

The use of imagination, as stated previously, is not recommended for working with energies. We will see later on that imagination can be used as a technique for leaving the body, but its effectiveness for working with energy is minor. Notice that imagining our hand closing and opening does not necessarily lead to it actually closing or opening. For this we need to apply our will.

We can imagine a white or yellow (or any color) substance coming into us, out of us, or circulating inside of us. Yet once we begin focusing on this, we will not have any other point of reference but the image. Furthermore, in some instances we may be imagining something happening, yet nothing might actually be happening. However, we might not even know this because the image in our mind is still the same. The effect is similar to mechanically repeating prayers, mantras, or anything else for that matter *while* thinking of something else. The repetition of the words will not have much of an effect; we need to focus our will, energy, and intention for effects to take place, and this is why directly using our will to send energies is more efficient.

The ideal is to work with energies using your will and paying attention to the sensations produced in the body. Bioenergy is a *real substance*, not an abstract concept or a model used to explain something. The sensations of moving energy are just as real. These perceptions will clearly tell you that something is happening with your energy—especially with practice. You will feel the sensation going in the direction you are commanding it to go. As with air, the physical eye does not have the ability to see bioenergy, but it can be felt. If you move your arm back and forth, you will feel the air.

At the beginning, the perceptions will not be as obvious as the sensation of placing your hand on paper, where you can feel the texture easily. Sensitivity and perception will be developed continuously over time (days, weeks, and months). At first, the sensations will more than likely be *very subtle*, but as you continue doing exercises with energy (paying attention to sensations), they will start to become clearer and more obvious. Try not to be in a rush to feel all of this, because being anxious disturbs our perceptions.

Here is a list of the most common sensations when working with energies. Some of these sensations you might have already felt when trying to leave the body.[42] They may be felt either in a specific region or throughout the entire body:

- Changes in temperature, either colder or warmer flows passing through the body.
- Tingling.
- Bubbling.
- Pulsations, especially in the regions of the chakras.
- Electric currents running through the limbs.
- Balloonment, or the sensation of becoming inflated, extremely large. This is also a sensation of leaving the body.[43]
- Oscillation, as if on a hammock or like spinning. This is also a sensation of leaving the body. What is occurring in this case is that as the energosoma becomes more flexible, the psychosoma inside the soma has more freedom to roam about and so it begins oscillating.
- Shivers. Aside from the common shivers running up and down the spine, they might be felt coming in different directions or in unusual areas of the body.
- Yawning and tearing, which work as a detoxification process.
- Small movements, tics, or jumps, usually associated more with the extremities.

Working with energy is a matter of perseverance and will. Everybody has bioenergy, and it is just a matter of time and practice before you start perceiving and controlling it. The effects of this practice will be immeasurable, and it will help you to become aware of many processes of the physical and extraphysical realities. The more you practice, the better the results and the greater the benefits will be.

It is important to note that these three exercises—absorption, exteriorization, and VELO to reach the vibrational state—can also be performed while outside the body, and their effect is the same as when inside the body.[44] Therefore, the VS can also help us regain our *extraphysical* balance and lucidity.[45] Furthermore, we will usually have better control and greater efficiency in using these exercises when outside the body, since we are outside the restriction of the physical body/matter.

From the very beginning, try to get used to not using your physical body for working with energy. A tendency when working with the VELO is to follow the flow of energies with your sight or to synchronize it with your breathing. The physical body is one thing, and the energosoma is quite another. Try to separate both things. You want to perform the energetic exercises using only the energosoma as much as possible.

Eventually, as the months go by, you will be able to work with energy even in non-ideal conditions, such as in broad daylight, or while walking, eating, or speaking. Likewise, after some practice you will need less time to achieve good results. For example, you may start reaching the VS in a matter of minutes in broad daylight while performing other physical activities. Once you have reached this condition, you can practice moving the energy several times a day, perhaps while warming up food in the microwave or waiting at the supermarket, post office, or doctor's office. There is no limit to your energetic development, and the ideal is to become like a professional energetic athlete.

In the following chapters, the practical extraphysical applications of many of these energetic concepts will be studied. In chapter 4 we will discuss the actual sequence and application of these exercises with projective techniques to produce OBEs.

Summary of Key Chapter Points

- Energy is the fuel that makes all systems run.
- Bioenergy is classified as immanent energy (IE) and consciential energy (CE).
- Immanent energy (IE) is energy that comes from nature, unprocessed and without perceivable information.

- Consciential energy (CE) is the energy the consciousness uses and manifests.

- A thosene is the unit of manifestation of the consciousness and is composed of *tho*ughts ("THO"), *s*entiments ("S"), and *ene*rgy ("ENE").

- Intellectual energy, with a greater emphasis on the *tho*ught aspect, is more balanced and subtle, while emotional energy, with a greater emphasis on the *senti*ment aspect, is denser and less stable.

- A holothosene is a collection of similar thosenes that have accumulated in a place or object or that characterize a specific person.

- Holothosenes have an influence on the individual, and there is a feedback mechanism that sustains and makes them grow.

- The energosoma (or holochakra) is the collection of chakras, which are centers for processing energy (absorption, circulation, and exteriorization). We have about 88,000 chakras, though seven of them are the main ones typically studied.

- A greater exchange of energy between two parties can lead to an auric coupling, and when reinforced, it becomes a sympathetic assimilation.

- The basic mobilization of energies is composed of absorption, exteriorization, and the VELO (Voluntary Energetic Longitudinal Oscillation) to reach the vibrational state (VS).

- Reaching the vibrational state (VS) is a technique for leaving the body. Furthermore, it is also fundamental for energetic cleansing, development, and protection.

Chapter Notes

1. Alegretti, 2004, p. 55.
2. Ibid., p. 56.
3. Vieira, 2002, p. 575.
4. Ibid., p. 575.
5. Ibid., p. 580.
6. Vieira, *What*, 1994, p. 165.
7. Aparicio, 2001, pp. 49–51.
8. Vieira, 1999, p. 76.
9. Vieira, 2003, p. 288.
10. It is important to clarify that sentiments and emotions are not the same thing. This point will be addressed further in chapters 5 and 7. For our purposes at this moment, we can think of them as being synonyms.

11. Vieira, *Homo*, 2007, p. 209.

12. Monroe, 1985, Glossary.

13. Alcatraz was a famous and active prison in the San Francisco Bay in California.

14. Vicenzi, 2005, p. 24.

15. Alegretti, 1996.

16. Ibid.

17. Nascimento, 2004, pp. 231–38.

18. Balona, 2004, p. 229.

19. Vicenzi, 2005, p. 23.

20. Vieira, 2002, p. 257.

21. Ibid., p. 301.

22. For more information, refer to Trivellato, 1997.

23. Vieira, 2002, p. 584.

24. Ibid., p. 267.

25. Ibid., p. 600.

26. Montenegro, 2000, p. 95.

27. Vieira, 2002, pp. 584–87.

28. Ibid., pp. 590–91.

29. Alegretti, 2004, p. 58.

30. Vieira, 2002, pp. 591–94.

31. Alegretti, 1996.

32. Worrall, 1989; and Vieira, 2000, p. 592.

33. Vieira, 2000, pp. 587–89.

34. Trivellato, 2008, p. 165.

35. Alegretti, 1996.

36. Balona, 2004, p. 245.

37. Farina, 2001, p. 127.

38. See chapter 7 for more information on penta.

39. Alegretti, 1996.

40. Rogo, 1986, pp. 95–97.

41. Trivellato, 2008, p. 165.

42. Vieira, 2002, p. 841.

43. Ibid., p. 495.

44. Peterson, 1997, p. 161.

45. Dries, 2006, p. 35.

CHAPTER 3

Out and About

The fundamental concepts from chapter 1 and the ideas regarding energy covered in chapter 2 will allow us to discuss extraphysical reality in detail. Once we start practicing the energetic exercises, we will begin to feel takeoff sensations during the night, will be more predisposed toward having OBEs, and will gradually start to have projections. Going one step further, we will focus in this chapter on describing the process and the perceptions of disconnection from the body as well as the reality we will find outside the body as projectors.

In trying to study the extraphysical environment, it is important for us to understand what our level of awareness is and how we perceive, move around, and feel while we are projected. Aside from studying the internal modes of perception, it is necessary to comprehend the surroundings in which we manifest; the concept of extraphysical dimensions and how they work; and the characteristics of the psychosoma—the body we mainly use during our projections. Later on in this chapter we will cover projections of the mentalsoma and the mentalsomatic dimension as well. This will help in understanding the full range of extraphysical possibilities.

Exiting

Working with energy will make our energosoma looser, thus facilitating the disconnection of the psychosoma from the physical body. As previously explained, this separation occurs through the division of the energosoma, part of which remains with the soma while the other part goes with the psychosoma. This process can be initiated by simply relaxing the physical body.

Likewise, the process of falling asleep slowly, after having worked with energies, will also lead you to feel the sensations of separation from the physical body. Something that can be extremely useful is to apply an OBE technique after performing the energy exercises. (We will study OBE techniques in the next chapter.) Consequently, we will start to recognize the beginning of the exiting mechanism because one or more familiar sensations of disconnection may arise.

Exit Sensations

Most of the sensations (not all of them) of leaving the body are caused by energetic repercussions from the division, or *stretching,* of the energosoma. In this section we will discuss the most common exit sensations. It is important to mention that we will not feel all of these sensations. There are certain specific sensations that we will have the tendency to feel with greater frequency depending on our physical and energetic constitution. Likewise, there are some sensations that we may never feel, even though they are very common for other people.

Some sensations have a lighter impact on the person, and others have a heavier one. We, as lucid-projector candidates, have to understand that any new activity carries new and different sensations with it. However, simply because they are different does not mean they are negative. Sensations are neither inherently positive nor negative, but through our *interpretation* we can classify them as positive or negative. For example, the sensation we feel on the soles of our feet when we walk is neither positive nor negative. It simply tells us something is happening—it is a consequence of an activity.

The same is true of exit sensations. They show us that something is occurring. Nevertheless, it is important to be familiar with them so as to be able to interpret them properly and not to be surprised or taken aback.

The unfamiliarity with exit sensations prevents many people from leaving the body. Thus, understanding and becoming comfortable with these exit sensations is an important part of being able to produce lucid projections with regularity. Refer to figure 3.1 for a list of the most common OBE sensations people reported in an OBE survey of more than 3,000 individuals.[1]

Some of these sensations are also felt when working with energies, as described in the previous chapter. It is extremely common for people to feel the vibrational state (VS) before leaving the body. As you can see, roughly one in three individuals reported feeling the VS before takeoff. Reaching this condition is a very good sign that our development through the energy work is going well. When leaving the body there will be many instances in which the VS will occur spontaneously, even when we are very relaxed. This starts to occur once the energosoma is already in good shape.

Some sensations are self-explanatory, such as floating or itching. Here is a description of other important sensations felt during the transitional exit phase:

Falling sensation with (or without) a jerk awake.[2] In most instances the falling sensation is a combination of dream images of falling with the actual sensation of lightness of the psychosoma. We become aware of this condition many times after having been falling for several seconds. As we usually become startled at this realization, it causes the psychosoma to rapidly enter the body with a jerk movement.

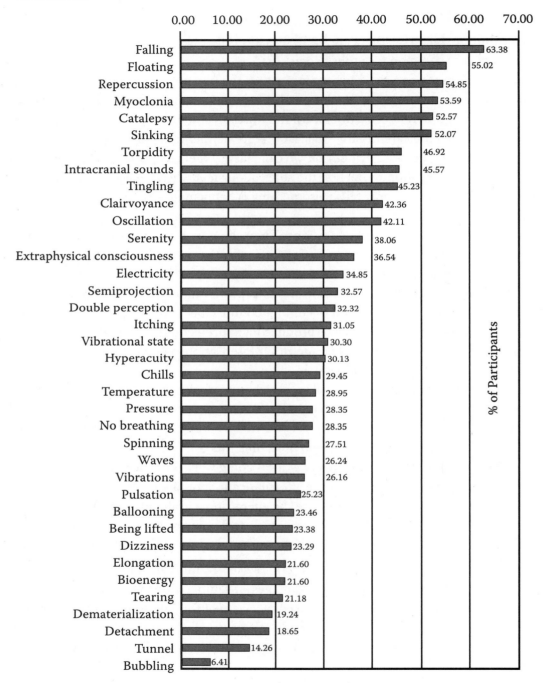

Figure 3.1: Typical OBE Sensations

Numbness or torpidity.[3] Numbness or torpidity naturally happens when the person is no longer able to feel the physical body. What can produce this is a partial or full disconnection from the body and the transfer of sensations to the psychosoma. In certain instances the soma may feel extremely heavy, as if it were made out of lead—so much so that the person feels that to even lift an arm or leg would be impossible.

Floating and/or oscillations.[4] Projectors, once slightly disconnected, may feel a sense of floating. In some cases there might be a swaying sensation. This can be similar to the sensation felt when the person has spent a day on a boat, in a pool, or on a hammock and then lies down to sleep. In other instances the person may feel fast spinning sensations.

Myoclonia.[5] These are twitches or small involuntary movements in areas of the physical body, mainly the extremities. They occur when the psychosoma, which has disconnected slightly, comes back into the body due to a change in thought or focus of the person.

Projective catalepsy.[6] This sensation of not being able to move can easily and erroneously be interpreted as negative. Usually once we become aware inside the body, oftentimes when waking up in the morning, we realize that we are not able to move our body. The body is completely immobile and rigid, causing panic in many instances. This sensation, if not understood and interpreted correctly, can cause fear or phobias in individuals.

This condition is caused by the following mechanism. We disconnect in this specific instance a little more than usual, to the point that the silver cord forms—and so we lose the connections to the muscles. Now, upon returning, even though the psychosoma is very close to or even in alignment with the physical body, the energy connections to the motor functions of the physical body have not yet formed—so the psychosoma is more disconnected than connected. As a result, the person is unable to move their muscles. There are basically two techniques to overcome this condition.

First, stay calm (it is hard to accomplish anything while in a panic) and try to make one *small* movement. Usually a slight movement of the head or an extremity (like a foot or finger) will cause the person to fully reconnect again. Each person should move that part of the body that seems easiest to move at the moment. Once this small movement has been achieved, the person will have regained normal mobility of the physical body.

The second and more productive thing that can be done, since in this case the psychosoma is still more out of the body than in it, is to decide to go out of the body. We should will ourselves outside the body by rolling out or installing a vibrational state to fully disconnect. The catalepsy is the easiest condition from which to leave the body. When we come back into the physical body, more than likely we will not feel the catalepsy again.

To clarify this, the analogy of a stuck drawer is useful. The more you push the drawer in, the more stuck it gets. Instead, it is easier to pull the drawer out and then push it back in.

This energetic irregularity that produces the catalepsy disappears as individuals work with energy and improve the overall condition of their energosoma. Therefore, this sensation is much more common in the first months of OBE training. It is sometimes popularly called "sleeping paralysis" or "waking paralysis."[7]

Intracranial sounds.[8] These are sounds heard inside the head of the person. They are usually very intense and can surprise the individual the first few times. They can be heard as loud, dry, repeated noises, such as "pow!" or "bang!" They can also sound like a strong engine or machine working—similar to a loud buzzing. There are several other possible sounds. Intracranial sounds sometimes can be so loud that we may think the entire neighborhood must have been awakened by the noise, when in reality they are heard only inside our head.

These sounds seem to occur due to the speed of disconnection of the para-head[9] (head of the psychosoma) from the physical head. In reality, if close attention is paid, the entire body makes these disconnection noises. But we usually perceive only the ones occurring inside the head. It is important to emphasize that these noises are not negative and have no undesirable consequences on any of the vehicles of manifestation. However, we need to get used to them so as to produce a projection with greater ease.

Double perception.[10] This sensation occurs during the transitional phase when the psychosoma has already disconnected from the body but is still relatively close. For a brief moment the person is able to simultaneously perceive both bodies. The sensations are usually tactile: energies, extraphysical consciousnesses, and others for the psychosoma; and the bed, pillow, sheets, and position for the physical body.

In some instances, or if we decide to leave the physical eyes open (no advantage to this), the double perceptions are visual. The psychosoma sees the bedroom, extraphysical objects, or even an extraphysical dimension from its vantage point, while the physical body sees the normal physical bedroom from its position. The two images perceived are sometimes superimposed, one on the other. This is similar to when the film in a camera does not advance and two different pictures are captured in the same negative. This condition occurs only while the psychosoma is close to the body; as it moves farther away from the body, the only perceptions that remain are the ones of the psychosoma, which is where the consciousness is seated at that moment. Because of the perception of these double sensations, it is believed by some that the consciousness divides in two.[11] Yet the consciousness does not divide or split. Observations from thousands of projectors and tens of thousands of projections verify that the consciousness stays in only one body at a time.[12] The experience, however, of being in one body and place at a time changes depending on the body of manifestation we are using; for example, the psychosoma or mentalsoma. This will be further clarified in later chapters.

Smelling or auditory hyperacuity.[13] As the psychosoma starts to disconnect from the soma, the energies and perceptions expand and we become much more sensitive. The two senses that expand the most are those of smell and hearing. Either one or both can expand during the same projective attempt.

Regarding the sense of smell, the person can start, during the transitional period, to smell things that are either very far away or that the normal human sense of smell is not usually able to perceive. We may become surprised to find out that even our holothosene has a characteristic smell that we can feel! This smell is not bad nor necessarily uncomfortable, but it is different.

The auditory hyperacuity is normally more distracting. The person, while disconnecting, can all of a sudden start to hear the voices of individuals who are having conversations in the surrounding residential blocks. Likewise, the person can start to hear extraphysical noises and voices as well (clairaudience).

Cranial pressure.[14] This is a sensation of something or a substance putting pressure on the person. It is usually much more common to feel the pressure around the head. The moment the projector fully disconnects from the body, it is felt as if this pressure—like a bubble—around the person had been pinched with a needle, and the psychosoma escapes as the pressure flows outward. As we develop our energetic capacities further through energy exercises, this sensation tends to disappear.

Balloonment.[15] This is a condition of expansion of the energies that we perceive as if we were a balloon that is inflating. We may feel very big in this situation, as if we have expanded to the size of the room, house, or even further.

RENEWAL / RENEWAL

It is important to mention that certain individuals like to have background or "relaxing" music and/or smells (such as incense) for leaving the body. Background noise can aid in drowning out other noises. Yet, for the most part these items do not necessarily help us to leave the body and they are certainly not a requirement. Care must be taken with both—especially with smells. If the person experiences the smelling or hearing hyperacuity, the smell or sound will increase and in certain cases might become unbearable for the individual. This can become a distraction for the projection. As a general rule, the fewer number of external stimuli we have, the better. Ideally we want to provide the fewest number of stimuli for any physical sense (smell, touch, sound, etc.) during the projective attempt.

Tunnel effect.[16] The tunnel effect can be felt for various reasons. This a sensation commonly reported by individuals who undergo a near-death experience. The most common cause for experiencing the tunnel is due to the changing of dimensions. When changing from one dimension to another, even when already outside the body, we may perceive a tunnel linking one dimension to the other.

There are two conditions that commonly occur when we have just disconnected from the soma: the slow motion and the blackout condition.

Slow motion.[17] The projector feels sluggish and heavy. As a result of this heaviness, the psychosoma moves very slowly. Usually, awareness is equally diminished in this condition.

This slow motion occurs because of the density of the energy enveloping the body. There is an area surrounding the body—with a radius of about thirteen feet (four meters) from the head—where there are more of our dense energies. This area is called the *extraphysical sphere of energy* (figure 3.2).[18] As a result of this added energy close to the body, the psychosoma moves slower than normal.

INDICATIONS / INDICATIONS

The mechanism of return to the physical body is very sensitive. Inside the *extraphysical sphere of energy,* this mechanism is even more sensitive. It is recommended for projectors to move outside the extraphysical sphere of energy (which has a radius of about thirteen feet, or four meters, from the head) as soon as they gain extraphysical awareness, so as to stabilize themselves and to avoid a premature return to the soma.

Figure 3.2: Extraphysical Sphere of Energy

Blackout.[19] The blackout is a lapse in lucidity that we generally experience as we disconnect from the body. Normally, when the full projection is about to begin and we are perceiving the transitional process, everything goes dark. We lose our awareness and there is a blackout. After a few seconds or minutes, we regain awareness already outside the body.

The blackout seems to be related to the extraphysical sphere of energy. The projector needs to learn to lucidly perceive during this transitional phase, which is just a matter of experience. During the first projections, the blackout is quite common. Yet as the energetic development continues and the projective capacity increases, the blackout occurs increasingly less. Eventually, all our projections can happen without a blackout.

The takeoff itself can occur in many different manners. The person may sink into the bed or disconnect by floating upward. A popular favorite for many individuals is rolling sideways out of the body. Once the person is fully outside their body, there are some common sensations that are noticed immediately, such as the lack of weight, the fact that the psychosoma does not breathe, and the characteristic sensations of freedom and well-being.

Extraphysical Lucidity

Every extraphysical experience is affected by our lucidity, or level of awareness. We are very conditioned by the intraphysical dimension, since this is normally the only reality perceived. Therefore, it is not surprising that when the soma goes to sleep, the consciousness goes "offline" as well. Being able to have extraphysical lucidity entails breaking an old habit (of many lives) and creating a new one.

The word *lucidity* is usually used to describe clarity of thought. By "awareness" people normally mean perception. Though this is generally correct, being lucid implies much more than these two characteristics. Thus, it is important to explore and expand on all the aspects that make us conscious (for example, when in the ordinary waking state).

Being "conscious," "lucid," or "aware" implies a plethora of mental faculties. The following is a list describing some of the more relevant aspects of lucidity.

1. *Clarity of thought* is the capacity to think clearly, linearly, or unimpeded—without major obstacles or hindrances. External pressures—such as holothosenes, noises, or stress, as well as internal doubts or preoccupations—can diminish it.

2. *Perception* implies being aware of the environment and is not dependent on only the conventional five physical senses. Our personal interests also affect what we perceive. We can focus our perception only on certain aspects that interest us and thus we might miss others. An example of this would be an individual who does not perceive that a colleague has been wearing braces for the last month.

3. *Decision-making ability* is the capacity to discern: to understand and distinguish options, and to select one of them. This is also the internal processing capacity of being able to "read between the lines." Seeing something written is perception, yet how deeply we understand what is written is the individual's processing capacity.

4. *Control* is the individual's capacity to execute a decision, the ability to put will into action, and to exercise control over the holosoma. In certain cases we are able to understand what is happening but we are not able to carry out the necessary steps to act on it.

5. *Memory* is the ability to recall past events. Without memory, we do not have an identity. Basically, everything we currently perceive is understood by comparing it with previous experiences. This is one of the aspects that shows up the least during dreams. Usually during dreams, individuals do not recall details like their work phone number, their mother's address, and so on—in other words, there is no detailed memory.

6. *Ethics* is the capacity to understand and behave according to our moral principles. We perform or choose not to perform certain actions because we think they are either morally correct or incorrect. In normal dreams, when our awareness is low, in many situations we do things that we would not do if we had a greater level of awareness.

Having extraphysical lucidity entails all of these aspects and more. In the ordinary waking state, the physical body can basically be awake or asleep. These two states offer us very different levels of lucidity.

When the body is awake, it gives us a certain support, or the "hardware" helps us to maintain a relatively stable level of awareness. However, when we are projected, this support is not there, and it becomes up to us to have greater lucidity and to be able to maintain it.

Naturally, it is important to stress that all of the aforementioned capacities do not depend on the brain and are not produced by it.[20] In order to understand the possible

- 0% Lucidity: Unconsciousness

- 20% Lucidity: Semiconsciousness

- 40% Lucidity: Doubt

- 60% Lucidity: Certainty

- 80% Lucidity: Self-consciousness

- 100% Lucidity: Superconsciousness

Figure 3.3: Extraphysical Lucidity Scale

lucidity levels a projector can enjoy outside the body, let us introduce the extraphysical scale of lucidity,[21] shown in figure 3.3. The percentages are based on an individual's total capacity for being lucid.

Extraphysical lucidity is an attribute that can fluctuate from experience to experience, even within the same projection. Thus, let us describe the generalities of what happens at each level.

0% Lucidity—Unconsciousness. This state naturally occurs when a person is sleeping, without dreaming. Also, for practical purposes, it can be said that a person who does not remember anything in the morning about their dream had 0% lucidity during the night. When individuals have a normal night—they dreamt some and remember a little—this could be classified as around 2%–3% of extraphysical lucidity, since they paid little attention to the images projected by the physical brain.

20% Lucidity—Semiconsciousness. This state is equivalent to having a lucid dream. As we sleep, in this case we enjoy a certain level of awareness, enough for us to notice that a dream is taking place and to be able to control the dream. In this condition, the psychosoma is usually floating close to the body, separated by a few inches most commonly—though not always. A person dreaming of flying may, in some instances, actually be extraphysically flying.

If one night we have a very lucid projection and meet someone with 20% lucidity (or less), the interaction is going to be similar to a person who is awake trying to communicate with a sleepwalker. The sleepwalker is focused on their dream and in most instances will not remember meeting the other person afterward.

In this case, we are meeting an extraphysical sleepwalker.[22] In certain instances, acquaintances mention that they saw us in their house projected. Many of these cases are due to a projection with a 20% level of awareness, in which we, projectors, were unable to remember anything.[23]

40% Lucidity—Doubt. At this level, because the level of lucidity is still low, the perception of the environment is "cloudy" and we are in doubt as to whether we are having a dream or a projection. Since lucidity is only at 40%, our perceptions and understandings are partial. In this condition, extraphysical perception is still somewhat mixed with the dream—a more physical activity taking place in the brain. As a result, some aspects of what the person remembers in the morning come from the dream and others from the objective extraphysical reality; the person will tend to have doubts about whether the experience was a dream or a projection.

Normally in this state we do not have control over our emotions. Projectors with this level of lucidity tend to be very prone to emotional reactions, either positive (euphoria) or negative (fear). This condition is somewhat confusing overall due to the intermediate lucidity level. The person is usually at a good distance from their soma.

60% Lucidity—Certainty. At this level we are sure that we are experiencing a lucid projection because of our own internal condition of lucidity. At this level we already enjoy a decent level of rationality, association of ideas, comparison of extraphysical and intraphysical dimensions, and others. We have no doubt about the fact that we are projected, in the same way that we have no doubt about our condition when in the state of ordinary wakefulness—right now.

80% Lucidity—Self-consciousness. This lucidity level is *equal* to the one we enjoy in the ordinary waking state. In other words, while projected we have the same level of faculties and attributes we have while in the intraphysical life, including thinking, analysis, and

Comparing yourself with the average person, and trying to understand what your 80% will feel like, you can evaluate your level of normal awareness by reflecting on the following questions:

- How good is your memory compared to others'?
- How good is your attention?
- Do you usually fail to notice things?
- Are you more distracted than others?
- How strong is your will?
- How emotional are you?
- Do you find yourself losing your emotional control frequently?

lucid decision making. Since 80% is the topmost level of lucidity we can currently enjoy intraphysically, this means that the level of lucidity can be even greater extraphysically.

100% Lucidity—Superconsciousness. This is the level of lucidity achieved in projections with the mentalsoma. In this condition, the mental capacities of the individual far surpass those in the ordinary waking state. Everything from the capacity of perception to the mechanism of communication is increased. In contrast, all prior levels of lucidity occur while projected with the psychosoma.

This scale can serve as a guide for projectors to measure their level of lucidity. Extraphysically, lucidity is inversely proportional to emotions. In other words, the more aware and lucid we are, the better we are able to manage and control our emotions; on the other hand, the more emotional we become, the less awareness or lucidity we have.

Notice that this condition is actually the same as in the physical dimension. When individuals have an attack of anger, they may say or do things they do not mean. When they become overly euphoric (become too *emotionally* happy), they may promise too much or buy things they cannot afford. When the emotion diminishes afterward and they are able to think more clearly, they recognize these overreactions and in most cases regret both scenarios.

Extraphysically, this relation between lucidity and emotions is even more accentuated and clearer (again, because we do not have the physical body as a buffer). Therefore, as our emotions increase, we lose our lucidity and end up returning to the body—in most cases we do not even know how the return occurred.

While projected, we can become too emotional or excited for a number of reasons. We may become too happy upon encountering a relative who is now an extraphysical consciousness. We may become afraid in a situation or dimension that is very different. In some instances, during the beginning phases, we may become surprised by small, natural extraphysical occurrences, such as not having a shadow, or seeing how different objects look when they are seen by the psychosoma.

Notice that at 60% lucidity, even though the person is aware, they are more prone to losing control over their emotions. At 80% lucidity, the person remains more mentally and emotionally stable.

It is important to point out the relative individuality of this scale, meaning at 80% there is the same level of control over emotions extraphysically as well as intraphysi-

> Ideally we would like to remain balanced and in control extraphysically (as well as intraphysically). However, those experiences where we lose our emotional balance and return to the body serve as a training process, providing us with opportunities to develop our level of awareness. Because projectors will naturally strive to gain more control, they will tend to improve this ability over time, and ultimately this will lead to greater alertness, awareness, and/or sharpness both outside and inside the body—resulting in a greater level of lucidity in regular daily life.

cally. This is *relative* to the individual and varies from person to person. There are individuals who lose their emotional control more easily than others.

As mentioned previously, lucidity can fluctuate from projection to projection, as well as during the same projection. We may be projected at 75% lucidity, and as we become surprised by something, this can result in our lucidity dropping to 55%. We can then rebalance ourselves by recuperating some lucidity and getting back to 75%—all within seconds, in the same projection.

There are many techniques individuals can use to raise their lucidity outside the body. Some of them entail using affirmations such as "I want to be lucid," while others are based on focusing the attention on body parts or on certain objects.[24]

It is important to try to establish a good level of lucidity once separated from the body. A useful technique for doing this is studying the vehicle in which we are manifesting. By looking for our legs or arms, we are forced to focus and activate our concentration. This will have the effect of raising our lucidity level.[25] If we can perceive our para-arms and paralegs, we are obviously manifesting with the psychosoma.

One of the best techniques for improving lucidity and stability at any time during the experience is to work with energy, as described in the example on the next page, "Extraphysical VS." Energetic exercises work both extraphysically and intraphysically. The effects are actually greater and more easily achieved outside the body, because bioenergy has a stronger effect in the extraphysical dimension than in the physical dimension; it flows with less resistance. As a result, the benefits of the VS, such as regaining equilibrium, energetic self-defense, and sympathetic dissimilation, work more efficiently outside the body.

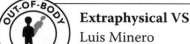

Extraphysical VS
Luis Minero
July 27, 1996, around 2:00 AM, Miami, Florida

… I regained some lucidity and was in the living room/kitchen of my apartment. My perceptions at that moment were confused, indicating that my lucidity was not very high (perhaps 30%). For some reason, maybe because of experience, a thought came into my mind as I stared at the front door of my apartment: "You cannot leave without lucidity." I was not able to fully make sense of this information because my awareness level was minimal, yet I somehow understood that I needed to have this thing called "lucidity" before leaving the house. I looked around and began trying to find this "lucidity" throughout the house—somehow thinking that I was going to find an object called lucidity without really knowing or understanding what it was. As my searched progressed, I started moving about the room, passing through some objects, and entering various rooms. When I arrived at my bedroom, I was able to see my physical body with all the energies around it. That is when a second intuition came: "Work with energy."

I started moving my energies up and down and reached a vibrational state (VS) almost instantly. My level of lucidity increased fairly quickly. When it reached a good level (around 80%), I started to think about what had just happened. I realized that I had been looking for lucidity as if it were an object and thought about how funny and ridiculous I must have looked doing this. I also realized that during my search I had passed through several objects without becoming aware of this. At that moment I thought about both intuitions and concluded that I had arrived at the information probably because of my previous experience.

Since my lucidity was now at a good level, I thought, "Now I can go." As I thought this, I moved across the bedroom and went through the sliding glass door in my room …

Lucid projections also work to improve the overall awareness of the individual both intraphysically and extraphysically. As we develop our control outside the body, we will notice that when manifesting as an intraphysical consciousness, we become more aware of the environment, and vice versa. In addition, as our perceptions of energy increase, we tend to become more psychic. In many instances, in addition to having increased intuitions, individuals may develop capacities such as clairvoyance and precognition.

It is valuable to write down the awareness level of the projection on paper. This will help us to become more aware of our level of lucidity during the projection, and will also help us in trying to improve it.

Internal Factors

As we start to project with awareness, we will realize that several important mental faculties have an expanded role extraphysically. How much we control them will determine the level of richness and depth of our experience.

Will, for example, is the key to any action outside the body. If a person has the intention of doing something and applies energy to accomplish it, then the action will take place. This energy can be applied in the form of an affirmation (with words) or simply by thinking about it. Extraphysically, going from one place to another is a matter of willing it.

Attention determines the scope of what we perceive. There are reports of certain projectors who after many experiences have never noticed their silver cord. This is not because they do not have one but because they have not paid attention to it; they were not looking for it.[26] An example of how will and attention affect the experience is when we try to go to a different place, such as our office at work. We need to focus our attention on the target, and keep our attention focused until we reach it (usually fairly fast). If our attention deviates from the goal, we may end up doing something different or going somewhere else.[27]

Intraphysically, when we are going to work (whether driving or riding in a bus or metro) we are usually thinking about many different things. These thoughts will not stop us from reaching our workplace, because the inertia of matter will keep us moving in the same direction. Yet if we were traveling to our workplace extraphysically, if we were to begin thinking about our mother, we might end up visiting her house instead of the office.

The manner in which we *perceive* things depends on the attention we place on them. Extraphysically, our senses are not limited to a particular organ or region in our psychosoma, the same way they are in our soma. In other words, our sight is not dependent on the para-eyes (eyes of the psychosoma), nor hearing on the para-ears (extraphysical ears). The psychosoma perceives through the perception of the information in the energy, namely through intuition, through the capturing of thosenes.

Holothosenes carry information and are everywhere, and this is what the psychosoma perceives. Capturing of this energy-information can be performed with the entire body. Extraphysically, we can easily perceive the holothosene of the environment and of other individuals we encounter. It is such a natural process and comes so easily extraphysically that we do not realize at the beginning that it is different from the physical process.

The process of intuition is a very efficient and clear mechanism for acquiring information.[28] Projectors use it whether they know *how* the mechanism works or not. It is similar, for example, to intraphysical vision. A very small percentage of individuals in the world know the mechanism by which an image forms in our minds, but all seeing people enjoy the benefits of this sense. Likewise, intuition is the basic tool of perception for the projector.

Let us give an example of perceiving through the entire body: vision.[29] Each area of the psychosoma can perceive and capture visual input; in other words, sight can be 360°, up, down, around, all over, or spherical. With even greater lucidity a projector can perceive several dimensions at once *and* with global or spherical vision!

Furthermore, the senses of the psychosoma do not work like the physical senses, as they are not as readily open to diverse stimuli. If we are walking and somebody behind us calls our name, this sound will come into our ears and will get our attention; we will then turn around to find out who is calling us. Even though we were not paying attention to who called us, because the ears are continuously receiving sounds, stimuli continue to come in, independently of where we are focusing our attention at that moment. Nevertheless, extraphysically, it is mainly our attention that guides our senses. If we are very focused on something, a lot of other things can be happening all around us and we may completely miss them.

Conditioning is a very determinant factor extraphysically, since perception is more subjectively dependent. Even though it is possible to see globally or spherically, most projectors do not enjoy this capacity because they are conditioned by the intraphysical fact that images are perceived only from the front—as occurs with the physical body. Projectors find themselves repeating unnecessary actions, attitudes, and postures from the physical dimension, meaning there is a natural tendency to want to use the psychosoma as if it were the physical body. Here are some examples of this:

- Trying to grab doorknobs to open doors

- Passing through doors (or windows) more often than through walls or ceilings

- Moving the legs, as if to walk, when going from one place to another (extraphysically there is no friction and we advance by means other than by pushing ourselves from the floor with our paralegs and parafeet)

- Trying to grab things with our hands or smell through our nose

> If we are going to fly outside the body, in which position will our psychosoma be positioned as we do this? Like a superhero? Aerodynamically? With our arms stretched out like wings? There is no contact with the air while projected, so this is unnecessary. If we think while outside the body, in which language will we do this? Will it be in our native language? Is our native language the official extraphysical language? Is there an official extraphysical language? We will explore these ideas further in chapter 5.

Extraphysical understanding is the result of what was comprehended, concluded, and generally observed from the overall experience. The quality of this *understanding* will be affected by the level of lucidity, interest, experience of the projector, amount of dense energy being carried (energetic load), conditionings, and others.[30] Furthermore, the level of education and knowledge will have an impact as well. The following examples can give us a practical idea of how these elements come into play.

> **EXAMPLE** Larry has a room in his house that he recently painted white. While outside the body during one of his first lucid projections, he realizes that the color looks very different from his "intraphysical conception of the color white." After briefly looking at it from different extraphysical angles, he comes to the conclusion that the color he is perceiving is not actually white, and furthermore that this second color is new to him. He has never seen a color like this and wonders if this color even exists in the physical dimension … Afterward, when back in the body, during the recording of his experience, he writes in his notebook that the color he perceived was *white!*

Let us try to understand this relatively simple experience by first addressing the difference in color perception. Color is the manner in which we, as intraphysical consciousnesses, perceive different wavelengths of light. The physical eye has a certain range of perception; this is called the visible spectrum. However, the psychosoma is not limited to the same perception range as the physical body, and extraphysical vision is also not based on light. Larry, while manifesting with the psychosoma, is therefore able to perceive more colors, and as a result notices that what intraphysically appeared white to him seems like a different color to him extraphysically.

However, Larry is unable to bring this knowledge back into the physical dimension, so he ends up writing in his notebook that the wall was white. A couple of reasons for this are his physical conditionings and biological mechanisms. Once inside the body, he has no physical point of reference for that color from his previous experiences. His brain has no way to "get hold of" this memory, and as a result, that specific detail is harder to "recall and interpret."

The physical brain can be compared in certain instances to coin sorters, which are usually cylindrical. As coins are placed on top, they start spinning and are sorted into pennies, nickels, dimes, and quarters (in the case of a coin sorter designed for U.S. coins). What happens when a 1 euro coin is thrown into this machine set up for U.S. coins? The machine that does not have a slot for euro coins will have no way of isolating or recognizing this coin. As a result, it will either place this coin in the wrong slot or the coin will become stuck. If the coin is placed in the quarters slot because it has a similar size, then the machine is interpreting the euro as a quarter. This is the equivalent of Larry saying the color is white, because he does not have any other "slots" in his mind to "fit the color into." If the machine gets stuck, it is the equivalent of Larry not being able to remember—lending evidence to the idea that this detail is harder to "grasp" than others.

From this simple example, we can see the importance of keeping an open mind with regard to extraphysical events. Larry's degree of experience also plays a role in this. If he leaves the body a few more times and notices this fact, he will start to get more acquainted with an *extraphysical point of view*. Through repetition, his brain will be able to "interpret" this condition and it will become easier for him to recall.

Another important factor is the strength of his will. If Larry is lucid and has a trained will, he can make a mental note to remember something. As he does this, he applies energy—as a result of his will—and will remember this fact with greater ease and/or in fewer experiences.

Notice here that once Larry remembers this extraphysical color, he will have it in his mind, though he will be unable to share it with anybody, explain it, or draw it. This is *intraphysically subjective* knowledge. It is very real indeed, yet it cannot be physically described to anybody else. Another problem Larry will have is in writing this down in his journal, because no language has a term for it. The easiest and most practical thing to do in this case is to make up a word and use it to represent this new color.

Let us use another example to understand internal extraphysical processes.

> Five friends decide to meet each other outside the body. They agree on a time and place. Two of them are unable to leave the body. Joanne is twenty minutes late and therefore does not find anybody else there. Don and Amy are there on time and are able to meet each other. Where they are meeting, there is a coffee table in the middle of the room with an object on top of it. The object is a man riding a horse—a decorative ornament.
>
> The next day they meet to discuss what happened. Don and Amy remember meeting each other, and Don remembers what they were talking about well, because, specifically for him, it was very important to make contact with somebody else extraphysically. Amy does not remember the

(continued) communication with Don with as much detail as he does, but she remembers this ornament on the coffee table. She knows it was a horseman who had a uniform similar to the one a friend's son uses in a school band. Don missed the object completely and is about to argue that there was no such object when all of a sudden Joanne starts describing the object enthusiastically and in detail. She noticed not only the uniform of the horseman, which in her mind was a military uniform, but also the fact that the horse seemed tired—something Amy missed completely.

We can see from this example the way the same reality can have different effects on different people, and also how their different individual personal interests affect their overall experiences. In joint projections, very commonly the accounts do not match 100 percent as a result of all these factors.

In certain cases, individuals may not even understand what they are seeing, and this is dependent on their level of intraphysical and extraphysical knowledge. It would be the same as if an indigenous man from the jungles of Africa, who has never seen or experienced technology, was put inside a complex virtual machine game. What would he explain to his tribe when he went back to his community afterward? Thus, greater knowledge will give projectors a greater "database" to rely on to understand the experience.

Morphothosenes

Morphothosenes are the elements that form extraphysical objects, and with which projectors interact when they are in the extraphysical environment.[31] The word *morphothosene* is a composition of the Greek word *morph-*, meaning "form," and the word *thosene*. Another term that has been used to describe these elements is *thought-form*. Yet thought-form does not describe the entire reality, because morphothosenes are much more than simply thoughts acquiring a form.

Morphothosenes are extraphysical forms, elements, and realities created through or with thosenes.

Morphothosenes are the building blocks of extraphysical dimensions; all extra-physical structures are created from morphothosenes. In a sense, morphothosenes are the extraphysical equivalent of intraphysical matter.

All objects, structures, cities, and so forth observed in the extraphysical dimensions are constructed out of morphothosenes. They are concentrations of thosenes that acquire a form. Their density can fluctuate from relatively solid, like extraphysical walls, to relatively fluid, like the extraphysical semi-materialization of people's dream images.

Morphothosenes can be consciously or unconsciously created. A projector mani-festing in the extraphysical dimension can create objects by consciously focusing their thosenes on a specific form. Likewise, an extraphysical consciousness that desires an object with relative constancy—a table, for example—can make this extraphysical object appear. Intraphysical consciousnesses can also create extraphysical morphot-hosenes without realizing it; here is an example of this.

An intraphysical person may have an object, such as a vase, on top of the coffee table in the living room. Energy coming from individuals is collected as they (people who live there, visitors, and others) look and admire the vase or simply pay attention to it. As the vase is kept in the same location for some time, the energy, unconsciously sent out in this case, begins to accumulate extraphysically and take on the shape of the vase. Eventually the extraphysical form is created. If, for some reason, after some time the physical vase is moved from the coffee table to another place, the extraphysical form will remain. A projector can leave the body and see the extraphysical object still on the coffee table. This specific morphothosene was created without any individual being aware of the process—even though they still provided the energies for it.

The exteriorization of energy can remove or reinforce morphothosenes. The sta-bility and durability of a morphothosene comes from the amount of energy it holds (similar to holothosenes). Some morphothosenes are more malleable than others, and even a mild exteriorization can make them lose their shape.

In some other cases, extraphysical "structures" are so dense and have been estab-lished and reinforced (energetically, thosenically) over such long and unknown peri-ods of time that it seems as if absolutely nothing or anyone can alter any little part of their formation. Thus, some morphothosenes were created with so much energy, by so many people, and for such a long period of time, while constantly being "fed" the same thosenes, that they can withstand even very strong exteriorizations of energy.

Extraphysical Dimensions

While most intraphysical consciousnesses live their life aware of only the physical dimension, there are many other extraphysical realities that have been observed, experienced, and studied by researcher-projectors. These are different realms or planes of existence where extraphysical consciousnesses coexist.

The analogy of radio frequencies can be used to explain dimensions. A radio can detect a large number of station frequencies. These frequencies all occupy the same space and do not collide with each other because of their different characteristics. In this same sense, dimensions are not separated by frequency or distance; they simply exist at different *levels.* An analogy that can be used is a radio that does not need to be moved to another room to tune in to a different station because, as all the radio frequencies are found in the same room, it is just a matter of changing the dial to reach a different station.

Like a radio, a consciousness can access a large number of dimensions or realities—it is just a matter of *tuning in to them.* The soma (physical body) influences us to such an extent (intraphysical consciousness) while physical that it has us rigidly tuned in to the physical dimension. However, individuals that have clairvoyance, clairaudience, near-death experiences, and lucid projections, among other multidimensional phenomena, experience, observe, and report these other nonphysical realities.

Dimensions, in general, vary greatly in terms of density, malleability, appearance, characteristics, and native inhabitants. Therefore, they can be classified into the following four groups of dimensions:[32]

1. The *physical dimension* is the reality in which intraphysical consciousnesses (human beings) manifest. There are several well-known physical aspects of this dimension that are important to point out, including, but not limited to, the constancy of space, time, volume, and distance. At a human level, these characteristics tend to remain unchangeable, immutable. Another aspect to consider is the acting law of gravity, which gives us a point of reference for what is "up" and what is "down" and also keeps individuals bound to the ground.

2. *Tropospheric* or *crustal extraphysical dimensions* are the planes closer to the earth's crust.[33] It is in these dimensions that the majority of initial lucid projections take place. Some tropospheric dimensions are almost exact replicas of the physical dimension. A projector will recognize known physical places, landmarks, and cities in these dimensions. Some other tropospheric extraphysical

districts have dissimilar characteristics from the physical dimension and do not have a specific likeness to known physical locations.

In all these dimensions, characteristics such as distance, time, and volume still have a fair degree of validity and similarity with their physical counterparts. Even though certain perceptions may be different, as projectors, we will notice these dimensions having coherency with our experiences in the physical reality. These dimensions are inhabited by extraphysical consciousnesses with a lesser degree of lucidity.

3. *Proper extraphysical dimensions* have less association with the physical dimension.[34] These dimensions are also more malleable, "passive" to manifestations of energy from consciousnesses. Proper extraphysical dimensions constitute a wide range of realities, from less lucid planes (but more lucid than the tropospheric dimensions) to highly evolved ones; from dimensions with many objects, such as tools, houses, buildings, different types of equipment, and others, to dimensions with few apparatuses and edifications as well as few similarities with our concepts of form and shape.

The physical sun does not have an effect on these extraphysical dimensions because the physical dimension is not perceived; therefore, night and day do not exist.[35] The native inhabitants of each extraphysical dimension can also vary greatly according to the dimension. For those consciousnesses that are about to be reborn and/or that are returning from a physical life, many of these dimensions are similar to "transit stations." The psychosoma (albeit in different states of "density") is the body used to manifest in both the proper extraphysical and the tropospheric extraphysical dimensions.

4. *Mental dimensions* are reached with the mentalsoma.[36] Reaching these realities requires an expansion of the consciousness. These dimensions no longer present any characteristics of the physical dimension, such as distance and time.

Extraphysical dimensions, in general, are "conditions" or "places" in which consciousnesses with an interrelated affinity meet and coexist. The affinity that draws them together is the similar holothosene that they all manifest.[37] Furthermore, it is this specific holothosene that separates one dimension from another.

In other words, it is the thosenic quality, or energetic information, that differentiates one extraphysical dimension from another. As was explained in chapter 2, thosenes can be modulated. There are thosenes with greater intellectual

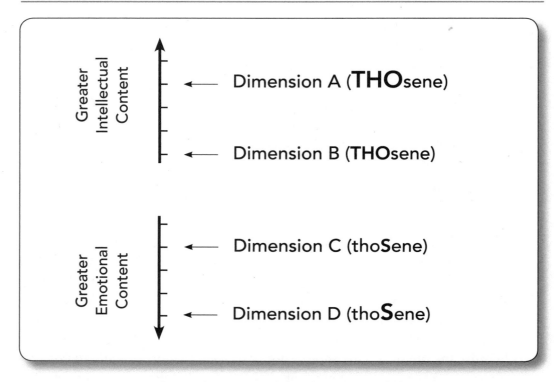

Figure 3.4: Dimensions' Thosenic Quality

content (**THO**sene), and others with greater emotional content (tho**S**ene)—see figure 3.4.

Furthermore, there are more than just these two states of information manifested through energies—**THO**sene and tho**S**ene. There is, in fact, an enormous gradient between them. The exact number of dimensions is unknown but there certainly seems to be a very large quantity.

Most of these planes have a characteristic level of holothosene that is quite old (millennia of years). The energy of hundreds of thousands of extraphysical consciousnesses—which have an affinity with a particular holothosene and "live" in it—continues to feed these holothosenes. This energy creates morphothosenes (structures) in the form of houses, roads, mountains, buildings, cities, and many others. Any object the extraphysical consciousness desires (or thinks it needs), whether consciously or unconsciously, will, with time, be created morphothosenically.

As a result, extraphysical dimensions that have inhabitants that are not very lucid can present objects that are unnecessary according to the natural extraphysical capacities of the psychosoma but necessary for them. For example, there are dimensions (tropospheric) where apparatuses for moving around and flying—somewhat similar to cars and planes—still exist. The psychosoma has the ability to fly, yet these extraphysical consciousnesses that live in these dimensions that present morphothosenes of transportation equipment do not know how to fly.[38] This condition is similar to intraphysical individuals who do not know how to swim, though the physical body has the ability to learn to swim.

Likewise, in certain tropospheric dimensions there are extraphysical consciousnesses that believe they need to eat and therefore create morphothosenes of food, or that still communicate extraphysically by moving their mouths (verbally). These dimensions are less evolved because the extraphysical consciousnesses inhabiting them have a lesser emotional balance and *still manifest many intraphysical conditionings.*

There are dimensions, in the *proper* extraphysical realms, where all the consciousnesses within that reality are able to fly; therefore, there are no car or plane analogues—since there is no need to create them morphothosenically. In general, *consciousnesses create the morphothosenes of the objects they still need to compensate for their limitations—whether consciously or not.* As a result of the differences in mentality and evolution between consciousnesses, as well as the "like attracts like" holothosenic condition that groups individuals together,[39] the number of existing dimensions is quite vast.

In some *proper* extraphysical dimensions, even the reality of "ground" does not exist.[40] This is because the extraphysical consciousnesses that coexist in that dimension—as a result of being in the in-between-physical-lives period—realize that they do not need the reality of ground. The reason ground is unnecessary is that they realize the psychosoma can fly and does not get tired—so in essence it does not need to "stand" anywhere. Other "lower" dimensions have ground because the consciousnesses coexisting there have not lost the *physical* conditioning of requiring ground that comes from their physical lives.

Certain morphothosenes, like the ground reality in many dimensions, are very stable and real. This ground morphothosene is quite old and has been created with the energies of millions of consciousnesses over eons of time. As a result, a projector will not be able to dematerialize this particular morphothosene in the same fashion as a less psychologically essential object created with much less energy.

Generally, when we are projected in the proper extraphysical dimensions, we will have the tendency to be in a dimension that has a similar characteristic holothosene to ours. In order to travel to very different dimensions, we will need to tune in to their characteristic holothosene.

As a result of this, it is observed that *more than a place, dimensions are a state of mind, of consciousness*; meaning there is no address to dimensions, but only a pattern of energies (state of mind) that we, as projectors, need to generate *within* ourselves so as to arrive there. Nonetheless, that pattern of energies is in fact very real, objective, and independent of us—since it already exists.

Individuals, when further developed, can perceive more than one dimension at a time. Intraphysical consciousnesses that have clairvoyance, for example, perceive not only the physical dimension but also extraphysical occurrences. Likewise, projectors can find themselves outside the body being able to perceive more than one dimension at once. Projectors' range of perception is increased as a result of their own development as well as their quantitative and qualitative experience.

Characteristics of the Psychosoma

A greater understanding of the psychosoma will provide further insight into the workings of the extraphysical dimensions. The following is a list of characteristics of the psychosoma and pertinent explanations for each one.

Self-Luminosity

Bioenergy is perceived as a certain luminous substance. Even physical rocks glow when observed through extraphysical vision. The psychosoma, which "houses" a consciousness, glows and radiates light,[41] which is a derivative of bioenergy.

The level of luminosity in an extraphysical dimension is a reflection of the holothosene of that dimension. Luminosity is not dependent on there being a light on somewhere in that extraphysical dimension. Extraphysical dimensions have an energetic pattern that is naturally lighter or darker. If while projected in a darker dimension we enter a room, we can illuminate the entire room with our presence. However, when we leave the room and go out into the "extraphysical open" in that dimension, we will not illuminate the entire dimension, though we will easily see and perceive everything because extraphysical perceptions, even visual, are not dependent on how much light a dimension has.

Everything is made from energy, and energy is seen outside the body and glows. A novice projector or an individual who underwent a NDE can say, "I saw a being of light, with a lot of light around him," or "A great light spoke to me." Yet, since everybody is luminous, the fact that there is light is not a good criterion for determining evolution. In these cases, it was not necessarily an evolved being that was present. Furthermore, if you already control the exercises of energy that were presented in the last chapter, you can control the level of luminosity you display outside the body. Of course, this may be a nice trick, but it does not mean we are instantly more evolved. As we understand the extraphysical dimensions in more depth, our criteria develop as well, becoming more profound and accurate.

Self-Permeability

The psychosoma is able to permeate "denser" dimensions and structures.[42] Therefore, a projector can pass through physical walls, objects, doors, cars, and other things.[43] For the most part, we will be unable to open physical books or doors or ring bells, among other things, while we are projected.

However, the psychosoma cannot go through structures of the same "density"; for example, when we try to go through our para-arm with our other parahand, we are unable to do so. We are able to touch our psychosoma and feel sensations of "density" and "substance" when grabbing it. Likewise, while projected in an extraphysical dimension, if there is a morphothosenic wall there, we will be unable to pass through this wall, again because we are at the same level of energetic "frequency" as the wall.[44]

The level of lucidity also affects the condition of self-permeability. When we are projected with a high degree of lucidity, it does not even occur to us that going through a wall may not be possible since we are very aware that it is the normal capacity of the psychosoma. Yet, when the lucidity is weaker, the *intraphysical conditionings* are stronger. In these cases, projected individuals may be standing next to a physical wall trying to consider whether they will be able to pass through it. This is similar to when children sit around on top of a ten-foot diving board in a pool thinking about whether they can (or will) dive off it. Extraphysically, the greater the doubts, the fewer the chances are of being successful; and in many instances, the projector loses lucidity altogether and returns to the physical body.

On *rare* occasion we can condense or materialize the psychosoma, even to the point of being able to have an effect on physical objects.[45] This is done through a type of energy called ectoplasm. Though this condition is possible, it is extremely unlikely and difficult. It is important here to understand the difference between something being possible and it being likely or common. The study of ectoplasm goes beyond the scope of this book.

Weightlessness

The psychosoma cannot be weighed and therefore can fly.[46] This condition is dependent, however, on how much dense energosomatic energy the psychosoma is carrying.[47] In certain instances, when this occurs, we notice that we do not elevate as expected. Individuals sometimes have "dreams" of not fully flying per se, but of jumping over houses, several trees, or mountains at a time; or of trying to fly but staying close to the ground (a few feet), sort of like walking underwater and struggling to advance. These types of dreams many times are OBEs with a greater amount of energosomatic energy accumulated in the psychosoma, making the projector heavier, loaded, and less lucid. Because of the lesser degree of lucidity, individuals normally confuse these experiences with dreams.

The dimension where the projector is projected also affects how easy or difficult it is to fly. As was mentioned in chapter 2, energies that are more emotional are "denser," and intellectual energies are "subtler." In certain dimensions, flying, or even just moving around, happens as if in slow motion[48] because of the characteristics of the dimension itself—or its holothosene (being denser).

Invisibility and Inaudibility

Projected intraphysical projectors and extraphysical consciousnesses are not perceived by the normal physical senses.[49] However, an intraphysical consciousness that has developed clairvoyance may be able to "see" the psychosoma. If individuals have developed clairaudience, they will be able to "hear" extraphysical voices. If they have developed their intuition, they may be able to "feel" the projector. In practical terms, the psychosoma is invisible and inaudible to physical eyes and ears.

On the other hand, if projectors are able to condense their psychosoma, they can reach a state of density that can allow intraphysical consciousnesses to see and/or hear them. As noted, this condition is rare and very unlikely. Yet, phenomena like bilocations,[50] parateleportations,[51] half-materializations,[52] false arrivals,[53] telekinesis,[54] farewell projections,[55] and others are usually accomplished using the previously mentioned denser type of energy called ectoplasm.

> Projectiology studies these phenomena (bilocations, teleportations, etc.), as well as ectoplasm. Yet even though there is a large amount of related material on them, their particular details and descriptions— as was previously explained—are beyond the scope of this work. For more information, please refer to this chapter's notes and the bibliography, as well as the back of the book for IAC courses on the subject—both the regular courses (CDP) and the specialized (intensive) ones. Visit LearnOBEs.com for more details on the CDP.

Self-Transfiguration and Elasticity

The psychosoma is mutable and malleable and can change form at will.[56] Generally, the appearance of a projector's psychosoma is a copy of the projector's physical appearance; that is, the psychosoma has, among other features, the same shape, height, and hairstyle as the physical body.[57] Nevertheless, the consciousness has the capacity to change this visual presentation. We can decide to look like a different person, and the psychosoma will transform into this other appearance. These transformations remind us of certain comic book superheroes or science fiction movies; for example, the "T-1000" and "terminatrix" made out of liquid metal in the *Terminator 2* and *3* movies.

The reason the psychosoma looks like the physical body is because we are conditioned to think that our physical appearance is our "real" appearance—it is our self-image. Our physical appearance changes over time and over different physical lives. For example, the psychosoma of a boy has the characteristics of a boy (i.e., height, body structure, and so forth). A person who grows a beard will present a psychosoma with a beard—that is, after enough time has gone by to become accustomed to the beard. Furthermore, during a previous life, the psychosoma looked like the physical body of that life.

Moreover, the psychosoma of an individual who has recently lost a physical member (i.e., amputation) still manifests this same appendage. After some time, perhaps years, once the intraphysical person is conditioned to not having the appendage, the psychosoma they present also will show an amputated appendage. This example sheds light on the famous "phantom limb" condition of individuals who have undergone an amputation. Is it possible that they are feeling their para-appendage due to their psychosoma still transmitting some sensations?

With some experience, we start to recognize while projected other psychosomas (extraphysical consciousnesses or intraphysical projectors) by their individual, unique, and specific holothosenes and not their appearance. In other words, the self-transfiguration capacity of the psychosoma potentially allows any consciousness to present itself with any appearance in the extraphysical dimensions. This condition in turn leads consciousnesses to start recognizing others by something more permanent than appearance. Extraphysically, individuals are recognized by their "content," or thosenization (information in their energy), and not their form. We are the collection of ideas, knowledge, sentiments, intentions, and other qualities that we manifest—these are the characteristics we develop and refine from life to life. Appearance becomes secondary.

Here, too, it is important to refine our criteria according to how the extraphysical body works. Since the psychosoma can alter forms, we can wonder, how many extraphysical consciousnesses can we find outside the body that look like Elvis Presley? If there are already people who want to look like him inside the body—where the body is not self-transfigurable—we cannot be surprised to find certain extraphysical consciousnesses who also do this. Yet, if extraphysically we find someone who looks like Elvis, is it actually him? More than likely it will not be him. We see here how we *cannot judge a book by its cover* outside the body. Furthermore, if we find a glowing extraphysical consciousness with a halo, wings, and a white robe, is it an "angel"? It will be important to check the *content* of the energies, because any consciousness can present itself looking like an "angel," but they are not necessarily more evolved. On the contrary, evolved consciousnesses usually give very little importance to appearances and terrestrial mythologies and stereotypes.

The psychosoma is also elastic. The projector can elongate any part of the psychosoma. This is an attribute that is shared by the silver cord, which can seemingly stretch without limits. (This has been observed and experienced in projections going great distances from our planet—exoprojections.) Furthermore, we can make our psychosoma grow larger or smaller. This may even be practical to do in certain circumstances, as some dimensions do not have the same reference of size that we have here on Earth in the physical dimension.

Invulnerability

Strictly speaking, nothing can hurt the psychosoma.[58] The psychosoma does not bleed or feel pain, cold, heat, hunger, or fatigue, and does not need to breathe. These conditions pertain to the physical body. The physical body has organs, and the psychosoma does not. Everything that is understood and observed about the psychosoma confirms that it cannot be damaged.

However, there are other criteria to keep in mind here. Feeling pain outside the body is a psychological, mental, and subjective condition—since the psychosoma does not have a nervous system. We may fly into a physical wall at a high speed, and because of conditionings during our whole life, we may "generate" and feel pain, as this is how we understand this experience "should" be. This "pain" is very subjective and inconsistent, since perhaps during another projection with greater lucidity we may undergo the same experience and not feel/generate any pain. Extraphysically, pain is created by what we think. Yet, because no individual simply produces thoughts alone but rather produces thosenes (thoughts, emotions, and energy), this "thosenic creation" of pain produces an energetic pattern that in some instances can stay with us upon returning to the body. The way we release these thosenes from our psychosphere, in order to eliminate the sensation, is by producing a VS (vibrational state), causing a dissimilation.

The psychosoma is completely indestructible and will not be damaged by our OBE explorations. If we so desire, we can stay underwater for an entire projection, go to an active volcano and swim in lava, enter into a nuclear reactor, or even stand on a freeway and allow an eighteen-wheeler to go through us.[59]

Historically, there have been groups, individuals, and authors who state that the extraphysical dimensions are dangerous and/or that the overall practice of leaving the body is harmful. This position is not supported by the facts. Most fears that these individuals have can be explained by misinterpretations; that is, fear of the projective catalepsy sensation, fear of the unknown (lack of information), lack of experience, and a variety of their own subjective fears.

Exploring: Flight and Time

The psychosoma can fly and reach both physical and extraphysical targets that are far away. The projector can fly, turn in midair, accelerate, and stop, having arms stretched out or not, while sitting, standing, or in any position. Flying over vast bodies of water, such as the ocean, is recommended, as the individual directly absorbs large volumes of immanent energy (hydroenergy, specifically) from the water, recharging the person for several weeks thereafter.[60] The psychosoma's potential for exploration is wide-ranging. It could potentially be used by astronomers, physicists, archeologists, anthropologists, biologists, and other researchers.

The ability to reach the desired target is dependent on a combination of several factors: first and foremost, the extraphysical lucidity of the projector; second, how much dense energy of the energosoma is being carried extraphysically; and third, the level of affinity the projector has with the target. If the level of lucidity and control is high enough, then in order for us to arrive projected at a specific target, we have to focus our will on the target. We will feel ourselves moving toward that objective. The more focused our attention is and the better we know the target (affinity), the easier it will be. Therefore, the mechanism by which a target is reached is by creating a rapport or energetic connection with it, and then following this connection.

We can also reach places we have never been to before. This can occur in two ways: (1) projectors may stumble upon—through exploration—a previously unknown place or dimension; and (2) projectors make something or somebody else their target—aiming to arrive at this target and therefore at the intended place as well. Let us examine some examples of the second condition.

If a familiar person (a relative, for example) is visiting a city or country to which we have never been before and that is unknown to us, we, as projectors, can use our relative as the target and focus on them in order to arrive there. Or, if the projector has a picture of a part of the city or country, then the projector can memorize all the details of the picture. Afterward, while outside the body, the projector can focus on the memorized image to reach the place. The projector can also accomplish this with an object from that place.

The projector will need a *focusing element* in order to get to a specific location. We do not need to worry about getting lost, since by simply thinking about our physical body, or even just the bedroom where our body is lying, we will return.

The time it takes to arrive at a specific place may vary. During the first attempts, the projector might feel that some time actually passed by—some seconds. Yet as the experience and proficiency of reaching targets is improved, the projector will be able to arrive almost instantaneously at certain places. Affinity with the target and experience diminish the perceived time it takes to get there.

Time is very subjective extraphysically and basically does not exist in the same way it exists physically. Normal projections can last anywhere from fifteen to twenty-five physical minutes on average. It is less common to see experiences that last forty-five minutes or more, and it is extremely rare for individuals to project for more than one hour.

In the tropospheric dimensions, the sense of time has a closer relation to the physical one. Yet in many proper extraphysical dimensions, especially the more subtle ones, time starts to lose its meaning and becomes a more subjective experience.[61] There is, however, an extraphysical sequence of events that cannot be reversed (going back to change the past like in the film *Back to the Future*).[62]

The points of reference then become the projector's own experience and a sense of time. In other words, we may feel that we "experienced" events that are equivalent to thirty intraphysical minutes,[63] but upon returning to the body and verifying the time with a clock, we realize that only fifteen physical minutes actually went by. This discrepancy with physical time will increase depending on our condition (subjectivity) and the extraphysical dimension in which we are manifesting.

Time is a *real intraphysical illusion* (just like matter) that in evolved extraphysical dimensions has all but disappeared. Though these projections are rare, there are accounts of projectors who have had extraphysical experiences that were *subjectively worth one or two years* of life—when maybe only less than a half hour went by in the physical dimension.

Types of Projections

Lucid projections can be classified in the following fashion:

Partial projection. These are projections of only a part of the physical body (e.g., the head, or an arm). They are very common at the beginning. In certain instances the projector can even extraphysically sit up, disconnecting the head, shoulders, and torso without being able to fully disconnect the legs and hips (figure 3.5).

Leisure projection. These are projections in which the projector flies and goes to visit a friend or another dimension. This is the extraphysical equivalent of physical tourism.

Loaded projection. This is a projection with a large amount of dense energosomatic energy. This condition tends to diminish the lucidity of the projector and the level of mobility. In order to "shake ourselves free" of this loaded condition, we should exteriorize while projected (see chapter 2). This is the equivalent of "releasing the

Figure 3.5: Partial Projection

ballast," and after this we are much more aware and dynamic. By exteriorizing, we exchange the more dense physical energies we are carrying for more subtle energies being absorbed during the projection.

Educational projection.[64] This type of projection seems to have a lesson as an objective. In many instances it is a practical lesson, such as applying our energies to change dimensions, creating morphothosenes, controlling our thoughts, and flying, among others. In certain situations the learning comes from observing some extraphysical condition that will help us understand something more specific. These projections seem to be coordinated by a more evolved being, called a helper (spirit guide).[65]

Assisted projection. These are projections whereby we are assisted by someone else in separating from our physical body. In most cases this assistance is received from a helper, yet it can also be from another projector. When projected, trying to extraphysically wake up another person—who is sleeping—is fairly difficult in practice, but feasible. Yet usually it is easier for the other person to produce a lucid projection by themselves than for another projector to wake them up extraphysically.

Assistantial projection.[66] During these projections, the projector goes and assists others extraphysically. Usually this involves the donation of bioenergy to another consciousness, either intraphysical or extraphysical. (Refer to chapter 5 for more information on this type of experience.)

Joint projection.[67] These are projections in which the projector meets another projector, and together they undergo a common experience (figure 3.6). This type of projection can be planned by the projectors while inside the body, and afterward they can provide each other with confirmation of their experiences during the projection. The ideal is when both projectors have a good level of lucidity and recall afterward.

Joint Flight
Maximiliano Torres Haymann (2003)[68]

I lived in Vitoria, Espirito Santo, Brazil, and had heard about the projectiology and conscientiology courses but had not yet attended any of them. An acquaintance lent me the projectiology treatise from Waldo Vieira, from which I learned several concepts that I mention here as part of this account of a lucid projection I had on December 24, 1998.

(continued) During the day I remained very calm, more serene than usual. I went to the beach in the morning and slept approximately two hours in the afternoon. I went out with Ellen (my girlfriend) to the Paseo de Jacareípe and was out until 11:45 PM. I was still somewhat full from dinner at her house. Upon arriving home, I watched some TV and decided to do the energy mobilization exercises. I heard a sound in my ear and thought it could be a pre-projective signal.

The air conditioning was on, and the temperature was below 25°C (77°F). I was lying on a mat next to my bed, because I had problems lying in the dorsal position on my bed's soft mattress. I started doing the energy mobilization exercises at 12:40 AM, and I think this lasted for about twenty to twenty-five minutes. I was tired and turned toward my left.

I awoke extraphysically with a 60%–70% level of awareness, according to my analysis. I had the sensation of being really projected and thought that I should stay calm and try to increase my awareness. I started to look around in search of my spirit guide or helper. I could perceive the dark room but felt that I could see it brighter due to the psychosoma's luminosity.

Immediately I had a brief lucidity blackout. It seemed as if I had returned to the soma. I was perceiving the presence of Ellen, who spoke to me as if she was in the ordinary waking state: "Wake up, my love."

This surprised me, since it was as if she was lying on top of me, and I stood up with some difficulty. When we were "standing" next to the bed, she showed me her foot, complaining about something. That attitude seemed strange to me, but I did not give it any importance.

We went toward the bedroom door. I had perceived that Ellen was not conscious about being projected and then I told her, "Ellen, we are projected!" I looked toward the bed to show her my soma for her to understand that we were outside our bodies. However, my soma was not on top of the bed. I understood that this was because I had lain on the mat, next to the bed. At that moment I forgot this fact, especially because when I woke up extraphysically, my psychosoma was on top of my bed. I remained clear that I was projected.

Figure 3.6: Joint Projection

We went to the living room and walked toward the balcony door, which was closed. Ellen was trying to open the door, but her hand kept on passing through it. I told her that she did not need to open the door, since we could just simply go through it. We did this. I looked toward the street and it was dark. We went toward the end of the balcony and started flying in the air toward the right of the apartment. We continued to look around and observe what was happening on the street. Ellen suggested a target for us to go to. Initially as we flew, we were hugging, and afterward we were holding hands. I looked to the sky and saw many stars, which seemed to be grouped in conglomerates. I went through a high tension cable and was able to see a strong specific glow that seemed to be the electricity flowing through the cable.

(continued) I told Ellen that I was feeling the presence of a guide flying next to me. The three of us were flying. I could feel the long hair of the guide, and for this reason I thought that this extraphysical consciousness had a feminine appearance. I started to laugh out of happiness and I think this made me come back to my body. I felt that I was in the soma and then I opened my eyes. Some of the projective events were remembered *en bloc* and others came afterward.

The following day, when I spoke with Ellen, she told me that she had "dreamt" with me, and that the day before the projection she had hit her foot on the sidewalk and had injured a toe—something I was unaware of.

Projections in series.[69] This is a projection that is part of a series of lucid experiences outside the body, usually with a common objective. In certain instances, an experience with an educational objective may require several projections, which are usually "scheduled" by a helper. The full series of experiences can take place in one night (three or four OBEs) or they can span several months—for example, one lucid projection every month with the continuation of the same main topic.

Mentalsoma projection. This is a projection to the mentalsomatic dimensions manifesting with the mentalsoma; the condition of superconsciousness or cosmoconsciousness.[70]

Mentalsoma

The mentalsoma is the fourth vehicle of manifestation of the consciousness. It is the most subtle and the one that allows for the most lucid manifestation. The mentalsoma is arguably responsible for the main aspect of the consciousness: lucidity.

Projection of the Mentalsoma

Projections of the mentalsoma are an expansion in lucidity, awareness.[71] Mentalsomatic projections are much harder to produce than psychosomatic projections, and it usually takes longer (years or decades) for people to develop this skill. These are very different experiences because there is very little relation between the mental dimensions and the physical dimension, which makes the mentalsomatic reality harder to understand. To *fully* grasp it, this reality needs to be experienced, since language is inadequate to describe it.

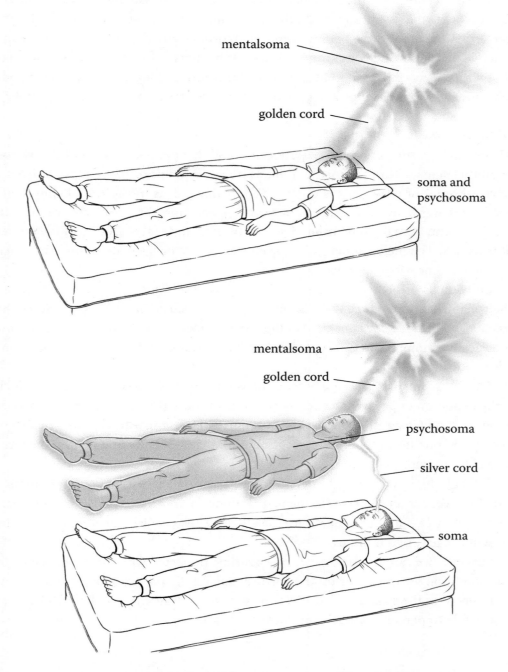

Figure 3.7: Direct and Indirect Projection of the Mentalsoma

The projection with the mentalsoma can occur in two fashions: in either a direct fashion or via the psychosoma.[72] In the first example, the mentalsoma projects alone and leaves the other three bodies (soma, energosoma, and psychosoma) aligned and inactive. In the second condition—via the psychosoma—the consciousness projects first with the psychosoma, splitting the energosoma and leaving the physical body inactive; and afterward it projects the mentalsoma from the psychosoma (figure 3.7).

Mentalsomatic Dimension

The mentalsomatic dimension is a "state of mind" that permeates the entire universe. Subdimensions within the mental dimension are difficult to make sense of from a physical point of view. This is due to the fact that we, as intraphysical consciousnesses, are normally biased due to our concepts of time, distance, and overall reality. The mentalsomatic dimension does not present any of the realities of the denser dimensions. The mentalsomatic dimensions are full of evolved ideas, some of which are incomprehensible to projectors.

Individuals projected in the mentalsoma have the utmost freedom in terms of their manifestations, since there seem to be no pressuring holothosenes. Since the "reality" of distance does not exist in the mentalsomatic dimension, the mentalsoma is basically omnipresent. Concepts like "size" have no point of reference in the mentalsomatic dimension.

The consciousness in the mental dimension can experience *macroscopy*, which is the condition of perceiving endless amounts of space (for example, many galaxies at once) in one instant, in one *perception unit*. This is similar to how we are able to perceive in one instant, in one perception unit, the understanding behind the term "chair," for example.

A reality like galaxies still refers to objects within space-time, a more tangible structure; yet consciousnesses in the mental dimension can also perceive in one perception unit vast amounts of justice, or ethics. These abilities go well beyond the present capacity of our brains.

Likewise, we can experience *microscopy* while projected with the mentalsoma. In this condition we can focus on the smallest subatomic particles and explore them as if they were the size of a galaxy. We are able to see differences and details that are impossible to perceive with the physical body. Likewise, going beyond matter, and focusing on ideas, we can begin to understand concepts like the smallest unit of compassion, assistance, or ethics.

Differences between the Psychosoma and the Mentalsoma

Let us start to understand the details of projections of the mentalsoma by comparing them with psychosomatic projections and analyzing some of the basic differences.[73]

As a general rule of thumb, *recalling* a projection is dependent on the level of awareness in projections of the psychosoma. Therefore, if, when we are projected with the mentalsoma, we are able to achieve 100% lucidity, then the recollection "should" be easier. In practice, however, the case is the opposite. Usually mentalsomatic projections are harder to recall than psychosomatic projections.

The reasons for this are twofold. First, it has to do with the mentalsomatic reality. The direct experience of the mentalsoma is so different from the physical dimension that the physical brain has basically no reference with which to interpret these experiences. Using the previous example of the coin sorter, imagine what would happen if, in this machine made exclusively for U.S. coins, only foreign coins (rubles, euros, and others) were thrown in. The coin sorter would not be able to deal with this efficiently, which is similar to what happens to the brain after a mentalsomatic projection.

Secondly, it has to do with the actual transfer of information from the mentalsoma. In the more common psychosomatic OBE, the experience is perceived by the psychosoma, and in order to remember it in the physical dimension, the energy containing this information needs to be "transferred" to the physical body. Yet in a mentalsomatic projection, everything is perceived by the mentalsoma, and for this reason, in order to remember it physically, the information needs to be transferred from the mentalsoma to the psychosoma and from there to the physical body (brain). Therefore, in order for the information to be recalled, it needs to cross two "bridges" (golden cord and silver cord) instead of just one (silver cord).

Not only is remembering a mentalsomatic projection harder,[74] but also physically reporting these experiences is a challenge.[75] Languages have words that have been created to describe what we normally see, namely the physical dimension; yet these words prove inadequate to describe the mental dimension.

The actual *projection process* of the mentalsoma is also different from the psychosomatic projection. Many of the sensations that are felt when the projector disconnects with the psychosoma are not felt when projecting with the mentalsoma. This occurs because many of the psychosoma's disconnection sensations are a direct result of the energosoma dividing. Strictly speaking, since in mentalsomatic projections the energosoma does not divide, many sensations simply do not occur.

A projection of the mentalsoma is more of an expansion of the consciousness, a tuning in to the mentalsomatic dimension, than an actual spatial separation from the other bodies. From the condition of being in a mentalsomatic projection, we are able to "reach" any corner of the universe, because there is no limit of space, distance, or time in the mentalsomatic dimension. Therefore, in these cases, there is not actually a "separation" of bodies in the physical sense.

The *level of lucidity* is something that can fluctuate wildly in psychosomatic projections. This happens as a result of emotional imbalances, lack of energetic control, and holothosenic influences in the extraphysical environments. However, in mentalsomatic projections, the consciousness does not lose its lucidity for any of those reasons because we do not manifest emotions in the same sense. There is also no heavy energetic load with us, and the mentalsomatic holothosenes are very stabilizing. Therefore, in mentalsomatic projections, projectors do not return to the body if they lose their emotional control.

Notice that the psychosoma is also called the emotional body, because it processes and produces emotions. The mentalsoma has its own means of "feeling," yet these "feelings" are much more refined than the raw emotions of the psychosoma. In order to make a distinction, two different terms are used. The mentalsoma has *sentiments*, while the psychosoma has *emotions*.

Emotions are feelings that can diminish the lucidity of the consciousness if they are too intense. Sentiments are sensations, feelings that do not diminish the lucidity of the consciousness—quite the contrary, in fact. Some examples of sentiments are universal brotherhood or sisterhood, lucid love, fraternalism, lucid compassion, and serenity. Notice the difference between these sentiments and emotions. We can have an attack of rage or passion, yet it does not make sense to talk about us having an attack of brotherhood or serenity. Since during projections of the mentalsoma, the psychosoma is not involved (was left behind), the mentalsoma does not have emotions and does not lose its lucidity as a result of them.

The *constitution of the body* is also very different between the mentalsoma and the psychosoma. While the psychosoma has a humanoid shape, the mentalsoma does not have any form.

It is theorized that the mentalsoma does not have a form because it does not need to have one. As the consciousness evolves, it overcomes physical conditionings—in this case, the conditioning of needing to present an appearance. As we go to more advanced extraphysical dimensions, there are fewer forms and morphothosenes, and appearance in the mentalsoma follows this same line of logic. The consciousnesses inhabiting the mentalsomatic dimensions realize that the psychosoma is already "obsolete" in many aspects and unnecessary for them in their evolution.

Upon analyzing the psychosoma, we arrive at this same conclusion. In other words, the psychosoma has paralegs, yet it does not need to run or walk anywhere. It presents parahands and para-arms, yet it does not need to carry anything or reach for anything. Additionally, in more advanced extraphysical dimensions, we also find increasingly less tangible forms. The psychosoma has a parahead, which exhibits para-eyes, para-ears, a paramouth, and parahair, yet none of the psychosoma's senses have anything to do with these nonfunctional areas. We do not smell with the para-nose. We do not need to talk or eat with the paramouth. We do not see with the para-eyes and we do not hear with the para-ears. Furthermore, the psychosoma has a trunk that does not need to hold lungs, heart, stomach, and other organs, because it does not have any organs. And, more importantly, the psychosoma does not actually need to have any appearance at all, because what differentiates one consciousness from another is the information in its energies, its holothosene.

Our psychosomas have a humanoid shape because of our self-image, our conditionings. It could be postulated that the psychosoma is a mold or a matrix of energy, and also has properties of a morphothosene.[76] Thus, we can also arrive at the conclusion that the appearance of the psychosoma is ultimately obsolete. Yet it is one thing to theoretically understand our conditionings and another thing to overcome those conditionings in practice. Consciousnesses who have reached such a stage of overcoming their conditionings, being free of physical rebirths and of the psychosoma, are the "natives" of the mentalsomatic dimension.

Characteristics of the Mentalsoma

The mentalsoma, besides allowing a broader manifestation than any other body, is also responsible for processing several consciential capacities.[77] The mentalsoma is responsible for all of our intellectual faculties. Let us explain some of the most relevant ones, since they are very present in our mentalsomatic experiences.

- *Discernment* is the capacity to ponder, discriminate, and differentiate between two or more conditions. It is the ability to reflect on problems in order to arrive at conclusions from different angles from which we can understand them.

- *Will* is the capacity to put intentions into action. Reaching the vibrational state is a matter of activating the energy of the energosoma beyond a certain threshold; it is just a matter of will.

- *Ethics* is the capacity to tell the difference between right and wrong, and to know to which degree something is right or wrong according to our current understandings.

- The *decision-making process* is the ability to choose one thing over another, based on certain criteria. Everything is open for analysis, yet the individual has to be able to formulate good criteria for this analysis.

- *Organization* is placing objects, tasks, and priorities in their proper order. Several activities can help the consciousness leave the body, yet we have to be able to apply the proper sequence and organize ourselves so as to be effective.

- *Discipline* is the capacity to combine will with constancy, so as to be able, for example, to repeat a task as many times as necessary.

- *Mentalsomatic* behavior is a more logical, analytical, rational, lucid, aware, self-controlled, or self-managed type of behavior. Ethics and discernment are part of every decision-making process.

An important aspect of the mentalsoma is the *holomemory*.[78] This memory, located in the mentalsoma, stores the record of everything that the consciousness has ever experienced in all its lives and intermissive periods. In certain schools of thought this is referred to as the *akashic records*.[79]

As a result of the holomemory access, individuals are able to have *retrocognitions*, or recollections of past lives. The mentalsoma registers in the holomemory every detail of our lives, whether we are aware of it or not. Therefore, even memories from our childhood that the brain has a hard time recalling are stored in the holomemory.

The mentalsoma, like the psychosoma, is not perceived by any of the physical senses. Likewise, the projector in the mentalsoma is not able to affect the physical dimension.

The mentalsoma is also the carrier of the consciousness and still uses bioenergy for manifesting. There is no current practical observation of the consciousness separating from the mentalsoma to manifest on its own. There is also no observation to date of any body or vehicle of manifestation more refined and/or evolved than the mentalsoma. In chapter 5 we will discuss in more detail the extraphysical consciousnesses that inhabit all these dimensions.

All the information accumulated on mentalsomatic experiences goes beyond the scope of this book. For more information, refer to the bibliography and to the back of the book for the CDP course by IAC. Visit LearnOBEs.com for information on the CDP.

Summary of Key Chapter Points

- Through relaxation and energy work, we can start to feel the disconnection from the physical body. Many of these sensations are new and may surprise us initially, but they are not negative.

- The extraphysical sphere of energy has a radius of about thirteen feet from our physical head and is responsible for the blackout sensation.

- Our level of extraphysical lucidity—which implies clarity of thought, perception, decision-making ability, control, and memory, among others—will determine the quality of our OBEs.

- The more aware we are extraphysically, the more we control our emotions, and vice versa.

- We stabilize ourselves and increase our extraphysical awareness by working with energy; specifically, by producing a vibrational state (VS).

- Will and attention are some of the main attributes we use to control our extraphysical experience.

- Extraphysical perception is based on the reception of thosenes, which can occur through the entire psychosoma.

- Morphothosenes are extraphysical forms, elements, and realities created with thosenes, and can be created consciously or unconsciously.

- Dimensions are different levels of energetic quality, or holothosenes.

- Morphothosenes in extraphysical dimensions are created to compensate for the limitations of the consciousness in that dimension.

- The psychosoma has several specific attributes—including self-luminosity, self-permeability, weightlessness, self-transfigurability, elasticity, and invulnerability—that help to interact with the extraphysical dimensions.

- While outside the body, focusing our will on a target allows us to reach it.

- Extraphysical time does not have the same meaning as intraphysical time, and in the mentalsomatic dimension there is no time.

- Projections of the mentalsoma are an expansion in lucidity and can be produced directly or via the psychosoma (indirectly).

- The mentalsomatic dimension does not have limits of size, form, shape, distance, time, and others.

- Mentalsomatic projections are harder to recall than psychosomatic ones; they do not produce any disconnection sensations, and the level of awareness is 100%.

- The mentalsoma is the body responsible for our awareness, discernment, will, ethics, decision-making process, organization, discipline, and also our holomemory.

Chapter Notes

1. Trivellato and Alegretti, 1999, p. 107.
2. Vieira, 2002, pp. 227, 472, 739, 841.
3. Vieira, *Conscientiology*, 1997, p. 14; Vieira, 2002, pp. 494–95; and Vieira, *Projections*, 2007, p. 55.
4. Vieira, 2002, pp. 211, 514.
5. Ibid., pp. 504, 741.
6. Vieira, 2002, pp. 130–33; Buhlman, 1996, p. 212; Muldoon and Carrington, 1992, pp. 55–56; Rogo, 1986, p. 42; and Thiago, 1999, p. 121.
7. Bruce, 1999, pp. 79, 87–98, 547.
8. Dries, 2006, p. 55; Vieira, 2002, pp. 512–13; and Thiago, 1999, p. 60.
9. *Para-* (prefix) = beyond or extraphysical. Parahead is the extraphysical head, or the head of the psychosoma.
10. Vieira, 2002, p. 508.
11. Bruce, 1999, pp. 44–72.
12. Alegretti, 2004, p. 101; and Minero, *Correspondence*, 2002, pp. 63–65.

13. Vieira, 2002, p. 808.

14. Vieira, 2002, pp. 253, 514; and Vieira, *Projections*, 1997, p. 195.

15. Vieira, 2002, pp. 495–96.

16. Atwater, 2000, pp. 12–13; Vieira, 2002, pp. 523–24; and Lutfi, 2006, pp. 46–47, 68–69, 72, 75, 80.

17. Vieira, 2002, p. 509; Thiago, 1999, pp. 63–65.

18. Vieira, 2002, pp. 553–56; and Vieira, *Projections*, 2007, p. 177.

19. Vieira, 2002, pp. 510–11, 735; Peterson, 1997, p. 152; and Martin, 1980, p. 26.

20. Vieira, 2002, p. 750.

21. Ibid., pp. 532–34.

22. Ibid., p. 216.

23. Ibid., p. 228.

24. See Castaneda, 1994.

25. Vieira, 2002, pp. 537–38.

26. Stack, 1988, p. 56.

27. Vieira, 2002, p. 567.

28. Minero, *Intuition*, 2002; Vieira, 2002, pp. 149–51.

29. Vieira, 2002, pp. 565–67; and Buhlman, 2001, p. 64.

30. Vieira, 2002, pp. 568–71.

31. Vieira, 2002, pp. 604–10; and Monroe, 1977, p. 75.

32. Vieira, 2002, pp. 542–44.

33. Ibid., pp. 545–47.

34. Ibid., pp. 550–51.

35. Ibid., pp. 536–37.

36. Ibid., pp. 552–53.

37. Vicenzi, 1999, p. 340.

38. Alegretti, 2008.

39. Vicenzi, 2005, p. 23.

40. Alegretti, 2008.

41. Martin, 1980, p. 27; Vieira, 2002, pp. 285, 289, 615–16.

42. Vieira, 2002, pp. 289, 617–19.

43. Vieira, *Projections*, 2007, p. 57.

44. Vieira, 2002, p. 551.

45. Ibid., pp. 158–66, 170–74.

46. Ibid., p. 620.

47. Dries, 2006, pp. 31–34.

48. Thiago, 1999, pp. 63–64.

49. Vieira, 2002, pp. 621–22.

50. Ibid., pp. 158–65.

51. Ibid., pp. 195–97.

52. Ibid., pp. 173–74.

53. Ibid., pp. 182–84.

54. Ibid., pp. 193–94.

55. Ibid., pp. 187–89.

56. Ibid., pp. 619, 640–44.

57. Muldoon and Carrington, 1992, p. 47.

58. Vieira, 2002, pp. 622–24.

59. Alegretti, 2008.

60. Ibid.

61. Vieira, 2002, pp. 534–36.

62. Alegretti, 2004, p. 101.

63. Ibid., p. 81.

64. Vieira, 2002, p. 816.

65. Refer to chapter 5 of this book for a detailed study on helpers.

66. Vieira, 2002, pp. 723–27.

67. Ibid., pp. 830–35.

68. Haymann, 2003, p. 227.

69. Vieira, 2002, pp. 835–37.

70. Ibid., pp. 133–39.

71. Ibid., pp. 312–15.

72. Ibid., p. 316.

73. Ibid., pp. 834–35.

74. Ibid., pp. 754, 816.

75. For an example of a mentalsomatic projection, please refer to Vieira, *Projections*, 2007, Chapter 60, pp. 214–20.

76. Vieira, 2002, p. 284.

77. Vieira, *700*, 1994, p. 374.

78. Vieira, 1999, pp. 57–58.

79. Akashic records are a deposit of information on the individual and everything else that exists. Specifying akashic records further, the information about the individual is in its own holomemory, the information about other places is in those places (including their history), and information about animals, plants, and others is in them as well. For more information, see Muldoon and Carrington, 1992, pp. 297–99; Bruce, 1999, pp. 411–23.

CHAPTER 4

How-To

With all the information from the previous chapters, the next step is to learn a methodology that will help you achieve the goal of leaving the body with awareness. The objective of this chapter is to explain how to start experiencing all the knowledge you have received throughout this book thus far, so you can evaluate the results of self-research through your own perceptions and direct experience. As Vieira (*Wha Conscientiology Is*, 1994) states, *the quickest link between theory and practice is a technique.*

Within the consciential paradigm, everything can be researched. We can consider ourselves our own guinea pigs for achieving self-knowledge. The methodology proposed for accomplishing this is self-research and experimentation through projective techniques. Projective techniques are methods that help to produce lucid OBEs through our own effort and control.

The ideal technique is the one that can be applied anytime and in the most circumstances, without too many requirements or a complicated setup. For instance, do you know a technique that can be applied while traveling on a plane? You cannot bring artifacts or crutches (for example, a pyramid, different perfumes, or candles) into such an environment to help you project. However, you can use a technique where all you have to use is your own mind. Such a technique is more universal in terms of conditions, requirements, and effectiveness. In general, the ideal technique is the one that gives us results, so it has to be efficient but also practical and healthy and based mainly on our personal attributes.

All of the guidelines given here are indications that will help you to develop your OBEs and increase the probability of success. It is also important to state that no technique is necessary. There are cases of people leaving the body while walking (momentarily, for a second or two at most) in completely nonideal conditions. Though this certainly happens, it is very unlikely. The more techniques and predisposing factors that we are able to integrate into our daily habits, the easier it will become to leave the body.

General Instructions

Let's present some principles or guidelines regarding the preparation for having projections:

1. *There is no OBE technique that will work for everybody all the time.* There are hundreds of techniques for producing OBEs or other types of altered states of consciousness that may lead to an OBE.[1] But in order to develop this capacity, we have

to try several of them so as to evaluate, within our own experience, which one will be the most efficient for us. The projective techniques are rooted in some internal attributes, traits, or elements that will be used to help us induce the OBE. Some attributes include, but are not limited to, relaxation, concentration, imagination, will, determination, and energy.

If a person has a good level of will, and this is one of their more predominant personality traits, then projective techniques based more on willpower or volition will probably be the best ones to start with. However, in certain cases we may even surprise ourselves because we end up with a technique that produces better-than-expected results even though it relies on an attribute we initially considered not to be one of our strongest. Therefore, we need to try as many techniques as possible, and in the end choose the one or two that we feel most comfortable with.[2] Afterward, the selected technique should be practiced for *at least* fourteen consecutive days, and the accumulative results will most likely begin to come as planned.

2. *Persistence*. It is important not to think that just because a technique was tried a few times and we did not have results that the technique or methodology is faulty. There are many other aspects that may interfere with achieving success.[3] Some of them will be studied later in this chapter.

In essence, if one person is able to learn something, then basically everybody else can learn it as well. The only difference is simply the amount of time it may take to accomplish it. Thus, in theory *all techniques work for everybody*, and millions of people all over the world have already had success with at least one of them.[4] For us, some of them will work faster and others may take much longer. So we should try to identify the one or two that will work best for us.

The key factor in learning to have OBEs is to persist and continue applying techniques until you are confident with the results you are getting. We did not learn to talk or walk in one week, so let us insist and persist. On some days we may feel tired and sleepy, and on others we may have eaten too much, be too excited, and so on. The effectiveness of the technique will be diminished because of these factors. Likewise, the holothosene we come into contact with during the day, as well as the thosenes we produce, will affect our energetic flexibility. We simply need to fight through these days and keep moving forward.

In theory, we can have a lucid out-of-body experience every night (and even more than one per night). Therefore, we should strive to try to leave the body every night.

We should create daily routines and habits that are simple and efficient in helping us to improve our projective capacity.

3. *Get used to the disconnection sensations.* Many disconnection sensations can be felt during the process, as described in the previous chapter. They can come as you work with energy, as you relax, or as you are doing your OBE technique. As you begin noticing them, you will progressively understand them better and this will keep you motivated.

However, OBE sensations can be a double-edged sword. On the one hand they let us know that the process has begun and we are on the right track, which is encouraging. On the other hand, they can distract us from our intention of leaving the body. Commonly, especially at the beginning, they can take us by surprise or call our attention to them so much that we forget about the bigger picture and stop doing the technique. Due to this, we need to get used to these sensations. They have to become "old news" for us. Feeling sensations is not our final objective. This is one of the reasons that it usually takes several attempts to be successful.

4. *Study the OBE technique.* Try to understand well the technique that is going to be applied. Do research on the technique's results and the dynamics of the disconnection process (rolling out, sinking, floating up, or another) as well as what sensations it normally produces. If possible, discuss the technique with others who have already applied it. Once you apply it, you will be better prepared.

While applying a technique, certain situations can occur, so here is a list of recommendations:

If you fall asleep at a certain point, start again when you recover lucidity.

If you finished the technique but nothing happened and you still have time, then start it again—sometimes the results can occur at the last minute of practice.

If you feel that you have disconnected a part of your body (such as a hand), or if you feel that you have already elevated yourself somewhat from your body, do not try to verify this. Trust your sensations. Many times people try to move or open their eyes to verify their sensations. The moment you start to tense some of your muscles to open an eyelid or move, your psychosoma will realign with your body and there will usually not be anything to see. Resist this urge.

If you start to feel you are leaving your body, do not stop doing the technique. This is not the time to begin to push or struggle to free yourself and forget about the technique. Do not become sidetracked by a sensation. Keep on applying the technique until you are fully out of body. Once you are out, enjoy the experience and then forget the technique.

5. *Focus on the technique.* It is very common at first for your attention to wander while applying a technique. Maintaining your concentration is key to projecting. As you repeat the technique and practice it with continuity and constancy, your concentration will improve.

6. *Mental saturation.* During the day we usually do not think about leaving the body or practicing with bioenergy. Thus, something that helps in this area is to try to develop a daily mental routine to keep ourselves more connected to these ideas. During the period when you are applying techniques, try to think during the day, as much as possible, about the extraphysical dimension and the targets you want to reach extraphysically; that is, the people you want to meet, the places you want to visit, the ideas you want to understand, and so forth.

In addition, you can saturate your mind by reading books about OBEs and related experiences. Try to establish conversations with friends or relatives who may know something about OBEs. The more you stay in touch with this information, the more you connect to a holothosene of projectability, thereby establishing such a holothosene in your room as well.

7. *Bioenergy exercises.* In several instances while in the transitional phase during a projective attempt, you may feel that you are floating just above your body. Though this sensation is more than likely correct, in some cases you will not go beyond this. One of the main reasons for this is the need for still more energetic flexibility.

The energetic exercises discussed in chapter 2 should be practiced every day and if possible several times each day. We should work with bioenergy particularly in our bedroom, where we are attempting our projective experiences. This will have the effect of creating a more shielded environment with a better quality of energies more conducive to OBEs.

Likewise, we should work with bioenergy before a projective attempt. It will prepare us for the projective experience and serve as a warm-up for the energosoma—which will stretch and divide itself at the moment of separation. *Energetic flexibility is essential for leaving the body,* so any effort we put toward it will be beneficial.

Remember also that the vibrational state (VS) is already a projective technique in and of itself (see chapter 2). You can lie down on your bed and start moving energy within your body (VELO), trying to achieve a vibrational state. Once you reach the VS, focus on the vibrations and, using your will, increase the intensity and volume until you leave your body.

8. *Results versus time.* After you have tried various techniques, select one and apply that technique for at least fourteen days straight. After that amount of time, you will probably know and control the technique very well. This condition will be ideal for achieving lucid out-of-body experiences. You might notice how, during the first several nights, your concentration is sometimes highly dispersed and hard to control. However, little by little your self-control and focus will increase. In some instances, although it is unlikely, people may have an OBE after only two days of applying a technique. Inducing OBEs with more regularity will usually take longer.

Persistence is the main attribute here. If you feel that after fourteen days the technique is not working for you, you can either attempt another technique or seek to modify the one you are trying. Normally after fourteen days you will know what is working in your routine and what is not. It is a good idea to review other aspects connected to the technique: place, time, comfort level, environment, and other factors that may be working as obstacles. These elements can be key factors here.

As a general rule, if you are practicing the energetic exercises several times a day, coupled with firmly trying to leave the body every time you go to sleep, then on average, within two to three months you should have your first experience. Remember, this is an average and it may occur earlier or later for you. Any effort invested in this regard will be well worth it in the long run. Very few life experiences can compare to the feeling we have once we produce our first lucid projection through effort and consistency.

9. *Physical conditions.* These are aspects regarding the physical place or location where you are going to practice the techniques. Therefore, before starting with the techniques, read the following guidelines and determine what you can incorporate from them to help you achieve OBEs.

The *physical base* is the place where you are going to actually apply the technique, leaving your physical body either lying down or reclining while your other body (the psychosoma or mentalsoma) projects.[5] Ideally, we could all have a *Projectarium*—the specialized laboratory for having OBEs located at the IAC Campus in Portugal[6]—in our house. However, since most likely we do not, then we want to optimize our surroundings as much as possible.

You can choose any place in the house that gives you privacy, where you feel comfortable, and where you will be not be disturbed. The bedroom is usually the most appropriate place for the majority of people. However, if there is another person sleeping in the same room with you (even if it is on separate beds), you may be less likely to be disturbed in another room.

If you have a partner and you don't have another place or room that can be used as a more constant physical base, then it is useful to have a sleeping bag or small mattress that can be used to apply the techniques. It can be set in a corner of the room or somewhere away from the bed. In doing this, we avoid physical interferences like touching, pulling of sheets, or any other external movement that may disturb us. If you have a king-size bed, it can provide you with more space to help partners avoid disturbing each other during the time a technique is being applied. In this second case, it is recommended to have individual bed sheets or linens (instead of king size, for example) for each partner.

Ideally, it is better to have a place you can always rely on to be ready for the application or practice of a technique—in other words, a consistent physical base. Pets should not be in our physical base at the time of the experience, as they may disturb us at inopportune moments and may become restless due to the energetic work.

Keeping in mind all the thosenic influences we studied in chapter 2, it is ideal to have *objects and furniture* with neutral energy or energy conducive to our projections in our physical base Generally speaking, if we have too many objects with various kinds of energy, this will create energetic confusion or saturation with unwanted thosenes in our room. Likewise, if we have objects that are loaded with emotional energy—like religious and/or mystical objects or antiques—they will not help, especially due to their denser emotional energetic load, among other factors. If you have doubts about an object, it is better to leave the object outside the physical base.

Therefore, any object or piece of furniture that has no use or attracts and/or evokes an undesirable thosenic or energetic pattern should be avoided. As a general rule, *fewer objects (or thosenes) mean less entropy (disorganization), or, in other words, more balance.* Naturally, to make ourselves more comfortable, we should remove all jewelry and personal effects we may be wearing.[7]

The following are some suggestions and comments about *useful objects* that we should have in our physical base:

- *Books or materials about projection.* These help with healthy mental saturation.

- *Pen or pencil, paper, notebook.* After returning from an OBE, you are going to want to document your experience. If you prefer to record the experience, keep a small tape or digital recorder next to your bed.

- *Digital clock—alarm clock.* A digital clock that does not make sounds as it goes from second to second is recommended in the physical base. This avoids distractions and is easier to see in the dark. Record the start and end times of your projection, since sometimes the period of time experienced can seem close to an hour when in reality it was shorter.

- *Bed linens and mattress.* Elements such as physical comfort level, cleanliness, and odors are important for the relaxation of the physical body. The goal is to avoid a premature return to the physical body in the middle of a lucid experience due to some physical discomfort. We want to provide conditions so that the physical body is able to remain in one comfortable position for as long as possible.

- *Personal clothing.* As already stated, the main point physically is to always pay attention to personal comfort. With this in mind, loose clothing is ideal because it does not cause any discomfort during the techniques. As a general rule, the fewer clothes, the better, to reduce stimulation on the skin.

With regard to the *illumination* of the physical base,[8] it is important to have a minimum of illumination, or indirect soft light, while practicing a technique. Total darkness is not the ideal. A state of semidarkness within the bedroom will help greatly with basic activities like walking to the bathroom, finding our projective journal and writing in it, being able to instantaneously recognize that we are in our room when we come back, and others.

Ideally, total *silence* is recommended.[9] Turn off the ringer on any phones that are kept in the bedroom, and turn off other electronic devices that may make noise, such as beepers, TV, and radio. There are other sounds that we cannot control, usually external sounds like dogs barking, car alarms, traffic, and so forth. In these cases, the most efficient technique is to not pay attention to them—tune them out. As we focus on the technique and on our objective, we become much better at ignoring and calmly overcoming the discomfort of these other sounds.

The ideal ambient *temperature* is around 72°F, or where it is neither hot nor cold for you personally.[10] In general, an air conditioning unit is recommended to control the temperature within the physical base. Another useful aspect of the air conditioning unit is that it may help you to drown out noises, since it produces a type of white noise.

10. Ideal time. Though leaving the body is possible at any time, the ideal time for an attempt seems to be around 3:00 AM.[11] The reasons for this are manifold.

- The best time to project is after at least four hours of rest. When tired, we have a harder time concentrating and remembering. We may also fall asleep while relaxing and working with our energies. It is good to allow our body and brain to rest for at least three to four hours.[12]

- At 3:00 AM, everything around us is usually quieter and calmer.

- When we (slowly and gently, ideally) wake up at this time, we are usually already disconnected from our daily problems, and it is therefore easier to concentrate on the technique at hand. Otherwise, when we go to bed, we may mentally disperse ourselves because our mind is still "bubbling" with ordinary daily worries.

- In the middle of the night, the production of melatonin and especially serotonin (two neurotransmitters that help prepare our body for sleep by relaxing it) is at a peak. When we wake up at this time, the relaxation (and therefore the nonalignment of our bodies) will take less time since these two substances are already working for us.[13]

- Finally, at this time, the generalized holothosene of society is less against us, since, as mentioned, most people are sleeping. The unfavorable holothosenic pressure from society toward OBEs—due mainly to lack of information—is diminished.

Ideally, we should try to wake up around three to four hours after we go to bed. Therefore, if we are used to going to sleep at 12:30 AM, then we should wake up around 4:00 AM (during the middle of our sleep cycle) to try our techniques; if we go to sleep at 10:00 PM, then waking up at 2:00 AM will suffice.

> When you wake up around 3:00 AM, it is ideal to stand next to the bed and work with your energies while standing. This will help you avoid falling asleep again before reasonably completing the energetic work and practicing the OBE technique. You can take advantage of the opportunity to go to the bathroom as well. Additionally, you can set your alarm clock to wake you up at this time to try your projective technique. (Low-volume soft music is ideal to avoid waking up abruptly.)

11. *Physical exercise.* Physical exercise, especially if it causes sweating, is positive and helps us with our projective performance. Our overall health, energy work, and mental agility will be greatly enhanced if we do regular physical exercise. There are cases where energy work does not improve simply because of the person's lack of physical exercise.

Beyond this, if on a particular day we are physically (not mentally) tired, we can use this to our advantage so as to exit the body. In many cases, when the muscles are very tired, the soma falls asleep faster than the consciousness, thereby producing a lucid projection. Another good opportunity to leave the body exists when we have just finished exercising, especially if it was done in the morning. For example, it could be effective to get a good night's sleep, wake up, go for a forty-five-minute walk, and then lie down and try to leave the body.

12. *Personal diet.* Ideally, you should eat a well-balanced diet. If your diet is sufficiently healthy, then you do not need to change the way you eat just because you are trying a projective technique.

However, if you do not have much physical energy, are always tired, or fall asleep each time you go to apply a technique or do any other activity that requires more concentration, or if your body is presenting any kind of symptom that catches your attention, then it is advisable to go to a physician to seek professional treatment. Check in with yourself to see if there is a need for a healthier daily routine—including diet and eating habits.

Generally speaking, a healthier person has a better memory, pays better attention, and is able to relax more easily. These attributes contribute to the process of allowing the consciousness to leave the body. So, a well-balanced diet is recommended.

Before applying the technique, avoid excessive consumption of food or beverage.[14] Ideally, the technique should be performed *after the digestion has run its course.* Solids will normally take two to three hours to be digested and liquids one to two hours, depending on the amount consumed and what type of food or beverage has been ingested.

13. *Necessities.* Before starting a technique, it is important to pay attention to any physiological needs. When you go to the bathroom, remember also to blow your nose. It is better if your breathing passages are open in order to breathe easily and stay relaxed during the OBE technique or energetic exercise.

14. *Physical position.* The ideal position in which to practice a projective technique is the dorsal position (figure 4.1), where you lie down on your back, with arms alongside the body and legs a little bit apart.[16] To further optimize this position, slightly flex your extremities, both elbows and knees. Placing pillows under your head, knees, and feet, and if needed under your hands (smalls pillows are preferable), is ideal. The dorsal position is itself already a projective technique. Here are the reasons that this is the ideal position:

- The dorsal position helps with blood circulation. While doing a technique, you will not feel any physical discomfort. If you leave your extremities straight, then as they relax, the muscles will become rigid and may begin to hurt. Note that this pain will show up only after some time has gone by. So even if at first everything may feel relaxed and comfortable, the real test will come after thirty minutes or so.

- This position can be held for a longer period of time without the need to move or any kind of discomfort. While practicing a projective technique, the physical body should be allowed to relax as much as possible, avoiding any unnecessary movements; this is to prevent our attention from being brought back to the

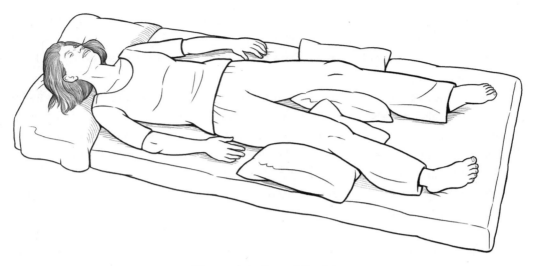

Figure 4.1: Dorsal Position

physical body and setting back, or in the worst of cases, losing the opportunity to project. This position should be kept for one to two hours.

- The dorsal position predisposes OBEs because it produces a slight hypoxia, or slightly reduces the amount of oxygen in the cerebral hemispheres, helping the physical body to relax.

- While the physical body is in the dorsal position, the psychosoma can disconnect more easily and in less time, helping the projector regain awareness at the moment of disconnection. From this position, the takeoff usually occurs as the person floats upward in a very forward and natural direction. This "forward" direction psychologically predisposes the person to regain awareness upon disconnecting, since we are conditioned to do everything in a "forward" fashion during our waking physical life (i.e., we walk forward, talk to others while in front of us, and so on).

It is important to mention that individuals ultimately can provoke OBEs in any position, even seated in a chair or sofa. Yet at the beginning, in order to maximize the probability for success, it is recommended that we cover these details so as to improve the quality, lucidity, and control of the experiences.

15. *Relaxation.* It is important to learn how to relax completely. The first OBE technique described later in this chapter can help you accomplish this. The ideal is

for us to reach a state of deep relaxation where we do not feel the physical body anymore. In this state, it seems to us that time has stopped and that we can stay there forever.

Always be very relaxed before any technique is applied, as well as before, during, and after having performed your energy work. As you practice relaxing more often, you will need less time to reach this state.

16. *Psychological conditions.* Thosenes can interfere while we are practicing a technique or an exercise to help us leave the body.[16] Uncontrolled or unmanaged thosenes can provoke many reactions, including the following:

- Lack of prolonged attention
- Continuous or sporadic daydreaming
- Edginess and excitability
- Intense emotions, whether positive or negative
- Difficulty relaxing properly

As a consequence of these reactions, the technique is compromised and it is harder to achieve productive results. It is important, therefore, to try to evaluate your thosenes. Assess if there are some ongoing thosenes that may be interfering with the process of relaxation.

Balanced thosenes help us on a daily basis, and not only while practicing a technique. To control thosenes, we should become more aware of them and constantly monitor or evaluate them to verify if something is wrong, and if so, to address and solve the problem.

Here is a list of some ideal thosenes, or psychological states, that are best to have before practicing a technique:

- Self-motivation
- Curiosity
- Open-mindedness
- Constancy and perseverance
- Concentration
- Calmness (free of fear or worries)

- Strong will
- Deep intention to leave the body

Reading material on OBEs or related subjects is a very productive activity that can help predispose us to leave the body.[17] While we are reading, our mind and intellect are active, yet our body and muscles are already starting to relax.

Likewise, we want to avoid certain mental and emotional states such as fear, insecurity, worry, anxiety, and so forth. Individuals should avoid engaging in exciting activities that pump too much adrenaline into the blood. So avoid violent, heavy movies or those that have a very exciting or intriguing plot that will keep you thinking about them later on.

> Meditation is a positive and productive practice in and of itself, especially when done *properly*—since there are many people who say they meditate but end up, in practice, simply falling asleep.[18] Some individuals may have out-of-body experiences through their meditations,[19] since meditation develops and trains several basic attributes for projecting, such as concentration, perseverance, physical and mental self-control,[20] and attention. However, as a technique for leaving the body, meditation is inefficient for OBE development. The main reason for this is the directionality of the intention. During meditation, the person wants to go *inward*, and during an OBE, we want to go *outward*.[21] For deeper and more efficient OBE development, it is best not to combine techniques for out-of-body experiences with other practices.

In terms of the mental approach toward OBEs, the two most common obstacles to leaving the body are fear and anxiety. The person is either afraid or too anxious to have a lucid projection. These are not necessarily big obstacles, but they are common. Individuals tend to present either one or the other. Therefore, let us address them both.

Fear is generally a result of not knowing what to expect, or fear of the unknown.[22] Individuals tend to be overly hesitant and cautious when something is not well understood. The topics of projectiology certainly fall into this category for the majority of people. Unfortunately, many times, movies and television shows are developed based on these topics where extraphysical realities are associated with and shown in a negative and fearful light, as this approach is more commercially viable. These portrayals are not fully accurate and tend to be skewed to one extreme, since there are innumerable dimensions that are extremely positive and benign. And, as was discussed in the previous chapters, there is nothing to fear and no risk in leaving the body.

The best solution for fear is to become more informed about this reality, or in other words to make the unknown known.[23] Reading and taking classes on OBEs is recommended. As mentioned previously, reading is an excellent activity before a lucid projection attempt, and it will have an even greater effect if the material being read is about projections. This will help you better understand the extraphysical reality, since you will be adding clear information about it to your "database." It will also connect you energetically to this type of activity.

Anxiety about leaving the body occurs when we cannot contain ourselves and want to leave the body right *now*. There are basically two conditions to be discussed concerning anxiety.

First, the person needs to relax more and just let the experience happen. Leaving the body is as much about using our will and perseverance to do the exercises as it is about relaxing and "allowing" ourselves to leave the body. There is a very fine line between putting effort into something and applying ourselves (pressing the gas pedal) and letting go and allowing the experience to happen. Where this fine line lies can be found only through experience.

An analogy of this is the clutch on stick-shift cars. The driver can understand when, how, and why to press the clutch pedal. Yet it will be only by feeling this in an actual car and testing it through many experiences that the person will be able to control the clutch pedal and, therefore, the car with ease.

The second condition with anxiety is related to expectations. In many cases individuals have the wrong expectations regarding the feasibility of having a lucid projection. It is important to mention that there are those more predisposed individuals who leave the body within their first few attempts. However, this is rare. For most people, leaving the body is a capacity that takes some time to develop. If we practice our energy work on a daily basis and try a specific technique for leaving the body, it should, on average, take us a few months to have our first OBE. Yet, as a result of the individual differences between each person, the actual time may vary.

Many people also commonly tend to relate their OBE learning period to other activities they may have learned in the past. For example, learning to play the piano provides a more direct and linear learning experience. In other words, a person can play the piano, even if it is poorly, from the first day; and they will then continue to improve progressively with more and more training.

Yet, there are some learning experiences where the progress is not as linear, such as learning to ride a bicycle. The child may fall on the first thirty attempts, yet on the thirty-first attempt they wobble a little bit but then continue on riding without falling. From this moment on, the child never falls again because of a lack of balance. In this case, it would seem that nothing was happening during the first thirty attempts, because the result was not obvious. Yet the child *was gaining experience with each attempt*.

Leaving the body follows this second trend, and we need to value the accumulation of experiences throughout the initial period. The first lucid projection is usually the hardest one to achieve. During all the initial attempts, it may seem as if nothing is happening. However, the person is gaining experience with each attempt and learning to control all exit sensations. Because of this, we should not expect a linear progression in our OBE learning process.

 The ideal would be for the person not to generate any expectations but to simply adopt the following attitude: "If I don't leave the body today, I will do it in three months, ten days, or maybe even tomorrow. Regardless of when it occurs, I will practice, learn, and enjoy all the nuances of the energetic work and the takeoff phase."

Projective Techniques

There are many different types of projective techniques, which can be categorized by the main attribute on which they are based. Some techniques are based on will, others on concentration or relaxation, and still others on imagination, creativity, evocation, passivity, or working with energy.[24]

So if you are a more visual person, choose the techniques that are based on this attribute as your main strategy. Explore your personal characteristics to help you in choosing the techniques. The following sections present detailed explanations of many projective techniques. Read them carefully and try each technique at least once. Then repeat the one that you feel works best for you.

Since you will learn several projective techniques, the tendency is to want to try them all in a relatively short period of time. However, try not to switch techniques every ten minutes. This will only disperse your efforts. Normally it takes at least thirty minutes for a person to begin to fully get into a technique. So to give yourself a better chance, practice one of them each day, for at least one hour. Do not change techniques in the middle of the hour!

Techniques—Attributes: Relaxation and Concentration
1. Psychophysiological Self-Relaxation Technique
Introduction

This is a technique that can be applied before any other technique, mainly because it helps with physical relaxation—an essential condition so as to have an OBE. The psychophysiological self-relaxation technique helps us relax our physical body as well as our mind.[25]

Instructions

1. Find a place where you are going to leave your physical body (physical base) while you experience an OBE. It is better if you can be alone, without external interferences. Lie down on something comfortable and wear loose clothing. It is very important to be comfortable.

2. Lie down (in the dorsal position) and close your eyes.

3. Begin the relaxation by choosing a group of muscles; for instance, the right foot. Focus on this foot and contract the muscles gently. Count from one to five, and then relax for a few seconds. Do it again with that muscle group or move on to another. You may continue to work with each group of muscles until you feel

they are well relaxed. Important: You don't need to firmly squeeze the muscles; gentle contractions will suffice.

4. To relax, you can use the method in step 3 or you can simply concentrate on a group of muscles and will them to relax—without contracting them. Experiment to determine which system works best for you.

5. You can start at your feet, moving upward through the legs, relaxing area by area. As you progress, you can cover your torso, arms, and finally the head. Always select small areas that are next to each other. If using the contraction system, there are some parts of the body that are more complicated to contract—for instance, the head—so each person has to find a movement that tenses and relaxes this group of muscles.

6. While you are working on an area, focus only on that specific area. This helps you to feel your body and relax it more deeply. As you focus only on one area, it also helps you to disconnect from the world.

7. If you desire, you can incorporate breathing into the process by contracting the muscles while you inhale, then holding your breath during the contraction while counting, and then exhaling while relaxing the muscle group. This provision can help the process for some individuals, although for others it is not as useful because the breathing may keep them more connected to their head and physical body. Evaluate in your specific case if you should include the focus on the breathing.

8. After relaxing all muscle groups, mentally observe your physical body and determine if there is any part that is still not fully and deeply relaxed, and if so, repeat the technique there once again.

9. Likewise, pay attention to your thoughts and emotions. Relax your mind and try to focus on your energies and any extraphysical sensations that may occur. Do not let other thoughts come into your mind. Be fully there in the moment, focused on nothing else but the process.

10. After a full pass through your entire body, you can do a second, third, and fourth pass, even continuing beyond until the end.

Disconnection

Continue the repetition of this psychological and physiological relaxation procedure to allow the psychosoma to leave the body. This technique will take you to the state of hypnagogia, which is the transitional state between being awake and falling asleep. The psychosoma will disconnect slowly in the same way it disconnects every night.

2. Mental Concentration Technique

Introduction

This technique helps us relax and relies on our concentration. Logically, it also helps to develop our concentration.[26] While we are focusing on a spot, our mental concentration increases and provokes a relaxed and comfortable sensation, which leads us toward the OBE.

Instructions

1. Isolate yourself in a room where you will be completely undisturbed during the technique. Dress comfortably.

2. Place a comfortable chair about six feet from a blank wall. Set a table against the wall. Light a candle in the middle of a large plate and place the plate on the table.

3. Turn off all lights, ensuring the candle is the only source of light in the room.

4. Sit in the chair, find a comfortable position, and avoid moving afterward.

5. Fix your attention directly on the candle flame and concentrate until you forget about everything around you. You want to memorize the entire scene, to mentally go to the candle, and to even *be* the candle. After some minutes, you may reach a point where you and the flame are connected—the flame begins to exist as an extension of your physical body.

6. At this point you may be deeply relaxed and perhaps feel the need to close your eyes. You may even perceive that you are disconnected from your physical body to some degree already. Keep the strong desire of leaving the body at the forefront, and use your will and determination to further increase that sensation, until you feel completely projected.

7. If you feel tired, do not struggle against falling asleep. In some cases, as we fall asleep, the OBE occurs.

Important: You are to be active during this technique; thus, use your will and inner motivation to keep your goal of leaving the body lucidly in mind, floating toward the candle. Full attention should be kept on the flame at all times. Distance yourself from any thought that distracts you from this goal. This is an exercise for your concentration and willpower.

Focusing on the candle flame serves to improve your concentration. Since the candle is the only source of light in the room, it will naturally attract your attention. The flame has a soft light that will not hurt your eyes—unlike staring at a light bulb. Since the flame makes continuous, small movements, it is easier to concentrate on, as opposed to something that is completely static.

Disconnection

As already stated, the disconnection can occur abruptly during the middle of the exercise as you close your eyes and nod off to sleep, or gently as you fully connect with the candle flame. Yet in some instances, as you are staring at the candle, you may disconnect suddenly even without closing your eyes—in a flash you may find yourself already projected, an inch from the candle. This sudden and swift takeoff is usually accompanied by intracranial sounds.

3. Projective Self-Image Technique

Introduction

Understanding that the psychosoma has the same appearance as the physical body will help in the process of leaving the body as well as in increasing our level of lucidity while practicing this technique. Many projectors do not perceive themselves; they usually do not try to see their extraphysical body, or psychosoma, when projected in it. In some instances this is because they have a greater interest in seeing the extraphysical dimension than they do in seeing themselves.

Instructions[27]

1. Select a place where you can be absolutely alone during the practice of the technique. Wear comfortable clothes.

2. For this technique you will need a large mirror, preferably one in which you can see your entire physical body reflected—the bigger the mirror, the better.

3. Sit in front of the mirror in a comfortable chair about six feet away.

4. Stare at your body in the mirror for several minutes while seated in the chair. Pay attention to the details of your appearance. Try to focus on every aspect of your body: shape, outline, type of clothes you are wearing, height, dimensions, and others. Evaluate your body at this moment in the most minute detail. Focus on the things that you usually do not pay attention to—your entire image reflected in this mirror needs to be memorized in great detail.

5. Try to saturate your mind with your physical characteristics. Focus on your reflected image and then try to feel as if that reflected image is you. Say your name a few times to your reflected image and look into your reflected image's eyes, feeling as if you actually are the reflected image speaking.

6. You want to be in the place of this image, transferring your consciousness to this image. If, while staring at the mirror, you start to become confused about where you are, actually doubting if you are in your body or in the reflection, allow this to happen.

7. There is no problem if you fall asleep. The important thing here is for your mind to be saturated by its own image.

Disconnection

Disconnection may occur either while sitting in the chair still conscious or later while sleeping. In both cases, the person disconnects from the body and adopts the position of the image. This technique works because of your strong-willed intention to transfer yourself to the reflected image.

Techniques Involving Imagination and Creativity

With imagination techniques, the key is to initially set your particular sequence of specific images and to then start their repetition. Afterward as this process continues, you increasingly add more detail to the images, so as to make them more realistic. As the images become more stable, solid, and real, the psychosoma has the tendency to start to follow these images, leading to a projection. Though the images in your mind may be unclear and fuzzy at first, through this pattern of repetition, your focus and the clarity of the images will increase.

1. Door Opening Technique

Introduction

The door opening technique is a mix of imagination, creativity, and concentration, allowing the projector to simultaneously test these attributes with the objective of leaving the body.

Instructions[28]

1. Dim the light and sit in a comfortable chair, with your body straight and hands on your legs.

2. With your eyes closed, use your creativity and imagine a white wall with a closed door in front of you. Take your time to create the door. Imagine and create all the details of this door: color, height, and special features of your choosing.

3. This is your door, so create it as you wish. You may also place a symbol or sign that has a connection with you on this door; for example, a star, a symbol, or a sign that says "exit," "extraphysical," or "projection." It can be anything that personalizes the door for you and increases your desire to leave the body. Try to make it a one- or two-word expression—do not make it too long.

4. Next, contemplate this door for a moment. Visualize yourself standing up from the chair and walking toward the door. Open it very slowly toward you, and imagine yourself passing through it. Follow these images closely, paying attention to the entire scene you are creating.

5. Take your time to finish this visual creation the first time. Then repeat all the steps from the beginning, intensifying each step as much as possible. With each full repetition, you will be able to visualize the entire scene better, adding small details to it (the ground on the soles of your feet as you walk, your clothes, the feeling of grabbing the door knob, and others). Your imagination will become increasingly more real and stable and you will be able to visualize everything better.

6. The idea is to liberate the psychosoma while you are imagining yourself passing through the door.

In this technique, the door represents a passage between the intraphysical and extraphysical dimensions. Some projectors use a tunnel, window, or any other possible way of exiting, serving to represent the moment the consciousness leaves the body.

Disconnection

Usually the disconnection occurs gradually in this technique. You may feel many disconnection sensations, yet keep on repeating your image again and again until you are fully outside the body.

2. Step Counting Technique

Introduction

The step counting technique integrates physical movements with concentration and imagination.[29] It takes advantage of the fact that on certain days, when we perform a very repetitive task, we often later find ourselves dreaming about that same task during the night. In certain cases, we are actually semiconsciously projected while repeating the same task.

Instructions

1. Create a path from your bed (or the place where you apply the technique) to the front door of your house (ideally), or to a balcony, window, or sliding glass door. Ideally, the path you select between your bed and your target will have between fifteen and twenty steps.

2. While physically awake, literally walk this path, counting the steps and focusing on the specific visual surroundings with each step you take. After each step, stop, focus, and visually associate something from your immediate environment with that specific step. Here is an example:

   - Step 1: You are standing next to your bed and the *mirror* in your room is the main object in front of you.

   - Step 2: Now, moving away from the bed, the room's *closet* calls your attention.

   - Step 3: You are approaching the door, so you associate this step with the bedroom *door*.

   - Step 4: You are outside your room, and now you can see the *shower curtain* inside the bathroom.

   - Step 5: ... (following the same pattern and so on)

3. Associate at least one thing with each step. The last step should be at a door or window. It helps if you put a sign on this door/window saying something

meaningful to you regarding your intention to have an OBE; for example, "Wake up!" or "You're projected" or "Raise awareness."

4. After you reach the last step, go back and repeat the exact same trajectory. Correlate the same objects with the same steps. Associate the last step with your sign.

5. Repeat and walk the physical trajectory as many times as you can. You can do this for thirty minutes to an hour.

6. Next, go to the place where you are going to practice the technique. Dim the lights, wearing comfortable clothes, and lie down in the dorsal position.

7. With your eyes closed, imagine that you are walking this path again, counting each step and looking at each object and image. Re-create the entire scene in your mind, step by step, until you reach your destination.

8. While you are counting steps, relax your mind. Forget the intraphysical environment in which you are actually lying down.

9. Keep on repeating this trajectory until the psychosoma disconnects. If you become sleepy, allow yourself to fall asleep while repeating the images in your mind.

Disconnection

The disconnection can occur while you are still awake and counting the steps. Yet in some instances, the person falls asleep and wakes up outside the body walking the path. The regaining of consciousness usually comes after step 7 or 8. This seems to occur because it is at this moment that we step outside the extraphysical sphere of energy and thus become more aware. The more concentration you apply to this technique, the better will be the results.

3. Projective Images Technique

Introduction

Projective images are scenes or visualizations that are related to an out-of-body experience and can be used to produce them.[30] Visualization techniques also help in the development of analysis, observation, memory, and many other skills.

The main idea in this technique is to make a connection between the visualization of certain physical situations and the disconnection of the psychosoma. Many activities from your daily life can be incorporated into a projective technique. If you already have a certain amount of creativity or imagination, this technique will probably work very well for you.

Instructions

1. Go to your physical base or the place where you are going to apply the technique. Wearing comfortable clothes, relax and lie down on your back in the dorsal position.

2. Close your eyes and relax your mind. Focus on the technique and on the objective of leaving the body.

3. Start by thinking about an image, a scene, an action, or an idea related to the projection you have in mind. Here are some examples of what you can use:

   • *Stairs.* Visualize a long staircase. Take your time to create it in your mind and imagine you are climbing it. When you reach the last step, you will leave the body.

   • *Playground tunnel-slide.* Imagine a long playground tunnel-slide. Several seconds pass as you slide down it. As you are sliding down, you have the sensation that when you reach the end, you will be disconnected from the physical body.

   • *Airplane takeoff.* Create the idea in your mind that you are inside an airplane's cockpit at the moment of takeoff. You can mentally connect this moment to the disconnection of the psychosoma. Try to incorporate all the sensations of the plane's acceleration and liftoff into your images.

   • *Tank.* Picture yourself floating in the middle of a gigantic water tank. The tank's bottom drain cap is removed, and consequently, as the water leaves the tank, it creates an enormous whirlpool, which takes you into its swirling circles. Once all the water finishes draining, you find yourself out of the physical body.

   • *Floating.* Imagine yourself floating in the ocean beyond the breaking of the waves. You float quietly and peacefully, only perceiving the gentle waves that calmly lift and lower you. As the waves keep coming, they continuously lift and lower you. As you get used to this motion, the psychosoma starts to follow this up-and-down movement while the waves begin slowly increasing in size (although still not breaking). Eventually, the waves lift you high enough that you project out of the body.

- *Rope.* Imagine you're climbing an endless rope.[31] You pull yourself upward with ease, your arms reaching upward for more rope while you push yourself up off the nodes with your feet. As the image becomes more real, the psychosoma starts to follow this upward motion. You keep climbing the rope until you eventually leave the body.

- *Well.* There is a deep, empty well. You are lying on the bottom of the well, looking upward. From this perspective, you see this long tunnel-like hole going up, and a small circle of light at the end of the tunnel—where the surface is. Suddenly, the well starts filling with water. You start floating in the water, and as the water level rises, you float upward with it. The small circle where the surface is starts to become bigger as you get closer, until you reach the surface and leave the body.

- *Elevator.* Similar to the well, you are lying on the floor of an elevator, in the basement of a skyscraper. The elevator does not have a ceiling, so you are able to see the elevator shaft going all the way to the top of the building. The top of the building is also open (has no roof), so you can see a small opening where light is entering at the top end of the elevator shaft (at roof level). Suddenly, the elevator starts moving up. You feel the sensation of going upward while the small opening of light, which was far away at the beginning, starts getting closer and increasing in size. When you reach the roof, you project.

4. While creating the projective image, try to fully feel yourself in that situation. Perceive everything as if you are actually experiencing that circumstance, and feel upon finishing that you can achieve an OBE. Continue repeating the scenes as many times as needed. As the images become more real, the psychosoma disconnects from the physical body. Do not let your mind wander.

Each one of these ideas is really a different technique. You can create your own technique based on an activity from your daily life that you usually repeat often. Your experiential familiarity with the activity will facilitate the realistic re-creation (and therefore sensations) of those motions, increasing your probability of success.

Disconnection

Many people find themselves projected while still thinking about and creating these images. The images are like bait for the mind, helping us forget about the physical body and physical sensations so as to focus more deeply on the nonphysical condition, allowing us to then detach more easily. The disconnection is normally gradual with these images.

4. Psychological Conditionings Technique

Introduction

This is the basic technique with a focus on imagination to induce an out-of-body experience.[32]

Instructions

1. Sit in a chair or lie down on a bed, and get as comfortable as possible. You can apply the psychophysiological relaxation technique before you begin to apply this one.

2. Once relaxed, concentrate your thosenes on the objective of projecting, avoiding any other thought not connected to an OBE. Set an extraphysical goal or target you want to reach during this technique. Think about this mental target for a few moments.

3. Forget any physical sensations as well as the physical body itself. Focus only on your condition of being a consciousness. Bring your attention to the extraphysical realm and forget all about the intraphysical dimension.

4. Pay attention only to your condition, in this very moment, as if no one else exists in this universe—just you. Block out all external sounds; they do not exist. Nothing else exists.

5. Imagine now that you are starting to disconnect from the physical body. At this point, visualize yourself slowly leaving your physical body and floating above it. Take your time in focusing on this. Imagine all the details of being suspended over the physical body. Spend about a minute on this image.

6. Repeat step 5 as many times as needed. Keep imagining yourself disconnecting slowly, rising, and then floating in midair. Do not change the perspective from which you are looking at your physical body.

7. Maintain your lucidity as much as possible. If you nod off in the middle of these steps, then start again. It is always worth reinitiating the technique to take advantage of the moment.

Disconnection

As your image becomes more real and you get deeply involved with the image, the psychosoma will gradually start to disconnect.

Techniques—Attributes: Physical Control and Breathing
1. Carbon Dioxide Technique
Introduction

The next two techniques are breathing techniques. These techniques will help you modify your breathing pattern so as to induce an OBE. Carbon dioxide (CO_2) is the main element in this technique. By safely increasing the amount of CO_2 in the physical body, the brain decreases its activity and allows the consciousness to disconnect from the physical body.[33]

These circumstances are benign and there are no side effects for the projector. To increase the amount of CO_2 in your body, you will breathe in specific patterns.

Instructions

1. Relax on a bed or any place where you feel comfortable in the dorsal position.

2. Remember that since this is a breathing technique, it is good to blow your nose and leave your nasal passages clean.

3. Close your eyes and relax. You can start this technique by applying the first exercise mentioned in this chapter, the psychophysiological relaxation technique. It will help you to have more control over your body.

4. The idea here is to work with your breathing. Start by inhaling air for two seconds, hold it in for eight seconds, and then exhale for four seconds. Once your lungs are empty, immediately begin the breathing pattern again. You can refer to the following table.

	Breathe in	Hold	Breathe out
Relationship/Ratio	1	4	2
Level A: Try to start here	2 seconds	8 seconds	4 seconds
Level B	3 seconds	12 seconds	6 seconds
Level C	4	16	8
Level D	5	20	10
Level E	6	24	12
Level F	7	28	14
Level G	8	32	16
Level H	9	36	18

5. As you become comfortable with one level of a breathing pattern, you can jump to the next one. You may remain at each breathing level for however long is necessary for you. Most people do about fifteen full inhalation-hold-exhalation sequences per level. Thus, after fifteen cycles at level A, move on to level B, and so on.

6. Notice that the ratio between the inhalation-hold-exhalation is always 1:4:2.

7. For most people, the ideal is to reach the 8:32:16 ratio (level G), though this varies depending on the size, lung capacity, and physical resistance of the person. Practicing the technique as much as possible will give you much more endurance in order to go further. If your body is of a smaller frame, reaching the 6:24:12 ratio (level E) may be enough.

8. At the beginning you may feel like you are forcing your breathing, but after some attempts you will get used to the rhythm and start to feel comfortable with the sequence. This technique should be extremely relaxing since, if you increase slowly from level to level, you will give your body time to relax into it, and it will naturally need less oxygen as time progresses. Thus, moving through the levels will be easier.

Observation: It is important to breathe in and out through your nose. Avoid breathing through your mouth. You will notice that you need to inhale and exhale very slowly. Nothing should be forced. Again, on the contrary, this technique should be very relaxing.

Also, leave your nasal passages open; do not tense and close your throat to hold the air in—hold in the air using your diaphragm. A comfortable pillow for your head may help you during this technique.

Disconnection

Normally the disconnection begins to be felt in the middle of the holding period. At first it will be a slight sensation, which by the middle of the exhalation will probably be gone as the psychosoma realigns with the body. In the next breath, during the middle of the holding period, you will feel it again. As you keep going, breath after breath, the disconnection sensation will become increasingly clear and stronger. Eventually, you will leave your body. Continue applying the technique until you are out.

2. Rhythmic Breathing Technique

Introduction

The rhythmic breathing technique involves controlling the rhythm of the breath, slowing it down through a simple routine.[34] Upon doing so, individuals can produce a disconnection of the psychosoma.

The key in this technique is to use the entire capacity of our lungs as we breathe; on average, we usually use only 70 percent of our lung capacity during our daily life. It is recommended to practice this technique on an empty stomach so as not to feel any kind of digestive somatic effects.

Instructions

1. Again, clean your nasal passages, put on comfortable clothes, and relax in a place where you will not be disturbed.

2. For this technique, it is recommended to be seated in an armchair, relaxed, with your arms placed over your legs.

3. Start by breathing slowly through your nose; don't breathe through your mouth.

4. Inhale through your nose and bring air deep into your lungs, trying to fill them from the bottom to the top. Do this by distending your abdomen—allow your diaphragm to do the work

5. Hold the air inside of your body for three to four seconds.

6. Then exhale slowly through the nose. Push the air out effortlessly by contracting your abdomen. Make sure you empty your lungs out completely, but do not force anything.

7. Inhale and exhale ten times in the same manner.

8. After the tenth exhalation, when your lungs are completely void of air, hold without breathing for about twenty seconds—or as long as you can without feeling uncomfortable.

9. Continue repeating the same alternating sequence: ten inhalations and exhalations using the entire capacity of your lungs, and then holding for twenty seconds without air. You will gradually feel that your breathing is very gentle and relaxed. Continue the technique until you fall asleep or leave the body.

Disconnection

The exit of the psychosoma usually begins during the holding period and continues getting stronger with each cycle. Even if you start to feel some sensations of disconnection, keep repeating the technique until you are fully outside the body. *For this technique, it is recommended to choose a place with good air circulation.*

3. Pineal Gland Technique
Introduction

This technique, though not based on breathing, is dependent on the physiology of the soma, whereby through the excitation of the pineal gland we can produce a projection.[35] The pineal gland is located in the center of the head. This technique is recommended for those without any ocular or ophthalmological problems.

Instructions

1. Make sure you have worked with energy (VELO and VS) before the attempt and that you are in a relaxed state.

2. You can use one of the following two methods to activate the pineal gland:
   • With your eyes open, extend your arm in front of you and look at your raised index finger—now at a distance of about one foot (30 cm). Move your index finger slowly toward the middle of your eyebrows and follow the tip of your finger with your eyes. Move your index finger back and

forth, from one foot out to almost touching the middle of your eyebrows. Keep repeating this exercise.

- Direct your eyeballs upward and toward the center of your forehead, as if you are trying to look at the middle of your forehead. Keep your eyes in this position for ten seconds and then return them to their normal position, relaxing all the muscles in this region for about thirty seconds. Keep repeating this exercise.

3. The limiting agent regarding how long you will do either of these methods will be the muscles of your eyeballs. After some minutes you will start to feel the area becoming somewhat heavy and tired. At that point, stop, relax, and continue the next day. There is no need to force the exercise.

4. The next day you will be able to do the exercises for a longer period of time, and this will continue to increase with practice. Be patient if at first you are able to do it for only a few minutes. Likewise, with some repetition, you will learn to coordinate the movements so they will not cause any discomfort and will be more relaxed.

Disconnection

The disconnection of the psychosoma will occur in a sudden and unexpected fashion. Usually the head of the psychosoma disconnects first. This exit is commonly accompanied by intracranial sounds. This fast and abrupt takeoff may surprise you at first, yet is harmless and causes no discomfort.

Techniques Involving Energy and Imagination
1. Elongation Technique
Introduction

This technique uses the elongation attribute of the psychosoma, which has the capacity to stretch without boundaries or limits.[36] This technique will stretch the psychosoma out of the physical body, provoking the disconnection of the vehicles of the consciousness. The energetic sensations during this technique can be very clear.

Instructions

1. Lie down in your physical base, wearing comfortable clothes. Set the room to the ideal temperature and close the door to avoid disturbances.

2. Apply the psychophysiological relaxation technique (the first technique in this chapter) to help you further perceive the extraphysical aspect of your reality.

3. Then initiate this technique by imagining that the feet and legs of your psychosoma (parafeet and paralegs) stretch (grow longer) outside your physical body by about six inches. Follow this elongation of your legs mentally, as they stretch out and then come back into alignment with your physical body. The entire movement of the paralegs separating and reintegrating should take about one minute—meaning it should not be too fast. You want to give yourself time to focus on it properly, feeling the energy in your legs and feet as well as the motion of the psychosoma as you do this. Repeat this elongation of the paralegs and parafeet three times.

4. Focusing now on your head and shoulders, try to sense the energy and even feel your psychosoma in this region. Imagine and feel the shoulders and head of your psychosoma stretching (growing taller) six inches beyond the physical limits. Then bring the parahead and parashoulders slowly back into the physical body. Follow this elongation mentally. Repeat this exercise in this area three times, spending about one minute with each repetition.

5. Now feel the energy and the psychosoma enveloping your entire body. Imagine and feel your psychosoma slowly stretching about six inches in all directions (inflating, ballooning). Pay close attention to your sensations. After a few seconds, bring the psychosoma back to its original size. Repeat this exercise with the entire psychosoma three times (about one minute each).

6. Next, do another cycle of stretching out the legs and feet, head and shoulders, and the entire psychosoma. However, this time stretch out one foot (instead of six inches) in each direction for each area.

7. For the next cycle, stretch each area out two feet, three times. Then for the cycle after that, elongate everything five feet, then ten feet, twenty feet, fifty feet, and so on. There is no limit for the psychosoma in terms of stretching.

Disconnection

You will probably feel the sensation of balloonment with this technique. Continue with the cycles of elongation until you are out of the body.

2. Rotation of the Psychosoma Technique

Introduction

This technique uses your ability to control the psychosoma and its movements of rotation to induce the disconnection.[37] It also takes advantage of the fact that most people sleep on their side—over one shoulder or the other—and that most people know very well the sensation of rolling over in bed from one side to the other. It is important to work with energies properly before attempting this technique so as to have a looser energosoma.

Instructions

1. Lie down on a bed for this technique. Wearing loose clothing, lie down on your side, over one shoulder, and relax. Placing extra pillows under the knees, hands, and feet may help the relaxation.

2. Focus on your psychosoma and mentally command it to rotate backward, so you end up facing the other side. You want your psychosoma to rotate or roll over, and end up on your other shoulder. Your physical body must not move. It is only a mental command that will make your psychosoma roll out of the physical body. Try to rotate toward the side of the bed that you usually get out of in the morning.

3. You can do this psychosomatic movement little by little, controlling it through your will and repeating the intention over and over again. Try to imagine yourself rolling to the other side while you incorporate the sensations that are common to you when physically executing this movement.

Disconnection

In many cases it may be relatively and surprisingly easier to leave the body by rotating the psychosoma than in a more conventional fashion. This technique commonly produces partial projections before generating a full disconnection.

Mental Saturation Technique

In the following account, we can see how this technique works.

Conscious Projections and Lucid Dreams
Cirleine Couto (2004)[38]

On February 2, 2001, I decided that for a period of at least one month I would use a technique to induce conscious projections. I chose a particular technique, known and used by many researchers studying dreams and conscious projections, that consists of conditioning our behavior during the waking state in such a way as to be able to reproduce a similar behavior the moment we are out of the body with reasonable lucidity. The technique works in such a way that, by repeating the pattern previously programmed, the moment the projector experiences a lucid dream, he acquires immediate lucidity and starts a lucid projection. Several researchers, such as Oliver Fox and Sylvan Muldoon, who contributed data from relevant investigations to the study of the projectiological phenomena, have obtained good results in inducing out-of-body experiences through techniques aimed at achieving extraphysical lucidity through lucid dreams.

I initiated the technique by repeating the following question to myself every time I thought of it: "Am I dreaming or am I awake?" Each time, I would thoroughly verify my condition at that moment and respond rationally to the question.

By repeating this technique often over a number of consecutive days, there existed the possibility that, at some point in time, I would experience a lucid dream, during which I would ask myself the question, increase my level of extraphysical lucidity, and conclude that I was in fact out of the body. In order to increase my chances of awakening in the extraphysical dimension, I conditioned myself to accompany the question with some specific movements, such as checking my hands to distinguish whether they are my physical hands or the hands of my psychosoma (in this case transparent and luminous) or touching the back of my head (nuchal chakra) with one hand to check for the presence of the silver cord.

(continued) On the afternoon of the first day of the experiment, I lay down for a little while after having eaten. As I relaxed, I fell asleep and immediately started to dream. Within the dream I clearly felt I was leaving the body. Still lacking better lucidity, the upper part of my psychosoma came out of alignment whilst my para-legs (legs of my psychosoma) remained in a state of coincidence with my physical body. By then I was sitting on the sofa, but I understood that my body was lying there, resting. It was then that I asked myself the question "Am I dreaming or am I awake?" I was able to verify my state and identify the vehicle of manifestation I was using at the time with lucidity, drawing the immediate conclusion that "I'm not dreaming. I'm projected!"

I was able to come totally out of coincidence with the soma and was happy about that. I then decided to leave the vicinity of my physical body so as to avoid a premature return. I went through the door of the room where my body was lying and felt the pressure of the wood against my psychosoma, a slightly unpleasant sensation. When my parahead (head of my psychosoma) went through the door, I felt some resistance, and from that moment I lost my spatial references. I felt myself being propelled upward at high speed. I stopped periodically at certain "places" where I saw some shapes that I shall attempt to describe. I saw a sky full of stars. When I saw this specific image, I wondered if I was looking at the cosmos. Next, I saw some really curious mobile geometrical shapes that opened to reveal new, inspiring shapes. The ensemble made me think of morphothosenes created by highly intelligent extraphysical consciousnesses, as the whole geometrical unfolding was synchronic, calculated, and beautiful. This vision triggered an intense absorption of extraphysical energy that left me in a state of contained euphoria. I could not determine if the vision was provoked by the fast takeoff of my psychosoma, followed by interiorization of my psychosoma into my physical body, or if it happened when I was being pulled back to my physical body.

Subsequently, I was aware that I was close to the soma and able to hear the rhythmic intracranial sounds indicative of the condition of realignment of my vehicles of manifestation. Immediately afterward, I felt a strong vibrational state confirming the projective occurrence. I could feel the beneficial effects of the extraphysical energy throughout the whole day.

After this experience I did not use the technique for one week due to events in my everyday life. Although I was not using the technique, I kept thinking of repeating the experiment, which I finally did after this break. The omnipresent memory of the technique and the results it had already produced likely prompted another projective phenomenon that happened on February 12, 2001, on the very same day I had scheduled to retry the technique. This time I had a semiconscious projection that took place during the early hours of the day.

I found myself in a place where people spoke English. I cannot say if I was in the United States, England, Scotland, or another English-speaking country. I was inside an ancient mansion whose interior was of dark wood. Other people were also there, including my partner in the evolutionary duo. The moment I looked at my partner, I noticed a thread stemming from the back of his head, but I wasn't able to see the other end of it. The thread was silvery in color and luminescent, reminding me of the light and color of lightning. At this point I gained some lucidity and told my partner I could see his silver cord. I then performed one of the conditioned movements I associated with the extraphysical awakening technique: passing my hand behind my head. With my left hand I felt around the space behind my neck, and after a while I felt a tubular structure there. This was my silver cord, of which I noted some characteristics: it was approximately two centimeters wide, it was silver-colored due to its luminosity, it was flexible and at the same time very strong, and it had a smooth texture. The silver cord seemed to be made of several small tubes all grouped together in one single beam, reminding me of the beam of collagen fibers that form a tendon, that strong structure that links muscles to bones in the human anatomy. Once I had proven to myself that I was projected, I tried to fly around a bit, with the intention of demonstrating to the other people present the phenomenon of projection. In fact, these people were surprised by my performance. I lost my lucidity while flying.

(continued) In light of the reported experiences, I concluded that for those researchers who wish to have more conscious projections or to further their studies in any given area, applying a projective technique can result in being able to collate important findings. Projective techniques promote the disengagement of not only the psychosoma but also the mentalsoma from the physical body. They also bring better lucidity to the projector, allowing for a more accurate collection of data from the extraphysical dimensions. Information acquired in this manner is relevant for the progression of projectiology, as this science presents ample room for investigation, calling for further data in many areas, such as paraphysiology of the psychosoma, silver cord, golden cord, mentalsoma, and others. Better-equipped projectors, by using projective techniques already trialed by other researchers, or even better by using their own techniques, will be able to collect additional leading-edge information that can be made available to anyone interested in the phenomenology of projection, thus actualizing and always refreshing the science of projectiology.

Recollection of the OBE

A projection, strictly speaking, is never forgotten. Even if we are not able to recall it while intraphysical, we can potentially recall it during another projection at a later date while outside the body. This is because the memory of the psychosoma (which is the holomemory—also called integral memory—in the mentalsoma) retains all of this information in its entirety. Yet in order to enjoy the full benefits of the projection during ordinary waking life, the person needs to recall the experience in this physical dimension.

On some occasions, projective recall will be quite easy. There are certain experiences that cause a greater impact on us, and these experiences are never forgotten. The first lucid projection usually falls into this category, yet most projections do not.

The intention after returning to the body is to register as much of the experience as possible, because in order to seriously develop lucid projections, we want to be able to study them afterward. Some experiences have details that make sense only after other experiences are had, maybe weeks or months after the original one. Yet if the initial detail is not properly recorded, an important association of ideas or a realization may not be possible.

The ideal condition for recalling an experience is to *wake up immediately after reentry into the body.*[39] If the projector is successful at doing this properly, then the memories of the projection will be clear and accessible for the person.

The way in which we come back to the body affects the quality of our recollection. If we come back without control, either because we were impacted by a strong emotion (such as surprise, fear, or euphoria) or a physical disturbance (the phone ringing, a knock on the door, and so forth), we lose awareness and come back to the body quite rapidly and without self-control. Yet if we are able to choose when we come back, we will return at our own pace, with a relaxed sense of control.

Before reentering the body, we want to remind ourselves, "I will wake up immediately the moment I go in!," so as to regain lucidity and remember our experience right away.[40] This is especially crucial after an important event in a projection to guarantee that we will remember the experience and get it all on paper. Usually, as we gain more experience with OBEs, we start to value and prioritize this more.

The main problem with recall occurs when we continue to sleep after we return to the body. In this case, when the recollection of the experience enters the body, more specifically the brain, it presents two problems:[41]

1. The memory of the experience, which is extraphysical in nature, will not be well received by the brain because the brain is in its own process of sleep. The brain is not biologically ready to accept an extraphysical memory. Therefore, this memory, which was not initially even perceived by the physical brain, has very little chance of being imprinted into physicality at this time.

2. If the person begins to dream after coming back, the experience of the projection in some cases will become mixed with the dream. Afterward, the recollection is not as clear because the elements are mixed.

During the initial stages of OBE development, projectors tend to return to the body and transition straight into sleeping afterward. Rarely do projections end when people want them to. Normally individuals will try to stay projected for longer, and something happens and they snap back into the body. The most common reasons for an abrupt return to the body are the loss of emotional control or a physical stimulus that disturbs the body. Because of the fact that in many instances we come back without control, it is important to know how to deal with trying to recall the experience in the morning.

First, upon waking up, we should try to create the habit to search our memories for projections that occurred during the night. The first thought that should come to mind upon becoming aware should be "What did I do tonight?" This should be done even before moving too much or opening the eyes; otherwise, the recollection may be "dispersed" by common morning motions. We should spend a few minutes making an effort to remember and trying to piece together all the memories, whether they are dreams or projections—it is better at this point not to discriminate or analyze too much.

Most times, when a projection has occurred, we will feel this upon waking up, even though the details of the experience may not be fully known. If upon some introspection we do not remember, then we should *slowly* try to shift our position in bed. Keeping our eyes closed, we should gently shift the position of our head or body. As we do this, the blood will circulate better through the head, and in many cases the memory will come rushing in.

Also, at this moment, in order to increase the efficiency of the recollection, we should do a VELO to reach a VS. The energosoma is the body that connects and communicates information from the psychosoma to the soma. Since the intention is to bring fresh information from the psychosoma to the soma, increasing the efficiency and *flow* of the communication bridge will help to accomplish this. Recalling an experience is similar to downloading a file onto a computer. If we have a "faster connection" (by doing a VS to connect better to the frequency of the psychosoma), then the recollection will be improved.

Once we have partially or fully recalled the experience, the ideal is to devise an outline, or some keywords, of the more important events of the projection. Then we should record these keywords. It is not wise to leave this task for later, regardless of how clear the memory seems or how much we believe we will not forget. In some instances, the recollection of a projection can be as elusive as a dream; with each second that goes by, we forget more details exponentially.

After these keywords are safely documented, we can now proceed to describe the projection in detail. The ideal, for most people, is to write about the experience.[42] The reason that this method (writing) is the best for recall is that the very act of writing activates our memory. We often will remember more details of the experience in the middle of writing about it. If a pen and paper are left on our night table, then going from the recollection of the experience to writing it down will be very quick—minimizing the number of events that can come in between and have an unproductive, distracting effect upon us.

Writing down dreams is already a technique for becoming more lucid during the night and thus producing OBEs. If we record our experiences—even if they are still dreams—this produces a healthy psychological self-conditioning effect. Basically, we are making a statement that what happens during the night is important to us, and that we want to be lucid and remember it. Naturally, the next night we tend to remain more aware, and then—through writing about it—the process is reinforced. The next night we have greater awareness, and the following morning more reinforcement, and so on and so forth. In one to two weeks, we will be recalling a great amount of material. In this condition, lucid projections will also be easier to produce.

Other means of documenting the experience can be used, such as a tape recorder and/or a computer. A tape recorder has the disadvantage that, even though individuals may have their tapes well labeled, it is still hard to find a specific experience afterward for self-study. The same is true of digital voice recordings.

If we are in a hurry, a voice recorder may work better to document the keywords in the morning. Before going to bed that same night we can listen to the keywords again and spend twenty minutes rewriting our experiences with details. By describing our experience from the previous night, we go to bed having the advantage of already being holothosenically connected with projections.

It is best not to leave the work of writing the details of a projection for another day. We run the risk of more than likely forgetting much of it.

After the Projection

There are certain events that may occur when we wake up after a projection. In many instances, we may experience a *shower of energies* that run through our body.[43] This works as a confirmation of the projection, and in many cases the recollection of the projection comes with these energies. This is a very positive sensation that can leave us in a state of well-being throughout the day.

Projections can also help to develop our *psychism*. Sometimes these effects will linger for days after the projection. We may feel the "looseness" of the energosoma. It may feel as if we are wearing long, loose, fine garments. The sensation is purely energetic. With this looseness of the energosoma, intuition and other energetic perceptions become more acute.

We may also feel ourselves being in a state of *waking nonalignment*,[44] as if we are semi-disconnected throughout the day. Sometimes we may feel as if our next step will be taken on thin air. This is for the most part a benign condition. Yet, if it (or any of this) becomes a nuisance, doing a VELO to reach a VS will help us regain better control over our vehicles. There is no way to emphasize enough the importance and usefulness of the energy work, and the VS will always tend to balance us.

Summary of Key Chapter Points

- Results of the OBE techniques are individual—what works for one person does not necessarily work for another.
- We need to get used to the disconnection sensations so as not to become surprised by them and to leave the body with greater ease.
- Always work with energy before a projective attempt, as this will loosen your energosoma.
- Pay attention to your environment. You want to prepare for it to be quiet and for you to be as undisturbed as possible.
- The dorsal position is a projective technique that in and of itself will help you to project.
- Learn to relax well.
- Try to be in the right frame of mind to produce the projection. Reading about OBEs before trying them can help.

- Do each projective technique for about one hour, and do only one technique at a time during this period.

- Once you have settled on your preferred technique, repeat it, if possible, for fourteen nights in a row. Your control over the technique will increase each time, and more frequent and consistent results will be achieved.

Chapter Notes

1. Vieira, 2002, p. 441.
2. Ibid., p. 442.
3. Ibid., p. 429.
4. Vieira, 1999, p. 9.
5. Vieira, 2002, pp. 401–6.
6. The Projectarium is a specialized laboratory for having OBEs. It was built at the IAC Research Campus in Portugal. For more information, see the appendix on the IAC Research Campus at the end of this book, and for technical details about the Projectarium, see Trivellato and Fernándes, 2002, pp. 3–30.
7. Vieira, 2002, pp. 420–21.
8. Ibid., p. 408.
9. Ibid., pp. 410–13.
10. Ibid., pp. 408–9.
11. Ibid., pp. 423–24.
12. Stack, 1988, p. 103.
13. Purchasing melatonin is unnecessary and not recommended. No positive effect has been shown to exist for OBEs by ingesting it.
14. Vieira, 2002, pp. 414, 853.
15. Ibid., pp. 417–20, 440–41.
16. Ibid., p. 415.
17. Ibid., p. 425.
18. Alegretti, 2004, p. 115.
19. Sarasvati, 1959, p. 328.
20. Ibid., pp. 47–50.
21. Vieira, 2002, p. 430.
22. Ibid., pp. 855–58.
23. Gutierrez, 1999, pp. 53–58.
24. Vieira, 2002, pp. 441–44.
25. Ibid., pp. 432–33.
26. Ibid., pp. 434–35.

27. Ibid., pp. 446–47.
28. Ibid., p. 444.
29. Ibid., p. 448.
30. Ibid., pp. 457–58.
31. Bruce, 1999, pp. 254–64; Vieira, 2002, p. 457.
32. Vieira, 2002, pp. 490–91.
33. Ibid., pp. 448–52.
34. Ibid., pp. 435–37.
35. Ibid., pp. 477–78.
36. Ibid., pp. 463–64.
37. Ibid., pp. 479–81.
38. Couto, 2004, p. 251.
39. Vieira, 2002, p. 757.
40. Ibid., p. 759.
41. Ibid., pp. 463–64.
42. Ibid., pp. 768–73.
43. Ibid., pp. 746–47.
44. Ibid., pp. 747–48.

Extraphysical Consciousnesses

The objective of this chapter is to clarify the mechanisms of how multidimensional contacts are established and maintained. Once we start having lucid out-of-body experiences, we will eventually come across other projectors and extraphysical consciousnesses. The idea is to discuss the many different types of possible relationships with the various kinds of extraphysical consciousnesses in a natural and pragmatic fashion. As the information builds, we will reach deeper, more complex and interesting topics, which will need to be well understood.

To a certain degree, leaving the body is like leaving our house and going for a drive (or getting on the metro). On the road, we encounter all kinds of drivers. Sometimes we encounter cordial ones, who always give the right of way and put on their turning signal. We also meet up with self-centered ones, who are not necessarily against anybody but want to get across the lanes or make their turn without any regard for others. We also find irresponsible ones, who may cause an accident at any moment.

Before we were born in this physical body, we were an extraphysical consciousness. Thus, thinking logically, the extraphysical consciousnesses who we may meet while projected are the individuals who passed away in the last months, years, and decades and are presently in their in-between-lives period. Likewise, once we pass away in this life, we will be one of those extraphysical consciousnesses that other projectors can meet outside the body. Thus, extraphysical society is partially a reflection of the intraphysical society, and just like driving, we may find different types of extraphysical consciousnesses.

Extraphysical Communication

Let us start by discussing the mechanism by which we communicate outside the body, whether with a projector or an extraphysical consciousness. There are three types of extraphysical communication:

- Verbal (oral)
- Telepathy
- Conscientese

Verbal, or oral, communication is similar to the speech we have in the intraphysical dimension—with articulation of words.[1] This method is used when individuals have a low level of awareness outside the body. This is the least effective means of extraphysical communication. It is still based on articulation as well as on a specific language.

When we are projected with a low level of lucidity, our physical conditionings tend to be stronger. This is similar to us wanting to walk while projected. Thus, we have the tendency to want to communicate while projected the same way we communicate when inside the body. If our native language is English and we project and happen to find somebody projected whose native language is Hindi, and neither of us speaks the other's language, then the communication problems we would encounter would be similar to what would happen intraphysically.

As the level of awareness increases, we start to use a more efficient means of communication. *Telepathy* is the transmission of energetic information; it is the transmission of thosenes (not just thoughts).[2] The moment we or somebody else thinks about something, it can immediately be "heard" by everyone else around.[3] In many instances, it feels as if somebody else's thoughts are forming in our head as the other person manifests them.

Telepathy can be divided into two categories, also according to the level of awareness. First, *minor telepathy*, though no longer articulated verbally, still has the conditioning of language. So even though we are thinking the information, we are still thinking through the use of our language of reference, and what we are thinking is transmitted with the specific "grammar" of our language.

Major telepathy, however, does not have the restriction of language. At this level of awareness, the conditioning has disappeared and we are able to think without symbols (asymbolically). At this point, since we are not thinking in any language, we are closer to our essence as a consciousness. Naturally, the consciousness has no official intraphysical language. At this level, when considering our previous example, there would be no communication problems between two individuals who are Hindi and English.

Conscientese is the highest form of communication we can use.[4] Since the system of communication we use is dependent on our level of awareness, we use conscientese when we are having a projection with the mentalsoma (100% level of extraphysical awareness). It is also known as *consciential language*, *cosmic language*, and *universal mental language*. The difference between major telepathy and conscientese is the difference between delivering and receiving ideas in a *retail* versus a *wholesale* fashion.

In major telepathy, though our communication is no longer dependent on language, we send one idea (the equivalent of a sentence), then another, and another. With successive ideas we build a paragraph, then a page, and then an entire book; yet the delivery throughout is made in a retail fashion, in small units—in this case, sentences. With conscientese, since we are more lucid, we can send the information of an entire book to somebody else at once (*en bloc*). The recipient, who is also at this level of lucidity, will be able to digest all the information in a fraction of a second. The exchange of ideas between us then becomes much more complete and encompassing. All cognition at this level is *super-amplified* (brainstorming, creativity, and others).

In the same way that our level of awareness can fluctuate outside the body, the means of communication fluctuate accordingly. For example, if we are communicating an extremely inspiring and interesting idea extraphysically with a projector from a foreign land, as we delve deeper into this idea, there will be an increase in the level of awareness of both of us (holothosenic influence) as well as in the level of communication, and both projectors could end up communicating with a high level of major telepathy during the same interaction.

Deactivation of the Bodies

Let us see how feasible it is for us to use these means of communication outside the body. The level of awareness and communication of extraphysical consciousnesses is very much tied to how many bodies they have discarded. Discarding a body is what we call "death." The more technically correct term for death is *desoma*.

 Desoma is a compound word formed from the words *deactivation* and *soma*. Therefore, a *desoma* is a somatic deactivation, the passing away of a body, or the process we call death.[5]

As we know, the physical body is not permanent. We experience and learn at certain moments attached to a physical body, followed by other periods in which we exist without one. For every human rebirth, we also go through a physical death. However, since we have four bodies, and not just simply the physical body, it means that we can experience more than just the passing away of the physical body—other bodies are discarded as well.[6] The level of awareness of an extraphysical consciousness will depend on how many of these transitions, or discarding of bodies, the individual has undergone.

It is important to understand that the discarding of a body is not negative, nor is it a punishment. Just like being born, it is a natural and common transition. We have already undergone many discardings, and we will undergo many, many more.

A death, or the discarding of a body, can also be understood as a transition from a condition of greater restriction to a condition of lesser restriction. As we shed bodies (which restrict us), our manifestation has the opportunity to expand, allowing us to have greater freedom of action. Unfortunately, because of cultural conditionings in societies, passing away is usually seen as something unpleasant and negative. We must notice, though, that this is a conditioning of particular cultures, since there are cultures on the planet in which death is celebrated and not mourned.

First Desoma—Deactivation of the Soma (Biological Death)

The deactivation of the physical body, or *biological death*, is known as the first death.[7] The deactivation of the soma occurs due to biological death, which in turn leads to the rupturing of the silver cord. Since the energosoma is the connection or bridge

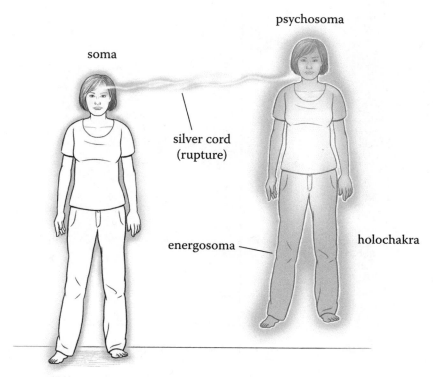

Figure 5.1: First Desoma (Deactivation of the Soma)

between the physical body (soma) and the psychosoma, a portion of the energies of the energosoma is also discarded with the biological death.

After going through the first death, we as consciousnesses stay with the remnants of the energosoma, as well as with the psychosoma and mentalsoma (figure 5.1). The first transition, or biological death, is also known as the final projection—from a physical point of view—and represents the irreversible disconnection of the consciousness from its soma (physical body). Without exception, everybody undergoes this transition. For consciousnesses unprepared for it, the deactivation of the soma is still a shock and trauma.

Second Desoma—Deactivation of the Energosoma

The deactivation of the remaining portion of the energosoma is called the second death. After deactivating the energosoma, the extraphysical consciousness remains only with its more subtle psychosoma and the mentalsoma (figure 5.2).

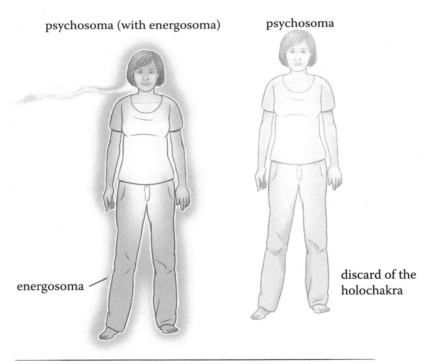

psychosoma (with energosoma)　　　psychosoma

energosoma

discard of the holochakra

Figure 5.2: Second Desoma (Deactivation of the Energosoma)

We observe that the human physical life is primarily an energetic manifestation of us as a consciousness through the energosoma and the physical body. In this fashion, the energosoma (energetic body) should exist only while we have a physical body. Ideally, therefore, every time a consciousness undergoes the first deactivation and discards its physical body, it should also promote the deactivation of its energosoma.

However, unlike the deactivation of the soma, the deactivation of the energosoma does not occur spontaneously or innately. The second deactivation is sometimes referred to by certain groups as the death of the third day. This deactivation does not actually, nor necessarily, take three days after the first deactivation to occur, since the time it takes to deactivate the remains of the energosoma can vary greatly. It can take a few minutes, hours, days, months, or in some cases years or decades.

In many instances, the consciousness does not pass through the second deactivation and is instead reborn. There are consequences for not passing through the second deactivation. Since the individual did not discard the energy from the previous physical life, the new energosoma in the next life "merges with" the old one, resulting in a person with a denser energetic condition.[8] The person's energy in the next life in this case will be less flexible, and achieving an OBE will be harder. Furthermore, for these individuals, even understanding the concept of an OBE will be much harder in most instances. These individuals will also perceive the energies to a lesser extent and will be less intuitive as well.

As was already stated, passing through *or not* passing through the second deactivation is an evolutionary issue. The level of attachments, conditioning, knowledge, and *practical application* of this knowledge is what will determine whether the individual passes through the second deactivation. Let us study this in detail.[9]

The great majority of individuals realize that they are "something" beyond the physical body—we call it the consciousness. Yet, in day-to-day life and in practice, we tend to ignore this fact and become very interested in, preoccupied with, and focused on our physical activities only—without keeping an eye on our broader reality. It is from these physical activities that individuals end up deriving the main reason for their existence. These reasons vary from person to person.

For some individuals, the main reason for their existence is having a happy or a big family, or both. Others basically live for their work, and their main goal is to achieve a specific position in the workforce and in society. A very important objective for many is to retire early and to live a comfortable life. For others, it is enjoying leisure activities and entertainment. For others less fortunate, maintaining their daily subsistence takes up most of their time. What needs to be evaluated here is where the energies of the person are mainly being directed.

As an example, some individuals have a nice family and good friends, and they are extremely driven and committed to their work. If they are asked, "Which do you prefer, your family or your work?," most of these individuals will answer "their family"—the politically correct answer. However, in many cases, the reality is that there is more effort, energy, and enthusiasm flowing from them toward their work than toward their family. In this particular case, their theoretical and verbal answer is not in agreement with their actual practice.

So, let us consider the following. If we did not have any obligations, and we were free to do whatever we wanted, what is it we would do? While living in the physical body, we are presented with many obligations in this dimension. First and foremost, we need to concern ourselves with the survival of the physical body. In terms of our most basic necessities, we are *obligated* to eat, go to the bathroom, sleep, and others. Furthermore, to maintain physical life and the conditions necessary to live well, most of us *must* work, pay bills, and so forth.

What occurs then when we undergo the biological (first) deactivation is that we free ourselves from all of these obligations, and are now free to think about and put our energies into whatever we wish. This is where any conditionings and attachments become more obvious. Many individuals will continue to dedicate their energies to what they understand to be important to them (i.e., work, family, sex, cars, food, friends, entertainment, and so forth) even though they no longer have a physical body.

If the person is too attached to something physical, then they keep the dense energy of the energosoma, which in turn attaches them to that physical element that is relevant for them. Thus, they do not pass through the second deactivation of the energosoma. Even though it would seem as if we could very easily choose not to be attached to something physical, what occurs is that while the person remains with the *dense* energies of the energosoma, the level of awareness is lower—similar to a loaded projection. The individual in this case remains at the equivalent of a 20% level of awareness (in some cases less), and thus they cannot judge their situation clearly.

Furthermore, it is not easy to simply explain to these individuals what their condition actually is, because how much they can understand depends on them (and on their level of awareness). Many times, they do not even pay attention or become aware of a projector trying to explain something to them. As was explained in chapter 3, the senses outside the body are not open; they are directed by the person's will and interests. So we can be screaming (using verbal communication in these cases) next to them, and they may simply not hear us because they are completely focused on something else (whatever interests them).

The person's conditionings and main interests take over by default. Some individuals are more lucid, and others less so. We ourselves can leave the body, observe this reality, and confirm it directly. Many extraphysical consciousnesses are sort of dazed and confused, with a low level of awareness. Their existence is *similar to our common dreams*, meaning not too lucid and not too clear. Just like in our dreams, we find ourselves acting in ways we know we would not act if we were more aware, while justifying the most irrational situations.

We have to realize that what leads the consciousness to such a condition is the person's level of maturity or how broad the mentality of the person is—in other words, it's an evolutionary issue. Let us use an analogy to explain this further. What would be the reaction of a three-year-old if he is eating his favorite chocolate bar, and then we take it away and tell him he can eat it after dinner in a few hours? Depending on how much he had focused on this activity, he may start screaming and throw a big tantrum. He may react as if his world has ended. Because he has a narrower mentality, the moment focused on eating the chocolate became his whole world. And so we literally took his world away from him.

However, what would happen with us adults if someone took our chocolate from us and gave it to a child? What would be our reaction? We may be fine with it, or we may actually split the chocolate in two and give the child half. We may think, "I'll stop by the supermarket later and buy one (or a full box of them)," or we may even just hand it over without any reaction. Since our mentality is broader, we will not react as if our world has ended, because our world is much larger than just a chocolate bar.

Unfortunately, for most people, their world—in practice—is basically *only* their physical life—and now, after the moment of physical death, it is not there anymore. This is like the child who is unable to see or understand that other possibilities exist (he can have the chocolate after dinner). Many individuals are unable to see or understand that other possibilities exist, like we will have many other lives and we are not physical beings. Even though the idea of having other lives is not a secret, for most individuals it is still only a theory—they lack the lucid personal experience or evidence of this. As a result, their main values are still mainly intraphysical and monoexistential (based on the current life only).

When someone does not pass through the second deactivation and stays focused on something related to their recently terminated physical life, they are usually unable to recall their past lives. Furthermore, they do not prepare or plan for their next life— since they are not even aware that their past life has ended or that they will have another life ahead. Over half of the population does not undergo the second deactivation. We can observe intraphysical evidence of this by simply considering the following question: What percentage of society is actually ready—or has enough practical understanding—to pass through the biological deactivation (to die) and handle it with calm and maturity?

On the other hand, individuals who do pass through the second deactivation (discard the remnants of the energosoma) are more lucid during their intermissive period (the in-between-lives period).[10] They are thus able to remember their past physical lives and realize that they are not just the product of the physical life that just ended. Their reality is broader. This also allows these consciousnesses to actively participate in the analysis of the life they just finished as well as help them to decide what tasks and activities they should get involved in to prepare for the next intraphysical life. In regard to evolution and the process of all of us being at this moment in a series of physical lives, the ideal would be to undergo the second deactivation every time we discard the physical body.

Everybody undergoes the first deactivation. Yet it is only after individuals have accumulated more development and evolution and have a broader mentality about their own reality that they start passing through the second deactivation as well. They will have many lives thereafter passing through the first and second deactivations and being reborn into physicality. After even more evolutionary growth, as well as many, many lives, individuals will eventually undergo the third deactivation as well.

Third Desoma—Deactivation of the Psychosoma

At the end of our long sequence of existences, there will come a day when we will have learned everything that we needed to learn from the physical experience as well as from the existence of our psychosoma. At that point, the consciousness will discard the physical body and energosoma for *the last time*, followed immediately by the discarding of the psychosoma as well.[11] This is known as the third death, or, in other words, the sole and final discarding of the psychosoma through the rupture of the golden cord (figure 5.3).

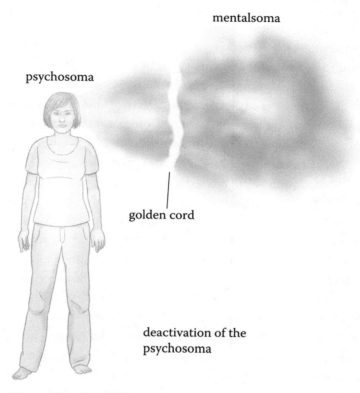

Figure 5.3: Third Desoma (Deactivation of the Psychosoma)

The third deactivation is like graduation from physical evolutionary school. After this, the consciousness does not need to have physical lives ever again. Due to this, these types of beings who have undergone the third deactivation receive the name of *free consciousnesses*, and they are the ones we meet in the mentalsomatic dimensions when projected with the mentalsoma.

Extraphysical Consciousnesses

When people pass away, they go to different dimensions. Their holothosene naturally determines the dimension they have an affinity with, which is where they will go. Thus, as explained in the discussion on dimensions in chapter 3, the *tropospheric* dimensions house individuals who have less information and less evolution. The level of overall stability and consciential maturity in the holothosene of individuals at the end of their life will make them go to higher (energetically more subtle) or lower (energetically more dense) dimensions accordingly.

Through physical lives we learn and refine our attributes and characteristics. This evolutionary improvement will allow us to go to increasingly more evolved dimensions during our intermissive periods. Eventually we will reach the highest extraphysical dimensions and be ready to pass through the third deactivation.

The consensus among the various conscientiological researchers is that right now, for each one of us currently existing as an intraphysical consciousness attached to a physical body, there are about nine nonphysical consciousnesses.[12] In other words, the extraphysical population is considered to be nine times larger than the intraphysical one. In round figures, if the human population is now over 6 billion people, then, applying a ratio of 1:9, this means that the extraphysical population is over 54 billion, for a grand total of more than 60 billion consciousnesses who right now occupy the multidimensional space on, around, and having to do with planet Earth.

The population explosion over the last hundred years has more than quadrupled the number of intraphysical consciousnesses on the planet. This does not necessarily mean that new consciousnesses are being created. It simply means that over the last hundred years there has been a significant change in the proportion between intraphysical and extraphysical consciousnesses. This gives us a very good reason to be optimistic about the evolutionary future of our planet. We have never had this many consciousnesses evolving with the human experience as we do right now; and given that evolution at our level and on Earth seems to occur as a result of our physical human experiences, this is a very good sign indeed.

Now let us consider the main categories of individuals (extraphysical consciousnesses) we may meet outside the body.

Helpers

Helpers are extraphysical consciousnesses in a very refined and developed consciential condition. They are lucid, well intentioned, positive, and much more evolved than the average human consciousness.[13] All helpers are focused on assisting consciousnesses, both physical and nonphysical, in the best possible fashion. We are certainly able to meet them outside the body. The communication with them is very direct and clear because they have been passing through the second deactivation after their physical lives for a long time now.

Helpers have been called by many other names, such as masters, spirit guides, illuminated beings, beings of light, and angels.

In some definitions of angels by different ideologies, they are described as being of a different *substance* than us. They are described as always having been angels, and we are described as never having been nor ever being able to become angels. This theory is not supported by the evidence. Experientially and in direct communications with them, we realize these evolved beings are usually much more conscientially or spiritually refined than we are, yet they once were at the level of understanding we are at right now. This also implies that with more evolution, we will eventually reach the stage of helpers.[14]

Though much information has already been accumulated on the evolutionary levels of the various consciousnesses observed during an OBE, explaining them goes beyond the scope of this book. For more information on this subject, please refer to the section at the end of this book on IAC, specifically regarding the CDP program. Visit LearnOBEs.com for details on the CDP.

Heightened Awareness

Helpers have a very developed level of awareness and understand the problems we face in a totally different light. Their mentality and vision are quite broad. This difference is similar to when a child in the third grade is having a hard time with his homework on long division and is helped by his older sister. The older sister, who is already in tenth grade, helps him, and since she naturally has such a strong command of math, the problem is easy for her.

Helpers have a developed sense of practicality and are committed to their assistantial tasks. The helpers' main intention is *to help individuals to evolve, to grow, to become more capable and self-sufficient.* We can be certain that every time a helper is close to us, it is because there is serious evolutionary work being executed. Since there is always much assistance to be given, helpers prioritize with whom, where, and in what they will invest their time, energy, and effort.[15]

Helping Us to Grow

Helpers know what our life task, or existential program (the main activities we planned for ourselves for this life), is. To understand their approach, let us consider what would happen if we left the body and asked them, "What is my existential program?" Helpers do not and would not say what our existential program is because part of accomplishing it is *us figuring out what it is*. In a sense, helpers want us to learn to make our own decisions, to make better ones each time, and to be responsible for their results, meaning to grow and to mature.

Notice that if helpers were to directly say what should be done, most people would then blindly go and follow their instructions. If for some reason what the person was trying to accomplish did not work, they might hold the helpers responsible for the failure—since they were the ones who so advised ("they told me to").

Helpers do not want nor need us to follow them. Wanting or needing others to follow us is a sure sign of immaturity, and helpers, being mature, do not behave in such a fashion. They lead by example. They want to help us grow as much as possible and to be more independent, not more dependent. In this sense, it is also important to realize that helpers do not force anything on us; they completely respect our free will in its totality.[16] Even in the unfortunate cases where we want to do something that is negative or unproductive for us and/or others, the helpers will not impinge on our freedom.

It is critical to realize that evolution comes from us, from within, by learning to evaluate what is best and carrying it out, and not just following something that somebody else said. Helpers also want individuals to realize that *we ourselves are the ones responsible for our own evolution*. We may have the best information available and the best helpers, yet nobody forces us to develop or grow, and at the same time nobody can develop or grow for us. We alone are the ones responsible for what we decide to do and how we go about doing it.

However, if we do pose questions, helpers will not allow us to leave empty-handed. More than likely, since they know us better than we know ourselves, they will be able to evaluate our evolutionary needs completely.[17] They will help us by providing information, perspectives, angles, and ideas that we had not considered, so as for us to make the best possible decision. They will be very assistantial in this sense, but the decisions actually made will be ours.

Unbiased

Helpers are unbiased and have a very developed sense of cosmoethics (cosmic ethics will be studied further in the next chapter). They *do not play favorites*. Thus, they try to help anybody who wants to evolve, as their criteria are more universalistic. They do not consider individuals to be from a specific race, social class, country, religion, or tradition that is any more or less than others. Most people usually have values and preferences that pertain specifically to a certain country, religion, race, or tradition, while helpers are already far beyond this.

Evolutionary Criteria and Priorities

Since helpers are concerned with our consciential evolution, this implies that they will not provide certain types of assistance.[18] In some cases, we might request aid for activities that are not too important from an evolutionary point of view, so, logically, considering the amount of serious assistantial work that helpers have, they will tend not to pay much attention to such things. Sometimes our requests are based more on physical comforts or pleasures that are not relevant or necessary for our consciential growth.

Likewise, helpers do not spend twenty-four hours a day "watching over" us. It is important to understand that there are much fewer helpers (evolved consciousnesses) in proportion to individuals that need help (lesser evolved consciousnesses). Therefore, helpers will prioritize being with us at the moments when we are more open to intuitions or performing activities that are directly or indirectly evolutionarily productive.

While we are doing mundane, routine activities, helpers will be helping individuals who are undergoing more critical moments in their lives. Likewise, when other people are doing more mundane intraphysical activities, helpers will help us at our more critical moments. At the same time, most of the physical activities we perform do not require a helper, since these are things we can do by ourselves.

Helpers are very interested in helping individuals grow. Yet, by looking at society, we see that most of the main interests of individuals revolve around intraphysical concerns and not necessarily inner growth. In some cases individuals tend to think that their physical problems are the most critical; and in other cases, for more selfish reasons, individuals think that helpers are there to serve them.

It is important to comprehend that helpers are not our possessions who can be summoned at whim. They are *evolutionary friends* willing to help us. Yet they are lucid, independent, and intelligent and very busy with many evolutionary endeavors.

The following may be a unique statement to make, but evidence shows that because of the average level of knowledge and understanding of most people, the relationship most intraphysical people establish during their physical lives with their extraphysical helper is similar to how they would relate to a waiter; meaning they only request things of helpers, and the relationship turns into a more paternalistic relationship (always asking). They treat helpers the way they would treat someone meant only to serve them. Although this is an unfortunate circumstance, helpers, thankfully for us, are extremely patient and understanding, realizing that most individuals do not understand how things work. Yet, evolutionarily speaking, those who relate better with helpers are those who nurture a more mature relationship with them, who are more concerned with their evolution and that of others—having the same types of concerns as the helpers.

Connections

There are two reasons that helpers assist us and we connect to them. Either we have a more personal connection with them, or we connect to them because of the activity we perform. We may have a personal connection with them stemming from a past life we had together. For example, maybe we were close brothers ten lives ago. So in the same way we would give a hand to a brother, they are giving us an evolutionary hand now. These types of helpers are the ones that "keep an eye" on us during our life.

Other helpers connect to us due to the activity we are performing. They are more technically specialized in a specific activity. Thus, a doctor who is looking for the cure for a specific disease may have a more technical helper who is giving him intuitions and trying to assist and safeguard him and his research. The main connection between them is the activity. If the doctor retires and someone else continues the research, the helper will then try to assist and safeguard the new researcher. This technical helper is keeping an eye on something bigger than the person doing the research; namely, on the effects and the number of people who will benefit once the research is concluded.

The way to connect or to be closer to helpers is for us to be more in tune with their holothosene. Thus, the way to bond more deeply with helpers is to be more interested in consciential evolution and in assisting others—just like helpers are. The opposite is also valid. If a person has a holothosene that is contrary to theirs, or mundane or hedonistic, in some instances such individuals can go very long periods without any type of evolved help. This is not due to the helpers' unwillingness to help, but to the fact that the person is not interested in what the helpers can provide in evolutionary substance—the person is looking for and interested in other things.

Energetic Refinement

As a consequence of having a subtler psychosoma, free of the dense energies of the previous physical body and because of their evolutionary level, a helper maintains a high level of energetic refinement.[19] Of all the extraphysical consciousnesses, more evolved consciousnesses like helpers are the hardest to perceive because of their subtlety. Even when individuals are projected, helpers are rarely fully visible, because they remain in a more subtle dimension. However, the communication with them, feeling their energies and support, is perceived more easily while projected.[20]

Likewise, when helpers are closer to us, our awareness generally increases.[21] This is the effect of their energies on us—*holothosenic influence*. In practice, this effect is felt significantly more while we are projected.

Functions

Helpers can perform different functions as they try to help us. They can work like a projective assistant, giving us intuitions and energies so we develop a capacity that they know can lead us to greater evolution. They can work as guides while we are projected. They sometimes act as a deactivation (death) expert, helping individuals in their transition through physical death. They work as protectors in many instances, helping us to avoid accidents but also protecting us from energies or influences that are negative.

Finally, the most common interaction individuals have with their helpers is not while they are projected but while they are intraphysical. Everybody already has a long history with their helpers, even though they may not have had lucid projections. Most individuals are unaware of their relationship with their helpers. Because of the dimensional difference, the helpers have the same difficulty communicating with us that we do with them. Yet we can minimize this gap through our development, especially through lucid projections.

Underneath the helpers in terms of awareness are individuals who have already passed through the second deactivation and are extraphysically preparing for their next life. These consciousnesses do not have the extensive experience of helpers and, since they are busy with their own evolutionary process, are not making a significant influence in the physical dimension. We can call these individuals *neutrals*. When we leave the body, we can communicate with neutrals (via major telepathy in most cases) and they will be polite and will seem like other normal people. Since neutrals do not initiate such deep and established interactions in the physical dimension, the relationship we usually have with them, unlike with helpers, is mainly only while we are projected.

Blind Guides

Below the neutrals we find the *blind guides*. Blind guides are consciousnesses who remain relatively confused in their intermissive periods, and most of them do not pass through the second deactivation. They have a narrower point of view and lack experience in trying to help individuals properly.[22]

> *Blind guides* are extraphysical consciousnesses who may have good intentions but have a low level of lucidity, and end up disturbing more than helping.

Since most blind guides do not pass through the second deactivation, they keep defending the interests of their recently terminated physical life. Their behavior is sometimes analogous to a confused *overprotective* parent.[23] They try to force their own will on others—the opposite of what helpers do.

For example, when a person with low lucidity passes away, they will try to keep on defending their family from any perceived harm. They actually want the best for their group and loved ones. So in an interaction between the son of the blind guide and a person external to the family, the blind guide will always favor their son. In an interaction between somebody of the same religion as the blind guide and somebody of a different religion, they will have a strong tendency to favor the individual of their group over the one from the other group.

The tragedy of blind guides is that they lack a broader awareness. They are unable to realize that the son they are defending at this moment was, for example, their son for the first time in this last life, while the person they are defending their son against (though in this life the person is external to the family) was perhaps the blind guide's son for twenty different lives before this one. In a broader sense, the blind guide has a richer history with the other person than with their son from this last life. Yet the blind guide does not realize this, and thus they can only defend the point of view they have, which is narrower because it is based on only one lifetime.

Blind guides become much more conditioned with physical life. So they can be born in religion A one life and will defend it by fighting against religion B with all their strength (sometimes even violently and sometimes, sadly, even with their life). Yet they do not realize that in their previous life, they were actually born into religion B and they did the same: defend their religion with all their strength—in some cases fighting against religion A. Going a step further, they do not realize that they have had many lives and thus many religions already. The same type of interaction occurs with nationalism and defending nations (or any other group for that matter).

Some blind guides have a higher level of awareness than others. They sometimes continue to repeat the same activities that gave meaning to their life while they were in the intraphysical dimension. They do this in a very mechanical and non-lucid fashion. Many times they actually continue to go to work, for example, and try to interact with the intraphysical beings there but are obviously unable to. They become frustrated and even more confused by their failure to interact.[24] Due to their low level of awareness, it is very hard to make them understand that they have already passed away; in most instances it is simply not possible.

An example is a soldier who passes away and keeps trying to attack their enemy outside the body, or the religious professional who keeps trying to recruit and indoctrinate others. Another is the parent who keeps trying to educate, control, and steer the life of their son but is unable to realize that the son is no longer a twelve-year-old, but is a forty-year-old man (and an independent person). We see in these examples how they keep repeating actions unnecessarily while investing energy in what they considered to be important in their life and/or on things that were left unresolved and had a deep impact on them. The influence they have is energetic. It is an energetic intrusion onto intraphysical consciousnesses.

The number of different types of blind guides is enormous. This is the most populated group extraphysically. We can understand the extraphysical population by analyzing physical society, since the extraphysical consciousnesses now are the ones that passed away in the last decades. We realize that the majority of individuals in societies have interests and values that are very specific to their momentary physical life and culture in which they find themselves. They are unable, in practice, to see a larger reality: the fact that they are more than just this physical life, that they are a consciousness in evolution.

Notice that most people do not have bad intentions toward others. In general, they actually even wish others well, but first and foremost come their own objectives. So in trying to accomplish their objectives (self-centered), they sometimes step on others.[25] Thus, when doing a simple business deal, individuals will try to negotiate the best possible price for themselves, in many instances without any regard for how this may affect the other person.

It is important to understand that although blind guides disturb, they are not monsters with a horror-movie type of appearance. They were actually normal individuals, like most of us. They can be our relatives who have passed away and will support us over anybody else because that is what they are conditioned to do. A blind guide sometimes behaves like our best friend who wants to go out with us. Even though we are busy with other priorities at that moment, they may insist so much that we finally give in—this is an example of their self-centeredness.[26]

Extraphysical-Intraphysical Connection
Luis Minero
August 7, 2003, Los Angeles, California

I fell asleep after working with energy for a while without feeling anything out of the ordinary. When I woke up in the morning, the recollection of the projection I had came to me. The recollection was not perfect and was only partial.

I had been in a classroom giving a class outside the body. As regular activities had started recently in the Los Angeles office, I had already had two or three other projections similar to this one. During the projection, I was giving classes to about eight to ten consciousnesses. The classroom was located at the top of a building that was about seven or eight stories tall. The environment felt extremely familiar and I knew I had been there before—yet not during the other experiences of teaching I'd had earlier in the year. The building was surrounded by an open area and by other shorter buildings basically encircling the one I was in. The place was like a campus for learning, and the structures were of very bright and lively colors—light green, yellow, red, and sky blue.

During the class I was lecturing about intrusion. I was using mainly speech and sometimes some basic form of telepathy to communicate with them, and the extraphysical-consciousnesses-students were also mainly using speech when asking questions. The language used was Spanish and the extraphysical consciousnesses looked decidedly Hispanic in their appearance.

I had never seen any of the extraphysical consciousnesses, and none of them seemed familiar to me. After a male extraphysical consciousness (dark hair with a mustache, white long-sleeve shirt, brownish skin, and about 1.70 meters—5'7"—in height) who was sitting in the middle of the room asked me a question, I tried to make it clear that the condition he was involved in was intrusion. My energetic intention was to make the consciousness aware that he was disturbing more than helping and that it was intrusion. As I mentioned the word intrusion, my energies flowed with some strength to reinforce the idea.

The projection was in a dimension that wasn't too evolved, as evidenced by the need for rooms and buildings, by the need for extraphysical consciousnesses to sit in chairs, and by the need to have to resort in many instances to speech (verbal communication). Likewise, the level of the information I was presenting was fairly basic.

After writing down this experience in the morning, I theorized that some of the consciousnesses that were in the extraphysical classes were eventually going to appear in physical classes, similar to the other experiences I'd had in which I was also giving classes while projected. However, none of those consciousnesses ever came to the classes—but the idea of wanting to find some of them physically stayed with me and I decided to keep my eyes open for the possible physical appearance of these individuals.

(continued) September 20, 2003, Los Angeles, California

About a month and half later I was teaching a class on the mentalsoma for two students. The class was given in Spanish and they both were Mexican by birth. I had already given two weeks of classes to them, and the classes were going as usual. As we were discussing the ideas on the mentalsoma, I mentioned that there was no intrusion in the mentalsomatic dimension. "C." then proceeded to ask me why that was so. The condition of energetic intrusion was something that we had covered the previous week and the question seemed to be the type of "leftover" question that is many times asked days or weeks later, after the information has been digested by students. As I was starting to answer it, I started feeling energies that had connected me with something extraphysically. In an instant I understood what was happening: the male extraphysical consciousness that had asked me about intrusion in the projection on August 7, 2003, had a close affinity with "C."—more than likely as a blind guide. The energetic recognition was fast and unmistakable, typical of intuitions associated with these events. I also realized that the objective of extraphysically teaching those consciousnesses more than a month ago was to try to educate them so that they would not place as much pressure on the physical person—in this case "C."

I felt in this case that such an objective worked, and the projection had helped so that "C." would have less energetic pressure on him from this extraphysical consciousness, and enough freedom and openness for him to be able to physically find information on the subject of OBEs and to be able to attend classes.

In certain instances the opposite also happens, where we as intraphysical consciousnesses can act as blind guides, and the recipients of those energies are extraphysical consciousnesses. Let us consider, for example, the case of a man who passes away and has the potential to pass through the second deactivation for the first time. This person already has the maturity and understanding to detach from physical life and regain his awareness extraphysically. However, once his relatives begin crying for him during the funeral and afterward (especially in many Western societies), they call him energetically, and this can have the effect of "anchoring" him to the physical dimension. This "anchoring" stemming from other people connected to the individual who recently passed away can be especially disruptive when it occurs for longer periods of time.

Thus, notice here that the intraphysical relatives do not have bad intentions toward the person who just passed away. On the contrary, they have the best intentions. Yet because their understanding of the process of death is limited, they end up disturbing more than helping—the definition of a blind guide. The person who passed away is a perfect candidate for receiving assistance outside the body, so as to disconnect energetically and be able to pass through the second deactivation (see the "Extraphysical Assistance" section at the end of this chapter). In this particular case, he already has one of the most important requirements for passing through the second deactivation: a higher level of awareness.

Intruders

Below blind guides in terms of awareness we find intruders. Intruders are different from blind guides in that they do not have positive intentions.[27] Intruders try to energetically force certain actions and have no regard for anybody else. They also have not passed through the second deactivation.

There are some intruders who are completely unaware even of their lack of awareness, and there is a minority of others who are aware of their negative intentions and actually enjoy it.[28] Both cases are extremely pathological and unevolved. The first group of intruders is composed of individuals who are mainly extremely needy and in lack.

An example of an intruder is a person who smoked most of his life.[29] The person underwent the first deactivation and no longer has a physical body. Therefore, he cannot grab a cigarette or a lighter and does not have lungs or air to breathe. Yet this person still has a strong craving for a cigarette. This need is so strong that it completely determines all of his behaviors and keeps him non-lucid.

The moment someone inside a body starts to smoke and manifest energies of smoking, the extraphysical consciousness will connect to the physical person like a magnet. The extraphysical intruder will start to smoke through and with the physical consciousness, performing a definitive vampirization of the energy of the physical one.

Extraphysical intruders are attracted by the energies they lack.[30] The way the connection is made is through an auric coupling (see chapter 2). Notice that in most instances the extraphysical consciousness has no idea who the physical person is. They are connected through the particular common activity—similar to individuals who only talk to each other on the street because one is out of cigarettes and is asking the other for a cigarette. As mentioned previously, our activities and our thosenes tune us in to different consciousnesses and energies.

The moment the physical person is finished with their cigarette, the intruder will create thosenic pressure for the physical person to light up another one, and another one after that, and so on. This is similar to a dog that begs nonstop for food at a table. Intruders are completely needy.

Notice that unaware intruders are also unbiased in many aspects. They do not care if the physical person is of a particular sex, religion, nation, or race. The intruder is there only because of their need. Naturally and logically, these types of intrusions occur with any and all types of addictions and vices—drugs,[31] gambling, violence, sex, food, alcohol, television, and others.[32]

The other type of intruder is the one who actually enjoys seeing others suffer. We can already see that because this is their defining characteristic, they have not even begun to comprehend evolutionary principles like respect for others or assistance. These are intruders who hang around and feed off the energy of activities like violent sports (i.e, boxing, ultimate fighting), spontaneous fights, crimes, and other thosenic patterns we may produce.[33]

When individuals become angry, these intruders take advantage of the opportunity and connect to people, amplifying their anger. Physical individuals later describe how "they lost their head" or that they do not know "what came over them." Intrusion does not discriminate; it occurs with people in all social classes, nations, and any type of physical group.

Some intruders act in specific places such as drug-related environments, night clubs, casinos, bars, and other drinking establishments. Some act on specific employment positions, like the influence and intrusion received by a corrupt manager. Some act through ideas, such as the businessman who gets ideas on how to carry out an unethical money-making " business strategy."

Some intruders act during a specific time of the day or night, like the nighttime actions of extraphysical consciousnesses who want to feed on energies (energivourous) or energetic vampires. Others act during special events such as weapons conventions, Halloween parties, and carnivals with many vices around, or around theaters that are playing certain types of movies that evoke negative energies.

While Intraphysical: Energy and Dealing with Extraphysical Consciousnesses

The relationships we have with blind guides and intruders occur much more frequently while we are in the physical body than when we are projected. Since blind guides and intruders are in the crustal or tropospheric dimensions, still very close to this physical one, with their interests and energies focused on what happens in the physical dimension, they produce all type of influences on physicality. Notice that it is from the physical dimension that they collect the dense energies they are looking for.

While projected, we rarely bump into these consciousnesses. As was mentioned before, while projected, we tend to go to dimensions that are closer to our holothosene, and because of this, during many experiences we might be in dimensions that are more subtle than theirs.

In theory, while we are in the physical dimension, we can become intruded upon at any moment.[34] The first thing we need to realize is that intrusion occurs because *we manifest a certain pattern of energy that intruders are needing or looking for and thus they attach to us* (like attracts like). Their influence in nature is energetic, or holothosenic.[35] Thus, in the great majority of cases, we are the ones who initiate the connection and make the contact possible—we prepare the field. The same energetic mechanism of "like attracts like" applies to helpers. If we manifest evolutionary and assistantial energy, then helpers find room within our holothosene to work with us and through us.

In the following example, let us describe a normal day to understand how the interactions between consciousnesses may work.

Say we happened to wake up early on this day. We slept well and had a good breakfast. We feel very well and are now calmly drinking coffee on our porch. We have enough time before we need to go to work. As we sip our coffee, we turn our head and happen to catch our neighbor getting ready to go to work. As we watch him, we remember that he just had a death in the family and he is having a hard time dealing with this. As we look at him, we think, "It's a pity. He is usually such an upbeat person. I wish there was something I could do for him."

The moment we think that, we did more than just think. We created (as always) a thosene in which we are stating that, if possible, we are available to help him. Our neighbor's helper captured that thosene, as did our own helper. At that moment, the intuitions start to flow. We remember that we received a book as a gift two years ago that dealt with overcoming such situations. We realize that we never even looked at that book, yet it must be on the shelf with the others. So the idea comes to us, "What if I find the book and give it to my neighbor?"[36]

In figure 5.4 we have a relative line of holothosenic balance. Level A represents our holothosene, the average of our energetic quality. When we started to produce thosenes about helping our neighbor, we were manifesting energy that is above our average. We are certainly capable of manifesting such energy, but it is not our average. At that moment, two helpers were able to connect with us at the level represented by level B.

We know we still have time before leaving for work, so we go inside to look for the book. Once we reach the book shelf, that book is the first one we see—what a *synchronicity*! We hadn't even seen or noticed that book in months! It is as if something was guiding us straight to it. So we go and give it to our neighbor. We quickly explain that he can keep it and that hopefully it will be useful.

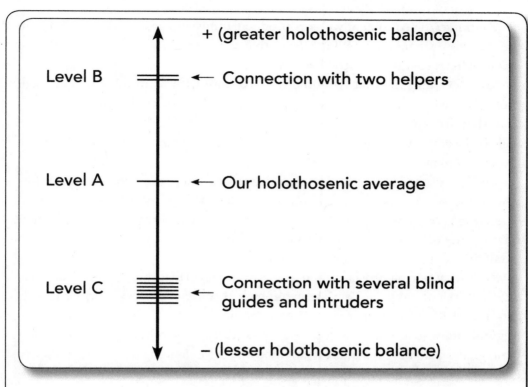

Figure 5.4: Holothosenic Quality

We get in our car and leave for work. As we are driving to work, a driver who is in a big rush cuts in front of us to get in our lane and we have to slam on the brakes. Our reaction is to produce aggressive thosenes against the other driver. We think how irresponsible it is to drive in that fashion. In some cases people will not just think about it, but they will show their frustration by screaming, making specific hand signs to the other driver, and in more extreme cases even getting out of the car to argue. The other driver is able to see us complaining through the rearview mirror, and since he is in a rush, he also answers back with a "sign" for us to see. He also starts to talk inside his car: "These people, can't they see I'm in a hurry?!" Obviously, nobody else knows he's in a hurry, but he is so self-absorbed in his own needs that he cannot understand anything else at that instant.

(continued) The moment we start producing thosenes against the other driver, we start to exchange energy at a level that is lower than our average. We are involved in an energetic quarrel with the other person.

Now, let's imagine that two other relatives are with us in our car. They will probably react to this event in the same fashion we did. They will support our position (they are our relatives) by telling us how irresponsible the other driver is and will also produce thosenes against the other driver (in some cases they will be the ones screaming at the other driver).

Now, let's suppose that in the other driver's car there are two relatives of his, who are also nervous and self-absorbed because they want and need to get to where they are going in a hurry. They will probably support the position of their relative (the other driver) because he is family and we are not. So they will also manifest energies against us and our party.

Now, what normally occurs (and in this example) is that these relatives are real, but they are not physical. They are extraphysical consciousnesses—former friends or relatives of ours. So there are some blind guides who have our best interests in mind and who are defending us. At the same time the other driver also has his blind guides who have his interests in mind and are defending him. We are already connected to our blind guides, sending energies against the other group, and vice versa, and everybody is connected by the energy of the quarrel. In a matter of seconds, we are connected with several blind guides. Some are against us and others are giving us support while amplifying our anger and indignation toward the other driver. At the same time, a couple of "independent" intruders who feed off this energy are connected to everybody and are helping to amplify the belligerent energy and thus feeding themselves from it.

This last interaction looks like level C in figure 5.4 (several consciousnesses connected). We are manifesting energy that is less than our average—since we do not spend the entire time in this condition.

We see how, during our daily interactions, we can become intruded upon at any moment. Even though we did not initiate the activity, our reactions helped to bring it to its final state. Our energy contributed to it.[37] For more evolved consciousnesses—e.g., helpers—the main pathology in the world is not AIDS, cancer, or any other physical illness; it is intrusion.

How do we deal with intrusion? First of all, by realizing that the energy *we* manifest is what attracts the extraphysical consciousnesses to us. We need to become more aware of our thosenes and reactions and try to improve on them every time. In the long run, what we are trying to do here is to distance ourselves from intrusive beings by improving the quality of our own holothosene.

Second, in the short term, we can use our energetic knowledge and capacity to disrupt these energetic connections. As was mentioned in chapter 2, the way to execute an auric uncoupling or a sympathetic dissimilation is by doing a vibrational state (VS). The VS will not only assist us in resetting our thosenes but it will also help us to balance ourselves emotionally, raise our awareness, disconnect any intruding energies, and prevent future intrusions.[38] Thus, the VS is the key to controlling energetic interactions.

Notice that the strength of our VS will be in agreement with our average quality of energy (line A in figure 5.4). So any connection weaker than our average will be disconnected. Naturally, if we already have greater experience arriving at the VS, producing it at this moment will be easier. Furthermore, if we practice it regularly, we will *prevent* many cases of intrusion, because our energetic defenses will be inherently stronger.

However, if we cannot yet reach a VS, then doing the VELO and activating our energy to the best of our ability will already disconnect most intrusions we have. Notice that a big part of the strength of the energy comes from the awareness of the individual—and we are more aware of what is happening than the blind-guide-extraphysical-consciousness is.

Note that we will not disconnect from our helpers by installing a VS. Yet they may have already disconnected and may be helping someone else in a critical moment. Of course, even during instances where they may still be connected, they do not put pressure on us. Helpers respect our free will. In the previous example, it was we (and the other driver) who chose to manifest those negative energies—though in most cases we are not aware of the consequences or the extraphysical dynamics involved.

In some instances helpers will be there to assist us in these situations. But in order for them to help us, we need to tune in to their "frequency" (again, we are the initiators). That means, if we are still angrily thinking about what we would like to do or say to the other driver, if this is still our intention, then there is very little the helper can do. We are choosing (through our thosenes) to focus on something else. Helpers do not force us to think in a positive and assistantial manner. We are the ones who need to start this cycle so they can help us along; they cannot do it for us.

While Extraphysical: Consciousnesses and Development

When individuals undergo the first deactivation and become extraphysical consciousnesses, they tend to go to a dimension that has the same holothosene that they do. So a consciousness with a more refined or developed holothosene (greater evolution) will tune in to a more stable and subtle dimension. Notice that there is nobody outside the body assigning these consciousnesses to specific dimensions. Individuals are already naturally *predetermined* to go to a specific dimension because of their own holothosene (holothosenic determinism).

Extraphysical consciousnesses will spend some time in their intermissive period (in-between-lives period) and will undergo rebirth (technically and more accurately called *resoma*, or the *re*activation of a *soma*) afterward. During the course of this new physical life, the intraphysical consciousness will have the opportunity to renew, refine, and improve its own ideas, attitudes, relationships, and energy (holothosene). As individuals do this, they may go to a slightly more evolved dimension during their next intermissive period. And so, from life to life as they continue improving, they keep on "climbing" dimensions and the evolutionary scale until they, after many, many lessons and many, many lives, undergo the third deactivation and become a free consciousness.

Very much in the same way, when we project, we tune in to a range of dimensions that are closer to our holothosene. In practice, it is not easy to go to highly evolved dimensions or to very unevolved dimensions because we have no resonance with either of them. Notice that our holothosene (the quality of our manifestations) determines who we are. We are not much less than that (making it hard to go to very dense, lower dimensions) and we are not much more than that (making it difficult to project to highly evolved dimensions). Normally, when we go to either dimensional extreme, a helper usually takes us to a highly evolved dimension for some specific educational purpose or to a very dense, lower dimension for an assistantial purpose.[39]

We have heard how some individuals are scared to leave the body because of encounters with certain extraphysical consciousnesses. In some cases, projectors talk about an extraphysical consciousness that sometimes is there to stop them from leaving the body (i.e., the gate-keeper, hitchhiker).[40] Also, sometimes there are stories of projectors who mention that they had to fight with an extraphysical consciousness outside the body.[41]

Thus, it is important to mention that if our energy is stable and positive, we will not have any type of experience of this nature. The reason that certain projectors have these types of experiences is because they still resonate with such activities. More balanced people do not have to worry about this.

Thus, let us pose some questions that can help us to understand this: Does my holothosene have any content of violence in it? Have I associated myself with a group that is defending a narrower interest (dogmatic or mystic)? Have I associated with energy from a group that is against another specific group?

This also helps to explain why, when individuals produce an OBE through drugs, their experiences tend to be strange and distorted. We can analyze this a bit further. What, in general, is the holothosene of the entire drug environment? What type of extraphysical consciousnesses are they evoking with such an activity?[42]

Again, it is important to stress that well-intentioned, normal projectors do not have to worry about having negative experiences while projected. Many individuals have had years and decades of OBEs, even projecting to evolved dimensions, without encountering any type of confrontation.

Similarly, for projectors who sometimes have had less-than-pleasant encounters, once they became aware of why this was happening and they renewed or recycled their holothosene, they stopped having such experiences.

There is an interesting consequence stemming from this "like attracts like" rule of holothosenic affinity. If our average of energy is not like the one of an intruder, then it is very unlikely that we will just bump into them outside the body.

It is actually much, much easier to meet intraphysical individuals who have intruder-like energy than to meet intruders extraphysically while projected outside the body.

"Normal" OBE Development

It is difficult to describe the possible trajectory that you will have as you start to have OBEs, because many individual factors can and will affect it. There is actually no such thing as "normal development" in terms of projections, just like there isn't an "average intraphysical life." Yet, to get a better idea, let us try to describe how the projective development, along with its extraphysical relationships, may progress.[43]

The first projections tend to end fairly quickly because we become too excited or surprised by certain elements; for example, the moment we pass through our first wall or the moment we jump off the first roof.

Our awareness can fluctuate quite a bit during these experiences. In some of them, we will feel the process of disconnection, have a blackout, and then regain awareness. In others, we will regain awareness during the middle of the night and will realize that we are outside the body.

As we start to control the extraphysical environment better, we begin to venture into projections where we go further. Individuals start trying to reach specific targets, like a relative's house. Projectors have experiences like flying and following the course of a river all the way out to sea, or spending some time underwater, or flying to another continent, or starting to learn about some of the different dimensions. In essence, even though these are mostly "tourist" projections, they are educational experiences as well.

In many instances (maybe after a couple dozen or so experiences), we may realize that we have not extraphysically met anyone yet. As the energy of this idea is on our mind, we may actually come across a group of individuals during one of the subsequent experiences. Perhaps we see them at a certain distance and decide to simply watch them—this being the first occasion we are seeing somebody else extraphysically. As we watch them, we realize that they do not have a silver cord, so they are extraphysical consciousnesses. In their communication, they are basically switching between minor and major telepathy—but there is no articulation taking place. The stability and normalcy of their "conversation" lets us know that they are individuals who have already passed through the second deactivation. As we think about all of these details, we feel energy (intuition) coming to us that confirms our conclusions.

Intraphysically, as we are thinking about the OBE after the experience, we realize that those consciousnesses looked very normal. We think to ourselves that we could have talked to them with no problem, and that next time we actually will. Therefore, two projections afterward, we see the group again. As we approach them, one of them realizes we are a projector and greets us. They ask us about the intraphysical dimension and we ask them about this extraphysical dimension.

As we had perceived before, they are consciousnesses who have passed through the second deactivation. Interacting with them using telepathy is something interesting and new to us, but we realize how much more effective telepathy is as opposed to speech. They are in that dimension finishing the preparation for their next life. They tell us certain characteristics about that dimension that we had not noticed. Eventually, we return to our body.

We continue to have a few more experiences with extraphysical consciousnesses, and our confidence and understanding of the extraphysical reality grow. We suddenly notice, however, after returning from an OBE, that there was a very specific energetic sensation surrounding us during this last experience. Also, some of the ideas we attributed to intuition and the reading of the energy of the environment seemed to have a different specific external source. As we think more about it, we realize that this specific energetic sensation that surrounded us and was so clear during this last experience was something we had actually felt several times before. What strikes us is the fact that it was so clear and obvious during this last OBE. Our sensitivity has increased a few notches.

In our next projection, we may feel that sensation again and decide to explore it further. As we concentrate on it, we exteriorize some energy to connect with it. It suddenly hits us what it is. It is our helper. As we realize this and connect more deeply with our helper, our awareness increases and in a few seconds we understand many ideas:

- That sensation has been with us during all of our projections.
- We have been receiving intuition from it during all of our extraphysical experiences. These ideas came so subtly that it almost seemed as if we were the ones producing or thinking them.

- The reason that we did not meet other extraphysical consciousnesses at first was because our helper had been guiding us through simpler things.

- The moment we thought about meeting extraphysical consciousnesses, it meant we were ready, and thus our helper guided us to the group we met.

- The confirmation of the conclusions we were arriving at while watching the group of extraphysical consciousnesses was coming from the helper.

- As we think about this further, we realize that we also felt the sensation of the helper on a few occasions before we were able to leave the body, when we were trying OBE techniques. The reason that we did not feel it on even more occasions was because our sensitivity was not developed enough.

- Furthermore, as our awareness increases, we realize that it was our helper who basically guided us toward certain books or materials on OBEs, before we learned how to have one.

- We realize that this sensation is not only from the last year; we also recognize it from our adolescence and even infancy during difficult and critical moments.

- Lastly, we notice and remember this feeling from our intermissive period as well, before we were born into this current life. Maybe our helper was the last consciousness to wish us well before coming into the current body, even sometimes reminding us at that moment that we would see each other in a few decades (now). So it hits us that our helper is a very old friend of ours.

Now that we are in better contact with our helpers and we know which intuitions are ours and which ones come from them, we develop a more effective communication with them. We can now ask them questions directly and benefit from their knowledge.

We also realize that because our helpers are at a higher evolutionary level than we are, they are basically always in a different dimension. Thus, actually seeing them outside the body is a rare condition.[44] They explain to us that we are so dependant on our vision in physical life that we too often look for this element alone, in order to feel supported and be able to create a better affinity with other things. Yet we must learn to pay attention to and to trust our energetic sensations and intuitions (which is a richer means of perception) more often as tools for interaction.

Evolved helpers do not value appearance and/or names very much. These are elements that are more relevant in the intraphysical dimension. Extraphysical recognition is based on the holothosene of the individual. Thus, we can analyze the level of the extraphysical consciousness based on whether or not we can see them. If we project many times and meet specific extraphysical consciousnesses who always seem to be there, then we can arrive at the conclusion that they are not that much more evolved than we are—and are probably not helpers. Since they are basically always in the same dimension that we are able to regularly reach, it means their holothosene resonates more with such a dimension, and the quality of their ideas is at that level as well.

Furthermore, if, even when projected, helpers are rarely visible, then we can imagine that their becoming intraphysically visible is an extremely rare occurrence. So we can ponder, what type of consciousnesses are the ones that have an easier time connecting with the physical dimension? The answer, naturally, is that the ones that are closer to the intraphysical dimension have denser energies that enable them to directly interact with this dimension. Thus, we realize that the great majority of consciousnesses that are channeled through mediums and that connect regularly to the intraphysical dimension fall into this category—especially in cases of psychography (automatic writing),[45] psychophony,[46] and others, where they are actually able to take control of a dense physical body. Denser consciousnesses are the ones regularly able to control physical bodies. In many of these cases, they seem to be well-intentioned extraphysical consciousnesses, yet, as the evidence shows, they are not evolved helpers.

The following is a list summarizing some of the types of assistance provided by helpers:[47]

- Efficient help during physical and extraphysical periods[48]
- Energetic support through the transmission of consciential energy
- Assistance in projecting or disconnecting from our physical body[49]

- Increase in extraphysical lucidity or extraphysical awakening
- Reception of inspirations and intuitive suggestions
- Assistance in reaching our main evolutionary life objectives
- Execution of visual didactic (learning) projections—including clairvoyance[50]
- Establishment of contacts with other extraphysical consciousnesses
- Extraphysical flying in group
- Mental body-to-mental body (mentalsoma) transmissions
- De-intrusions[51]
- Guidance toward productive, positive extraphysical experiences

Extraphysical Assistance

As we continue developing our projectability, especially as our mentality expands as a result of these experiences, we can reach the level of starting to do assistantial projections.[52] In these experiences, we project with our helpers to provide assistance to somebody else.[53] The assisted individuals can be needy intraphysical consciousnesses of the most varied kinds, or extraphysical consciousnesses such as blind guides and intruders.[54]

Notice that although blind guides and intruders can be very bothersome, we do not leave the body to argue or fight with them. Having this mindset is a sign of immaturity. Blind guides and intruders are the neediest consciousnesses. Extraphysically, helpers do not quarrel with them either; they try to help them grow out of their condition, in the same way they try to help us improve.

Projections of assistance (assistantial projections, or projectiotherapy)[55] begin when we are ready and when we make ourselves available for them. We ourselves always determine how much assistance we provide. This depends on how well each projector understands the evolutionary importance of assisting others—*both inside and outside the body*. It is interesting to note how assistance to others and evolution go hand in hand. In other words, the level of evolution of individuals can be ascertained by the quality and quantity of assistance they provide. The evidence points to the fact that there are no evolved beings who are selfish or self-centered; if so, they are not evolved.

From a phenomenological perspective, extraphysical assistance to an intraphysical consciousness can look like figure 5.5. Normally, the helper determines who is going

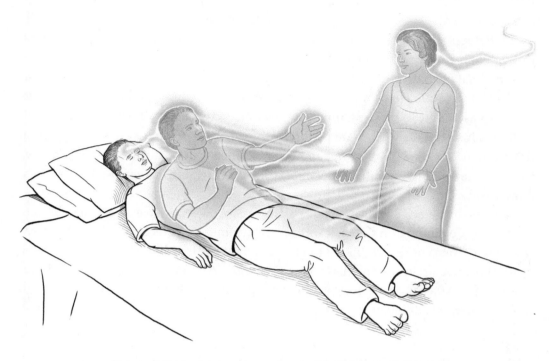

Figure 5.5: Assistance to an Intraphysical Consciousness

to receive the assistance and what type of assistance will be provided. Due to their greater awareness, they know what is the most critical and relevant assistance needed at that moment. Most of the time, extraphysical assistance for the projector involves the donation of energy.

Naturally, helpers already do these types of exteriorizations without us. Yet their energy is very subtle and the recipients are always fairly dense. As a result, the effect for the individuals receiving the assistance is very light and subtle, so they have a hard time feeling this. Therefore, as projectors, we are very useful in these types of interactions because we have dense energy.

When exteriorizing with helpers in an assistantial projection, we are usually the ones closer to the assisted person. Helpers exteriorize energy to the assisted person through us. Since they have the awareness of what type of assistance is needed, helpers are responsible for the information in the energy; that is, for the "THO" and "S" in *thos*ene. We are responsible for the energy ("ENE" in thos*ene*) that is reaching the assisted individual. Therefore, we act like a filter that condenses the subtle energy of the helpers, so that the patient receives the best information (from the helpers) through dense energy (from us).

One final aspect about assistantial projections is that in many cases they are usually harder to recall. Helpers normally help us to project with a greater load of energy in these cases. Due to this heaviness, our awareness tends to be lower and our recollection is hindered as well. In many instances, we only realize we are in a projection the moment we are finalizing our donation of energy. It is at this moment that we have finished giving off our load of energy and we are able to regain our awareness more easily.

In some instances during assistantial projections, we can have a very high level of awareness, depending on the task we are performing. If the assistance is more mentalsomatic, then more than likely the level of awareness will be higher. Assistantial projections that are more energetic tend to be more common (greater need) and thus more useful. Assistantial projections can vary greatly within the scope of that mentalsomatic-energetic gradient.

Extraphysical Rescue
Luis Minero
November 4, 2006, around 4:00 AM, Los Angeles, California

The day before (Saturday), I had seen "G." during a meeting we had at night. We had a discussion about scheduling activities. Even though the discussion was insignificant, I felt a lot of energy going back and forth between us.

In the middle of the night, when I regained awareness, I was already projected. I was in an extraphysical city, with streets, stores, and cars. The city had more the pattern of a horizontal widespread city (like Miami) than a compressed vertical city (like New York).

Through intuitions (from helpers), I knew I was looking for somebody. I had in my mind the picture of G.'s face, yet I understood that it was not specifically "G." that I was looking for. I knew I was supposed to rescue an extraphysical consciousness from this dimension, and that this extraphysical consciousness was related to "G." Using the abilities of the psychosoma of vision, I thought about him and zoomed into him in the middle of the crowd.

The sidewalks were half-full with extraphysical consciousnesses walking randomly—they seemed to be following what were their daily routines from when they were intraphysical. I understood from the intuitions of helpers and from other similar experiences I've had that I was not supposed to attract attention in this dimension. If the other extraphysical consciousnesses knew what I was up to, they would try to hide and/or protect the target so as for me not to get to him.

Due to this, I did not fly to catch up to G.'s "acquaintance." I decided to walk faster through the crowd trying to find him. At one point, I realized that the crowd was a little distracted with their routines, so I increased the size of my psychosoma to a height of about fifteen feet so as to be able to locate him from above the crowd. I was able to see him about a block away from me. Immediately, I diminished the size of my psychosoma to the normal size and kept on going as if nothing had happened.

I thought that I should not do that again and that I should be more careful. Otherwise, I could compromise the assistance, and the objective would not be met.

When I arrived at the place where G.'s friend was supposed to be, he was no longer there and I felt that he had gone into one of the stores. Helpers were basically giving me intuitions on where to go. I went in to look for him, and as I searched for him, I felt he had left the store and gone into the bar next door. I went out of the store and into the bar to look for him. The energies of this extraphysical bar were much stranger than the usual strange energies in physical bars. He somehow had left the bar through the back.

As I went out into the street, the instruction that came to me was "Stay put!" I waited a moment and after a few seconds I saw him coming in my direction. It surprised me that he looked so much like "G." He looked, however, very confused and disoriented; I would say he looked somewhat drunk. I approached him and told him I had been looking for him. Since he didn't answer, I asked him where he was. Again he didn't answer.

(continued) Because of his disorientation, it seemed as if he was going to step off the sidewalk. It also seemed as if he was starting to feel that there was something going on with me. So I decided to move in. I grabbed him by the hand and told him, "Watch out! You're going to get run over by the cars." Since we had not attracted any attention, I started to externalize as much energy as I could now that I was holding his hand and could not lose him. I immediately felt the helpers exteriorizing energies with me to him, and in a fraction of a second we all disappeared. I came back to my body, and he was taken by the helpers to another dimension, where I'm sure they will continue treating him.

In certain projections of extraphysical rescues, it is best not to reveal who you are because the rest of the extraphysical consciousnesses may try to stop you. They do not realize you are like a fireman entering to save a child from a burning house. They do not realize this because they are unable to see the flames; in this case, they do not realize the holothosene they are in. So in their minds, if you behave differently from them, they look at you suspiciously and act defensively.

Notice here how the helpers directed the experience and decided who was to be rescued. I think this extraphysical consciousness became disconnected from "G." during our physical discussion the night before. He was disoriented in part because he was no longer connected to "G.," as he had probably been for a long time. His similar appearance to "G." also was evidence that he had been close to "G." probably for many years, if not decades.

Summary of Key Chapter Points

- Extraphysical communication (communication outside the body) can occur verbally (orally), telepathically (major or minor), or through conscientese—this depends on the level of awareness of the projector.

- A desoma is the *de*activation of a *soma*, and a synonym for (physical) death.

- The first deactivation is the discarding of the physical body (soma).

- The second deactivation is the discarding of the energosoma.

- Passing through the second deactivation depends on one's level of evolution, as well as a lack of conditionings and unhealthy overattachment to physical life.

- The third deactivation is the discarding of the psychosoma, where afterward the consciousness does not need to have physical lives again.

- Helpers are evolved positive consciousnesses with increased awareness and unbiased, refined evolutionary criteria who want to help us evolve.

- Blind guides are extraphysical consciousnesses who may have good intentions but have a low level of lucidity; they disturb and intrude more than help.

- Intruders are extraphysical consciousnesses with a low level of evolution who are either needy and/or have ill intentions toward others.

- While intraphysical, our thosenes and intentions connect us with and evoke and call different extraphysical consciousnesses. We can use the VELO and the VS to uncouple from them.

- Once individuals pass away, they will spend the majority of their intermissive period (in-between-lives period) of time in the dimension with which they have a similar holothosene.

- The development of our OBEs, for well-intentioned individuals, will be assisted by our helpers, who will guide us through experiences that will help us to develop our capacity.

- As we develop further, we can arrive at the condition of having assistantial projections, whereby we cooperate with a helper in a more side-by-side manner to help other consciousnesses.

Chapter Notes

1. Vieira, 2002, pp. 648, 652.
2. Ibid., pp. 194–95.
3. Ibid., p. 647.
4. Ibid., pp. 649–51.
5. Vieira, 2002, p. 326. In conscientiology and throughout this book, you will find both terms—*desoma* and *death*—used interchangeably, since they are synonyms.
6. Alegretti, 2004, p. 68.
7. Vieira, 2002, pp. 327–31.
8. Alegretti, 2004, p. 69.
9. Minero, 2003, pp. 130–33.
10. The intermissive period is the intermission between two physical lives, or the in-between-lives period.

11. Vieira, 2002, p. 332.

12. Vieira, 1999, p. 12.

13. Vieira, 2002, pp. 687–91; Vieira, 2003, pp. 199–201.

14. Vieira, *Homo Sapiens Pacificus*, 2007, p. 233.

15. Monroe, 1997, p. 127.

16. Dries, 2006, p. 112.

17. Buhlman, 1996, p. 224.

18. Vieira, 2002, pp. 688–91.

19. Ibid. p. 687.

20. Monroe, 1977, pp. 127–28.

21. Dries, 2006, p. 111.

22. Thiago, 1999, p. 101.

23. Arakaki, 2005, p. 171.

24. Vieira, 1999, p. 90.

25. Almeida, 2005, p. 165.

26. Vicenzi, 2005, p. 102.

27. Vieira, *700*, 1994, pp. 376, 462–83.

28. Muldoon and Carrington, 1992, p. 295.

29. Tornieri, 1998, pp. 43–50.

30. Thiago, 1999, p. 96.

31. Vieira, 2003, p. 472.

32. Guzzi, 1998, pp. 26–27; Kardec, 1976, p. 198; and Vieira, 2003, p. 512.

33. Bruce, 1999, pp. 514–15.

34. Vieira, *700*, 1994, p. 341.

35. Daou, 2005, p. 42.

36. Minero, 1997.

37. Guzzi, 1998, p. 78.

38. Vieira, 2003, p. 811.

39. Vieira, 2002, p. 688.

40. Bruce, 1999, pp. 514–15.

41. Ibid., pp. 523–24, 526–27.

42. Razera, 2001, p. 169.

43. Minero, 1997.

44. Bruce, 1999, p. 480.

45. For more information, see Bonin, 1983, p. 667.

46. Psychophony is when an extraphysical consciousness speaks through the vocal cords of an intraphysical consciousness (usually a medium). For more information, see Vieira, 2002, p. 190; and Bonin, 1983, p. 666.

47. Vieira, 2002, pp. 687–88; and Monroe, 1977, pp. 127–28.

48. Nascimento, 2005, pp. 31–43.

49. Oderich, 2001, p. 357.

50. Cubarenco, 2002, pp. 191–93.

51. Machado and Paro, 2002, p. 169.

52. Taylor, 1998, pp. 33–51.

53. Vieira, 2002, pp. 488–90.

54. Presse, 2003, p. 156.

55. Takimoto and Almeida, 2002, p. 31; also study conscientiotherapy in this same article.

Consciential Maturity

One of the common uses for the word *maturity* is to reference something that is fully developed. In a first attempt to define this concept one could say that *consciential maturity* means being fully developed as a consciousness. However, like any indicator of evolution, consciential maturity is a relative term, and the question therefore becomes, what does "development" or "evolution" mean?

When leaving the body and observing the consciousness from an extraphysical perspective, we can understand evolution and spiritual development in a broader and deeper context. While inside the body, the consciousness is bound by physics and matter and thus we find ourselves restricted. Yet outside the body, we can observe ourselves free from this restriction and can study the consciousness in its natural habitat—in the wild, so to speak.[1] This is what allows us to understand concepts such as evolution more profoundly.

Exemplifying the advantages of the extraphysical point of view, let us pose the following question: How can we affirm what more evolution or less evolution actually is? Through behavioral observations, we can see the attitudes and actions of individuals that lead toward greater or lesser evolutionary results for ourselves and others. Yet in many instances it is difficult from a physical perspective to fully understand people's actions and their repercussions. Furthermore, many times we execute positive and/or evolution-promoting actions and they seem to not yield results (or do not seem to, from our perspective). So how can we be sure that the initial intention of certain actions was in fact more evolutionary or less evolutionary?

When lucid outside the body, we can clearly perceive thosenes and holothosenes; in other words, we can clearly perceive what other people think, and others can clearly perceive what we think. In many instances this process of perception is just as effective (if not more so) than vision inside the body—and it is just as clear (if not more so). So, just like we can see with relative clarity while inside the body that one person has a darker hair color than another, in the same fashion, outside the body we can distinguish with relative clarity when the thosenes of a particular consciousness (e.g., a helper) are more assistantial than those of another.[2]

Observations (which are the basis for any hypothesis—in any field of knowledge), inferences, or conclusions are clearer and deeper regarding consciential evolution when lucid outside the body. A person's holothosene already shows what the quality of their intentions, sentiments, knowledge, and ideas are. Comparisons can be made from this so as to arrive at relative terms such as "more mature" and "less mature," evolutionarily speaking. In essence, we could ask ourselves: What is it that makes an evolved helper more mature than I am? We can observe the thosenes helpers manifest so as to study and understand them, to use them as examples, and to eventually try to implement their strategies in order to reproduce their thosenes and grow from this as a consequence. The idea is not to follow a helper's behavior without discernment or just because they seem to be more evolved, but because we realize that there is more logic, common sense, and mentalsomatics in their strategy. In turn, this leads to more efficient evolutionary development.

Holomaturity

Consciential maturity and *holomaturity* are synonyms.

Holomaturity (*holo* = whole, integral, total + *maturity*): Condition of integral maturity within the consciousness—biological, psychological, intellectual, holosomatic, intraconsciential, and multidimensional.[3]

Holomaturity is not limited to only the characteristics developed in the physical world, but also includes multi-existential and multidimensional aspects of the consciousness. Furthermore, since the development of several attributes can take many lives to achieve, physical age is less of a factor in the development of holomaturity.

Maturity is associated with a good level of development, with being "ready to," and with having reached a condition of stability. Normally, it is the accumulation of experiences that leads to this,[4] as well as the "digestion," integration, and lucid incorporation of these experiences into our lives.

We can begin by discussing the four areas of holomaturity that correspond to how we *use* the four bodies (vehicles of manifestation of the consciousness): the soma, energosoma, psychosoma, and mentalsoma. Then we can move on to discuss the other aspects of the consciousness. From the myriad attributes that the consciousness must develop in order to reach the condition of holomaturity, there are some that are more prominent in determining the level of evolution of the consciousness. After discussing holosomatic maturity, we will focus on those more critical evolutionary attributes.

Maturity in the Use of the Holosoma

We can begin by analyzing how each consciousness *uses its holosoma,* or bodies of manifestation, since this use can be more refined and mature or more raw and immature. Having each one of the bodies well developed implies different things for each of them (figure 6.1).

Holosomatic Maturity

- Soma → Physical body
- Energosoma → Bioenergies
- Psychosoma → Emotions
- Mentalsoma → Discernment, awareness, processes, elevated sentiments

Figure 6.1: Holosomatic Maturity

Soma

Maturity of the physical body entails that this vehicle is physiologically developed to its fullest, or has become an adult body. At around twenty-six years of age, most people will have their physical body *fully* developed.[5] Normally there is not much we have to do to achieve this type of maturity except live long enough to reach it. Therefore, physiological maturity would be considered the easiest type of maturity to reach. With some rare exceptions, such as people with genetic anomalies, everyone eventually becomes somatically mature.

This concept can be expanded if we consider the integration between the consciousness and the physical body; in other words, how well the intraphysical consciousness understands and uses its physical body in a *healthy* and *productive* manner.

For example, we can learn how to "read" our soma to determine when it is tired or needs food, water, sleep (and how much), and so on. This can help us in the development of OBEs because we will know what it is that our body needs before starting a projective technique, or any other activity, for that matter. By the same token, we can classify the ability to deeply relax the physical body at will as an indication of a more mature condition related to the handling of this vehicle.

Energosoma

The energosoma is the vehicle of energies, our bioenergetic body. Maturity in the use of this vehicle is the condition where the consciousness can perceive, understand, and control energy at will, at any time and in any place.

To establish a basis for comparison, we can think of the low end of the scale (a less mature condition) being represented by people who are completely unaware of their bioenergies, with their energosoma blocked and unhealthy. On the other hand, we can find consciousnesses who have learned how to perceive energies, balance and unblock their energosoma, recharge it at will, avert external influences at will if necessary, and so on. If we use the exercises presented in chapter 2 as a reference, then a more energetically mature person would have the ability to reach the vibrational state anywhere, anytime.

A more energetically mature person would also have a refined sense of energetic perception. Three levels can be established in order to measure maturity:

- Perception of bioenergy.
- Ability to quantify this energy, or to measure how much energy a place or a person has.
- Capacity and experience to qualify this energy while extracting information from it such as thoughts and sentiments (thosenes). At this level, the person would have also learned to recognize specific individual energetic signals (psychic signals) that represent specific extraphysical events.[6] This allows the individual to have an easier time understanding and staying connected to the energetic and extraphysical reality.

Another aspect of energetic maturity is the mastery of the energosoma, which implies preparedness to face different (and often difficult) situations. For instance, a more energetically mature person would become less drained after discussions or arguments. Helpers have immense energetic endurance.

The same can be said of and applied to cases of intrusion. Though we may become intruded upon because of the energetic information manifested in a specific situation, we can also have a greater or lesser energetic capacity to become de-intruded. Even though the cause of the intrusion lies in the energetic information (thosenes), the actual detachment from intrusion in any specific moment is a matter of energetic capacity. Naturally, if our energosoma is more mature and better trained, several kinds of intrusions will not able to *crack our shell*.

A person with less energosomatic maturity will be more easily influenced by the energetic environment. A classic example is when we go out with a shopping list, get carried away or engulfed by the holothosene of the store or shopping mall (consumerism), and then come back with three times the original number of items, none of which were on our list to begin with and many of which are unnecessary.

Energosomatic maturity will also help us to achieve lucid OBEs. If we know how to control our energosoma, then we will be able to create an ideal condition to predispose and then allow for a liftoff with the psychosoma.

Similar to the situation with the soma, when we associate the energosoma with the observations of the consciousness, we can expand this maturity. When we understand that *we are not physical beings*, the more efficient and mature development of our bioenergetic control does not rely on *physical* elements (such as crystals, pendulums, physical movements, breathing, and others). When we are outside of our body projected or in between physical lives, the development we manifest extraphysically is due to our skills and the will we have nurtured—however, there are no physical objects to rely on. Thus, extraphysically we cannot use crystals, physical movements, pendulums, or other items to process energy. Extraphysical observations show that the more the consciousness matures, the more it uses its own will in a direct manner.[7]

These objects for working with energy can be seen as momentary or transient tools during certain phases—even though they are unnecessary in many cases. Such crutches are similar to a walker that a baby uses. This device can help when the baby is learning to walk (though it is not *really* necessary, since most people learn to walk without it), but it will take effectiveness away from the child if they keep using it beyond a certain age, or even worse, if they want to continue to use it always.

 Are we able to identify if we still use unnecessary crutches? How aware are we of how much we have become dependent on them? Can we already start to overcome them and leave them behind?

There is no average age for the achievement of energosomatic maturity. It could take anywhere from a number of years to several lives to go from total energetic unawareness to a good maturity level. The exercises with bioenergy presented in chapter 2 are great tools to increase energosomatic maturity.

Psychosoma

Psychosomatic maturity is more complex, because the upper bodies are more complex. The psychosoma is the vehicle of emotional actions and reactions. Therefore, maturity here means being prepared to recognize, understand, and deal with emotions—as well as being able to express emotions and sentiments in a mature and balanced fashion, without allowing ourselves to become overrun by them.

Observations of helpers and more mature consciousnesses demonstrate that they are able to maintain their level of awareness at all times by not allowing their emotions to rule their manifestations. This is very clear when we leave the body and we lose our awareness because of an emotional outburst. While projected extraphysically, we manifest the same holothosenic quality we manifest while physical. In other words, extraphysical helpers are exceptionally stable emotionally when they are in an intraphysical life; on the other hand, individuals who are exceedingly emotional while in the physical dimension have a much harder time keeping their balance (and therefore lucidity and continuity) extraphysically. Having OBEs and coming back to the body for emotional reasons becomes a form of training for the stabilization of our emotions.[8]

An example at the low end of the maturity scale is the person who is completely dominated by emotions, making all decisions in an impulsive manner, based on emotional reactions. Many times this person becomes blinded by the emotional content of any situation; for example, feeling rejected when receiving criticism at work, even if it is presented in the most polite and constructive way. A lack of maturity would prevent this person from seeing the difference between aggressive, destructive criticism and criticism that is constructive and presents opportunities to grow.

It is important to mention here that emotional evolutionary maturity does not imply repression of emotions or being cold and unfeeling. On the contrary, it is observed that evolved consciousnesses feel more deeply and more accurately, yet they remain in control and in balance through this experience—without losing their lucidity. Their perceptions are more refined and they are able to deal with them better. Helpers have a holothosene of maturity.

The immature holothosene of a person makes it harder for helpers to establish a closer rapport with them in order to provide assistance. A more mature person will naturally develop a closer relationship with helpers, who sometimes need to make us aware of certain areas where we may have to improve, or as a part of their effort to try to help us grow. Less mature individuals think they will always hear things that are pleasant to them, yet evidence shows that that is not the case. Similarly, in raising children, in order to educate them properly, we need to help them develop skills that may not be particularly likeable to them at first, especially when added to the fact that they may not understand why we are teaching them certain things that may only be of use to them in a future they cannot yet see.

Paralyzing guilt, energy-draining regret, constant bitterness, and regular drama-tizations of situations are also examples of the low end of psychosomatic maturity. Repressed, hidden, or unperceived emotions can hinder the development of psychic abilities and OBEs, because they will pollute and contaminate the individual's holo-thosene.

Psychosomatic maturity will also bring more confidence to the individual, who in turn will maintain a serene attitude when experiencing psychic abilities. By devel-oping control of our psychosoma, we can overcome *fear* (immaturity and/or lack of experience), when it exists, when we experience extraphysical perceptions. There are many cases where people consciously or unconsciously block their psychic abilities because of fear. In other cases, individuals eagerly seek psychic experiences, but upon having their first one, they block it out because they are scared of what else could be seen or the consequences of it.

Mentalsoma

The mentalsoma is the vehicle of discernment and the root of all thought processes. While the psychosoma is credited for the generation of emotions, the mentalsoma is the vehicle where the ideas and thoughts of the consciousness are first processed. Therefore, maturity of the mentalsoma is expressed by the ability to understand and formulate ideas and thoughts and be able to put them into practice, and to make bet-ter decisions.

More mature consciousnesses (e.g., helpers) are more mentalsomatic. This implies that they are lucid, organized, rational, ethical, knowledgeable, disciplined, and so forth (refer to chapter 3 for several of the attributes of the mentalsoma).

The mentalsoma is the most permanent body of the consciousness. The soma, the energosoma, and eventually the psychosoma will all be deactivated and discarded (will undergo desoma). However, all the evidence shows that the mentalsoma will not be discarded. In more mature consciousnesses, the mentalsoma is the body that is at the forefront of the individual's manifestations, managing their attitudes, reactions, and activities.

Are we able to see the level of impulsiveness in our reactions? How many times do we end up doing something because it is what we *like* to do, even though we *understand* we should do something else, because we *know* better? How many times a day do we feel anger, euphoria, lack of attention, anxiety, cowardice, and other emotions? Which vehicle predominates in controlling our manifestations in our daily activities, the psychosoma or the mentalsoma?

The application, prioritization, and use of the mentalsoma will help us to mature and evolve faster.[9]

The mentalsoma is also the body that brings balance and equilibrium to the consciousness. This is demonstrated by having projections of the mentalsoma, where, because of the fact that the psychosoma (the emotional body) is inactive during them, we do not lose our awareness due to an emotional outburst. Our awareness remains stable and constant during these projections.

Popular clichés such as "let your heart decide" or "listen to your inner child" are examples referencing the lack of priority toward the mentalsoma and are less mature attitudes. We realize that in many instances society tends to emphasize less mature conditions over more mature conditions—for example, emotions over ideas.[10] By simply analyzing TV channels or movies, we realize the abundance of emotions being broadcast through comedies, dramas, horror movies, and other types of films and TV shows. Mentalsomatic shows are very few in number, yet this is a direct reflection of what the majority of people want to see and of the level of the holothosene (and of the maturity) of the great majority.

Of course, emotions play a role in certain decisions—sometimes a larger role and sometimes a smaller one. If we want to pick the color of our next car, the decision can be 100 percent emotional. However, when deciding how to best apply our efforts to accomplish our life task (see chapter 7), the best strategy is to allow the mentalsoma to predominate. Thus, one of the aspects that needs to be developed in order to reach mentalsomatic maturity is to *understand* (a mentalsomatic ability) which decisions should be made by the mentalsoma and which by the psychosoma.

The application of the mentalsoma in every activity—whether intraphysical or extraphysical—is more effective and already demonstrates a certain level of evolutionary intelligence.

Evolutionary intelligence is the understanding that the physical life is a function of evolution, as well as the ability to utilize and *apply* any resource we may have for the consciential evolution of ourselves and others.[11]

An example that can give us an idea of our level of evolutionary intelligence is to determine the main reason that we want to leave the body. Among many possibilities, some people want to leave the body mainly to indulge in extraphysical tourism (not negative, but not too evolutionary); others want to spy on others (negative, unethical, and very immature); others want to find information about their own evolution or life task (evolutionarily essential, positive); and others want to help others (positive, evolutionary, and similar to what more mature consciousnesses do).

Discipline and determination are attributes of a mature mentalsoma. Some people follow through and implement their ideas, while others start many projects that "die" before their fruition because of a lack of sustained effort. The low end of the scale in this aspect is represented by mental laziness.[12]

The mentalsoma, the body of lucidity and clarity, is the one we use to shed light on any situation. Mature consciousnesses try to make everything more clear, not more mysterious or mystical. The word *mystic* (from the Latin *mysticus*, "of mysteries," or the Greek *mystikos*, from *mystes*, "initiate") implies that something is mysterious and unknown, surrounded by mist. The unknown is actually what we are trying to conquer by doing research and advancing knowledge and development.

It is less effective to repeat practices based on traditions whose results are unknown, mystical, or unclear and which were established by individuals who also did not understand them well—the reason for the name "mystic." Mystical elements are based on mysteries, the unknown, and essentially ignorance.[13] Even using the term mystic already promotes the holothosene of something being or (especially) remaining in the condition of being mysterious. Therefore, one intention in the application of the mentalsoma is to *demystify* aspects[14]—in opposition to merely thinking of them as "mysteries of the universe."

Main Traits of Consciential Maturity

The four types of maturity just presented, regarding the bodies of manifestation, give us an idea of how the process of maturation works. When observing the consciousness, we realize we have many traits, areas, and attributes that can be developed. In other words, the evolution of the consciousness is very complex.

Each one of us has developed certain traits more than others. This occurs because in the evolution of the consciousness throughout many lifetimes, we have been exposed to certain situations more than others, allowing us to have more experience in certain activities. Thus, we have strong traits and weak traits.[15] The weaker and less mature traits are not necessarily negative, but are just simply in a state of less development. This is similar to a child in kindergarten, who is less mature but not necessarily negative.

One of the best evolutionary strategies is to identify our strong traits in order to rely on them and use them to develop or overcome our weak traits. As examples, self-organization can help to overcome slowness of thought, and the ability to help others can be used to develop social skills and overcome shyness (where the energy does not flow naturally).

We realize here too that age becomes less of a factor, since the development of all our traits takes lifetimes. Naturally, with age, individuals have a greater overall understanding of life, yet in specific cases younger individuals may already express the development of certain traits better than older individuals do. We may find, for example, divorce cases where the person with the most mature attitude is the teenage daughter or son, who may offer effective advice to one or both parents to smooth out the process.

There is no set sequence for the development of maturity. One can present a relatively high intellectual maturity (referring more to the brain and/or materialism) and a relatively low emotional maturity. An illustration of this would be a Nobel Prize winner in physics who gets irritated to the point of screaming at a dog because of its continuous barking.

Altruism, Assistance

One of the important traits that define the evolutionary level of the consciousness is the level of assistance it is able to perform. The more evolved and mature the consciousness, the more altruistic it is and the more individuals it helps.[16] There are individuals who struggle to understand the reasons behind providing assistance and thus do not provide any. There are helpers of hundreds of individuals and there are even helpers of millions.

First of all, assistance is a measure of evolution because these consciousnesses (i.e., helpers) have reached a condition in which they need less and are able to produce enough to cover their basic necessities and also have a surplus (of time, energies, resources, etc.) from which they are able to help. Certain individuals struggle to even cover their own basic needs. Yet, as development continues, the consciousness is able to produce a surplus; it is this surplus that can be given—and rarely does evolutionary assistance imply money.[17]

Naturally, there are individuals who already produce a surplus but do not use it to help others. So the first issue is actually being able to help, and the second is then having the intention to help—which usually is less common. Manifesting altruism is a measure of how much we have overcome the tendencies and restrictions of the physical body—the more animalistic and immature influences. The opposite of altruism is egocentrism, which is when we think about, talk about, and work mainly for ourselves.

It is interesting to evaluate how much altruism individuals manifest in their daily lives. Sometimes the opportunity to help someone comes up, and a feeling grows inside of us that leads us to help another (whether outside or inside the body). This assistance—which is performed without any secondary intention or gain, without the expectation of reciprocity, and not because anyone else prompted us to do it (whether at that moment or before, in some congregation)—is rare. Here we are referring to this type of assistance, with this quality of purity, transparency, and authenticity. Yet more likely than not, we have already assisted in situations of this nature.

Helpers find themselves in such an assistantial condition most of the day, so their holothosene has a very obvious and high content of altruism. Remember that, when lucid and having a good level of awareness extraphysically, it is as easy to feel holothosenes outside of the body as it is to see the difference between two people with darker and lighter hair color inside the body.

> It is interesting to consider, what is the average amount of time during a twenty-four-hour day in which individuals manifest a high quality of assistantial thosenes?[18] Would it be one hour a day? Or maybe thirty minutes as an average? Maybe ten minutes? Maybe less than one minute? We can also consider here what our personal average is. How much of our day is still lived considering only our perspective alone? These questions can give us a idea of the assistantial thosene content in our holothosene.

Naturally the amount of assistantial content in the holothosene varies from person to person. However, the answers to such questions give us an idea of the difference in maturity between a more developed assistantial condition and common individuals. It can also help us to understand in what area we need to apply our efforts to evolve further.

Consolation and Clarification Task

In addition to the amount of assistantial content in the holothosene of individuals, we can also classify the quality of the assistance provided into two types: the consolation task and the clarification task.[19] Let us first explain the ideas behind these two types of assistance and then see how they apply to specific cases.

To *console* means to give support, time, and energies to somebody else. It implies "being there" for the person. The word consolation can refer to the act of (physically or emotionally) caressing and generally comforting somebody else. The consolation task implies giving something to someone. Generally, the person who provides consolation is well liked and received by others, and this facilitates things. The positive effects of consolation also tend to be more obvious and faster, and in some cases immediate.

The consolation task is easier to do, since it does not require any special skill. As a matter of fact, in some instances certain animals do a much better job at the consolation task (comforting) than certain humans. For example, in some cases the dog may be there to greet and give energy to the owner when he comes home from work, making the owner feel better, while other relatives may act completely aloof.

The consolation task has its disadvantages in that it can create dependency and complacency. In other words, individuals receiving consolation can get used to the resource that is being freely given. Once a condition of dependency has been established, another disadvantage that can arise is that consolers can abuse this so as to manipulate (either consciously or unconsciously) the other for their own personal gain or interest.

Naturally, when this occurs, the consolation stops being assistantial. This is what certain religions practice, whereby they console, but also want and need the person to be open to indoctrination as a tradeoff; in other words, needing the person to need them for their own survival. In some cases the underlying idea behind such behaviors is: "You do not need to understand the whys. Just be obedient (and in some cases fearful), and we will take care of you."

The other drawback of consolation is that it is temporary. Though the recipient may be comforted, in the long run this does not necessarily solve the root of the problem. It is similar to giving a homeless person food for one night—it may be positive in that it eases their hunger temporarily (which is a basic necessity), but just in and of itself, it does not provide any tools for the person's own self-sustenance, to be able to provide for themselves in the long run.

The *clarification* task implies educating, elucidating, and generally explaining or clarifying something so that the person will become more self-sufficient and grow.

The clarification task is more complex (1) because the person who does it has to know something (which requires mental effort and learning); and (2) because in order for the clarification task to bear fruit, the person who receives it also has to put some effort into applying and developing the ability. The clarifier can provide the seed, but then the clarified individual must actually sow the seed for it to grow into a tree and bear fruit.

Generally speaking, individuals normally prefer to receive something already finished than to put effort into developing something. This is the reason that many individuals prefer to take medication to become better instead of putting effort into living a healthier life to prevent illness in the first place.

The fact that clarification requires some work from the recipient makes the person doing the clarification less popular and less well received. However, when the clarification task is well understood and implemented, the lesson learned can act as a permanent solution for the problem(s) of the recipient—instead of a quick fix. Thus, using the previous example, it is one thing to give food to a homeless person (temporary and requires less effort from both parties) and quite another to teach the homeless person a skill to get a job that will cover their basic necessities in the long term (requires more effort from both parties). It is also much easier for people to ask for some sort of help or aid, and less comfortable—and less common—for them to put the effort into developing a skill. The same logic applies to the one providing the aid.

Helpers mainly perform the clarification task. Their aim is to elucidate situations so that individuals will be able to make increasingly better decisions. Naturally, the clarification task is a more mature condition than the consolation task—since it produces more permanent results. Thus, it is one thing to "clean" a person energetically (consolation) and quite another to teach the person how to develop energetically so they can clean themselves (clarification). There is a big difference between removing an intruder from someone and helping the person develop the capacity to de-intrude themselves regularly.

As consciousnesses mature, they start gravitating more toward the clarification task; they offer it more and want to receive it more. They look for strategies that produce longer-lasting results and are less superficial. They want to understand more, through emphasizing the mentalsoma in their manifestations. In so doing, they pursue knowledge that is more permanent.

The clarification task, however, can also become non-assistantial when it lacks lucidity or is abused. In order to properly apply the clarification task, the recipient has to have a decent minimum manifestation of mental, emotional, and energetic stability in order to be able to receive the information and lean on and maintain this stability until they reach the next step of growth. If the recipient is too unbalanced or fragile—either on average or at that moment in time—then the consolation task may be needed first, so as to help balance them. Afterward, the clarification task can be applied and have a positive effect. If the clarification is used first in these situations, it can be counterproductive for the purposes intended.

> Imagine you are at a funeral. Do you go with consolation or clarification? Most individuals unfortunately do not understand nor deal well with the processes of death and dying, and thus find themselves fragile at such moments. If we take into consideration their condition and their understanding, it would not be helpful if we go and say something like, "I was outside my body yesterday and your grandfather is not dead but is already preparing for his next life, where he will have a new family and new opportunities to grow." This could be true, but in this context it probably would not be helpful for people to hear. Thus, in a situation like a funeral with people mourning, it is more proper to gently apply the consolation task. Consolation works well in emergency and exceptional situations. Problems arise when it becomes a habit, used for its own sake.

Using this example, we realize that even after the funeral, clarification needs to be performed gently, slowly, and appropriately. Even then, certain individuals may never be ready in this life for *full clarification*. Therefore, when doing the more mature task of clarification assistance, it needs to be given in measured quantities, lucidly, depending on what the recipient can handle and is able to take advantage of.

Helpers use consolation with us when required, yet they try to use clarification whenever possible since it will benefit us more in the long term.

In the case of your own interaction with a helper, it is interesting to consider the following: What is it that my helpers should not clarify for me because I would not yet be able to handle it? Is there anything about myself that I *would not want to know*? You can also ponder whether you still primarily tend to use consolation or clarification.[20]

Cosmoethics

A developed sense of ethics is another hallmark of the high end of the maturity scale.

Cosmoethics (cosmo + ethics) is the set of personal principles based on the individual's own level of awareness and level of evolution. These principles hold true for the consciousness, regardless of where in the cosmos the consciousness is manifesting.[21]

Cosmoethics is something internal; it is not dictated by moral values and what is generally accepted by the societies in which we live during this life. It is an internal constitution, written by you. Cosmoethics is not a theoretical concept, like goals that we would like to achieve and write on a piece of paper. Instead, cosmoethics is what we present every day through our actions, priorities, and decisions. Our cosmoethical code is not static and may change to reflect what was learned through experience. Understanding the long-term benefits of cosmoethical behavior is a sign of mentalsomatic maturity.

More evolved consciousnesses are more cosmoethical. To understand this better, let us explain the opposite of cosmoethics: self-corruption. Normal corruption occurs when someone *knows* what should be done, or the proper way of doing things, yet the person perverts, distorts, ignores, and/or corrupts this idea and does something else. *Self*-corruption is when we know the correct thing to do and neglect to do it; in many instances it is equivalent to self-deceit. As with the example of smoking, even though the person who does it knows it is harmful, the person still does it (see chapter 5).

Notice how self-corruption is related to our level of knowledge and *knowing* what the correct thing to do is. When individuals smoked in the 1920s, though they suffered all the negative health effects of smoking, they were not self-corrupt because nobody knew that smoking was harmful. However, nowadays, this is well known, and thus it is a self-corruption. There is usually some sort of internal justification for carrying on with the self-corrupt activity, some sort of excuse, which individuals call "an exception," "one last time," "well, in this case…," or justifications (in the case of cigarettes) like "it helps me to relax" and so on.

Imagine that a doctor is on an international flight and another passenger has a medical complication. Depending on the severity of the case, the steward may page any medical professional in the plane for help. The doctor can choose to cross his arms and not do anything, or he can go and help. If he decides not to help, he is deciding not to use the information he knows and is thus denying his training, therefore behaving in a self-corrupt way. If he goes and helps, since he is the one with the medical training, he is acting knowledgeably with the information he possesses and is behaving cosmoethically. On the other hand, if other passengers who are not doctors decide to cross their arms and fall asleep, they are not committing a self-corruption, because they are not denying any knowledge of theirs.[22]

We can see from this example how cosmoethics is extremely individualized and works in agreement with the level of information and level of evolution of the person. Therefore, cosmoethics is not written in stone for everybody to follow; rather, *our level of responsibility and freedom* will depend on *our own internal level of maturity and degree of information.*[23]

It is observed that the fewer skills and less information and maturity we have, the less freedom this affords us and the less responsibility we have. By the same token, the more awareness, information, and evolution we have, the more freedom we enjoy and the more responsibility we have. For example, a child does not have much freedom or responsibility. A teenager ("intermediary condition") who can drive has more freedom and skills than a child, but is now responsible for driving correctly as well. Adults have even more freedom, information, and responsibility. The same analogy applies in an evolutionary sense.

For example, after reading chapter 2 of this book, we know that our thoughts are in fact thosenes that influence other people and places through the energies that are emanated. If we speak badly of somebody else, this energy will affect the person on some level. We are making an energetic attack upon this person. If, after knowing this, we repeat the behavior, then this would be a self-corruption, because we would be distorting the knowledge we now have. Note that individuals who do this but are not aware of the effects still produce a negative effect. Yet it is not a self-corruption to them since they do not know any better.

One of the reasons helpers assist us is because they are being cosmoethical—as more mature consciousnesses are. Helpers implement what they know. Similar to the condition of the doctor in the previous example, helpers have the ability to see our needs *and* the capacity to help. They are correct and coherent with their knowledge and maturity, and so they help.[24] They do not help because they follow any dogma or any line of knowledge. Helpers are completely independent in their actions, and their personal decision to assist is a sign of their consciential maturity.

We all have a very good capacity for understanding concepts and ideas; the (evolutionary) struggle is with putting these ideas into practice and being *coherent* with them. If we are *sincerely* trying to close the gap between what we know and what we do, then we are being cosmoethical. If we do not try and/or if the gap is big, then we are being incoherent, and we justify this incoherence in many ways. In many instances, we do not even say anything, but in our mind we develop an excuse (self-corruption) for the incoherent behavior.

When we perform certain tasks and the result is not positive, even though the action *looks good* intraphysically, many times the initial intention was already not clean, clear, or sincere. Sometimes a secondary (usually hidden) intention existed. Extraphysically, intruders and blind guides connect to the essentially self-corrupt energies. This does not occur because they are aware that we are self-corrupting but because the intention is not clean, clear, or sincere, so they unconsciously resonate with it. In a certain sense, experiencing (or being a "victim" of) intrusion is an indication of a lack of cosmoethics.[25]

In the previous example of the doctor, notice that the doctor may be outside the jurisdiction in which his license is valid. Though this may be the case, cosmoethics still holds true, since the principles go beyond physical laws or what may be techni-cally or legally correct. It would still be a self-corruption for him not to help—whether or not he is in his jurisdiction—even though, strictly speaking, it may not be illegal for him to choose not to help on the airplane in that case.

> **EXAMPLE**
>
> Imagine a person who goes hunting in Africa for sport (entertainment) and kills a wild boar. Even though the firearm is registered, and he is going during hunting season and shoots the animal within the allowed perimeter (everything legal), it is still anti-cosmoethical, because the person does not need to kill for survival but is doing so only for entertain-ment purposes. Contrast this with a native tribesman from that same corner of the world who kills a wild boar to feed his tribe.[26]

Notice that the problem in this case is not with killing the animal, but with the rea-son for killing it, the intention, and the thosene behind the killing. Energies work on a much subtler level than physical actions, yet they speak louder. Nature and the physi-cal dimension have a natural *food chain* dynamic. Within such a dynamic, the human body through its immunological system kills millions of viruses and bacteria each day; it is either them or us. In this case, it is either several wild boar or several tribesmen. It is the way nature works. So the issue is why the person is killing the animal. We can also see from this example how cosmoethics goes beyond physical laws.[27]

Notice that the hunter may be thinking, "I'm killing this wild boar to give to the natives so they will have something to eat." Yet he may also be thinking at the same time, "And I'll just stuff the head of this animal and hang it on my wall as a trophy." Does the intention lean more toward the first thought or the second? Physically, only the person manifesting the thought knows the real intention behind the actions. In some instances the person is concealing the real intention.[28]

Self-corruptions exist even at the level of a person's intentionality, as this is where the *self*-corruption begins in the first place. It has nothing to do with anybody else but us; we are the ones producing it. Beyond this, extraphysical consciousnesses (blind guides, intruders, helpers, and others) are permanent witnesses to our thosenes.[29] We are like a radio station transmitting our thosenes permanently to the extraphysical dimensions.

Naturally, being that evolved consciousnesses are cosmoethical, the way to connect to them more is for us to tune in as much as possible with their holothosene—for us to be more coherent with our own knowledge.

Here are certain general guidelines that are observed within cosmoethics:[30]

- May the best happen for all, even if the best in general (i.e., what assists the most) does not imply what is best or most comfortable for us.

- If we can already theoretically understand a problem, then we have a certain responsibility to work toward the solution. Most of us can understand many problems. This does not mean we are going to try to save the world (lack of discernment). Using our mentalsoma and our ability to prioritize, we can select which problem we are going to concentrate on, keeping in line with our assistantial capacities (coherent with our skills). Unfortunately, some individuals do not work on improving any situation, or are working below their assistantial means (i.e., they are being incoherent with what they know).

- Always choose the lesser of two evils. In a specific situation where there will be a loss either way, try to pick the condition where less is lost overall, choosing the "least worse" option available in that circumstance.

- Always select the greater of two positive conditions or of two goods. (Same as above.) Notice that these last two guidelines are independent of who is in which group.

Let's say we have a politician who obtains public funds for a new project. Instead of organizing a group of workers for the new project and passing on the profits to them, he decides to give the contract to his brother. The brother will administrate the project, and even though the workers will still have work, the brother (one person) will keep the majority of the profits. What would be the greater of two goods in this case?

Based on the example of the politician, it is interesting to consider what idea (self-corruption) the politician and the brother use to justify such action. Maybe their behavior is legal. We can see here again how cosmoethics has very little relation to what is legal and what is not.

Using this concept, we can understand the mechanisms of certain interactions outside the body. It is harder for individuals who leave the body with a negative intention (e.g., spying) to reach their target. This is because as the person emits thosenes with such an intention, less mature and energetically denser consciousnesses—the ones who resonate with that activity—connect to them. Likewise, the energy of the negative intention being manifested is also denser. With a denser energetic load, the person will have a harder time carrying out their objective. The individual will evoke and be surrounded by different energy if their intention is to provide assistance, for example, and thus the result will be different.

Imagine that a person goes to bed feeling very angry with a colleague due to a work-related problem. If, instead of thinking constructively and/or diplomatically about the problem and the colleague, the person thinks aggressively, this creates around them a holothosene that attracts intruders who feed on that and amplify their anger. Sometimes the internal speech they are rehearsing in their mind for the next day goes from bad to worse. Certainly, as they continue thinking in that fashion, they can be making an energetic attack on their colleague. However, on their side, since they have allied themselves with (connected themselves to) several intruders, the quality of the energy around them will be lower, and their night's rest will be compromised. Their energosoma will harden due to the dense energies around, and that night it will be much harder to have an OBE. Notice that nobody is punishing the person. It is simply the end result of their actions. Consciential development occurs more slowly when there is a lack of cosmoethics.[31]

In our evolution, it is observed that we are naturally learning and that we will still fall down at times and "scrape our knees" in the process. However, to develop further and more efficiently and productively, ideally it would be preferable for us to be *sincere* (coherent) with the information we do know.[32]

Universalism

Universalism is the philosophy of more evolved and mature consciousnesses. We can describe it as the opposite of prejudgments, segregationism, corporatism, parochialism, and many other kinds of dogma.[33]

> *Universalism* is the coherent (logical) behavior of the consciousness according to the broadest understanding of the universe.[34]

The reason that universalism is applied by more lucid consciousnesses is because it is the most logical (coherent) course of action. Let us discuss certain cases of anti-universalism so as to understand this in practice.

First, let us tackle the case of *racism*. We realize through observation that prejudging specific people by the color of their skin is very superficial, since in all groups there are individuals who are more or less developed, with more or less mature intentions and with a greater or lesser level of skills. Individuals who still manifest racism typically have the tendency to think that their own race is superior to others.

However, as consciousnesses start to have more experiences and start to understand more about the universe, they will come across the reality of us having more than one body (four bodies, in fact). The only one of these bodies that has a race is the physical body, the one that represents the least of what we are—since it is the most temporary. Thus, trying to judge the capacity of the consciousness and its mental-soma by the color of the physical body's skin is a most infantile criterion (like trying to judge a book by its cover). Notice that though this is an argument anybody can theoretically understand, as we experience this broader reality more often, it becomes an undeniable fact.

Furthermore, as we experience more of the universe, we realize that we have already had many physical lives; thus, we have already had many physical bodies with different skin tones: yellow, white, black, bronzed, and others. The fact that individuals think that their skin color is somehow better shows the high level of conditioning to just this one physical life and the narrowness of their perspective (immaturity). In contrast, the fact that more mature consciousnesses are not influenced by those ideas demonstrates the expansion and coherence of their understanding. In many cases, individuals are born into race A, and they defend it and show prejudice against race B. Yet they do not realize that during their last life they were born into race B and showed prejudice against race A. So the problem is not about race, but about the consciousness's perspective regarding themselves, others, and reality in general.

Normally most of us have no problem understanding the concept of universalism. Yet maturity is about what we think and do *in practice*, with our energy and our actions. So even though we may agree with the previous arguments about race, we could ask ourselves: In practice, would we marry a person of any race? The answer to this question and our deeper and subtle reactions to it can give us an idea of our level of developed universalism in this regard.

With regard to believing one sex to be better than the other (whether the male or female one), the same arguments apply. The physical body is the only soma that has a gender, and we have already been men and women in many other lives. The consciousness is not of the gender of this one life; we are much more than this.

By the same token, we can see that if in a past life we became very conditioned to being a man, for example, and we helped to promote the holothosene of machismo, now, in this current life when we are a woman, we could be experiencing the consequences of the holothosene we helped establish in a past life. This effect, put simply, is what is called karma, which will be addressed in more detail in the next chapter.

Now, let us think about universalism versus *nationalism*. From the moment we are born, we are conditioned to identify ourselves with our particular nation. As we grow up, we have to learn—and to love—our national anthem, poem, flag, and so on. Thus, we grow up defending our country and tend to romanticize it and put it above other countries. We are even conditioned to think that dying for a piece of land is correct or somehow noble.

Likewise here, we realize at some point that we were already born in many different regions and corners of the world. We have already defended—unfortunately sometimes with our physical life—many different lands. We may have switched sides (countries) in different lives, yet the pattern that keeps repeating of becoming conditioned to a certain country of our current life is still the same. As more experience is gained, the consciousness realizes how truly senseless nationalism is—and even more so the potential act of war that comes from it.

We can ponder how many people have died in wars because of nationalism. There are some conflicts on this planet that are so old that *in the same conflict the same consciousness* has already died fighting for both sides. Yet we can also ponder the following: If in this life we would have been born in a country on the other side of the world, would we still think that our current country is the best? Which values and beliefs would we be upholding (defending) at this moment? Would they be different?

Borders change over decades; they are simply an intraphysical consensus, having very little to do with broad universal consciential realities. Also, as more of the universe is understood, we realize that we are actually citizens of the universe and not of a specific region, country, or even planet.[35] Consciential evolution (even just considering the series of physical lives followed by nonphysical periods) takes an unknown number of lives; thus, we logically have already been born in many different areas. Furthermore, it is observed that we have been born on different planets before this one—so we (consciousnesses) are not even natively terrestrial.

Planet Earth, for example, can be considered a "consciential elementary school" at best. There are many "elementary schools" (planets with intelligent physical life similar to our level) in the universe. Moreover, when consciousnesses were at the previous level of "consciential kindergarten," they may have gone to a different "school"—were born on a different planet for many lives during their consciential kindergarten phase. Later they will also be reborn on many other planets (with similar levels to "consciential middle school," "consciential high school," and so on) as their evolution progresses—and logically, there are many of these types of planets in existence in the universe as well.

Lack of universalism is predisposed, supported, and exacerbated in most cases by ignorance. Some simple yet effective techniques that can help us to improve our level of universalism are to travel,[36] learn different languages,[37] coexist with and assist people from different cultures,[38] project lucidly outside the body to extrapolate the physical frontiers, and so forth. Individuals are then able to analyze their own culture better (more objectively) and become more cosmopolitan and international,[39] a step toward becoming more universalistic.

We can also discuss universalism as it pertains to *religions*. Individuals in most cases do not choose their religion, but are simply born into one, most not realizing that this is the case.[40] Just as with nationalism, the religious conditioning we are faced with from an early age makes us grow up defending our religion. In many cases it is defended to the point of complete lack of awareness or even fanaticism.

These religious affiliations can lead to discrimination, prejudice, and even hatred in some cases. In other likewise negative cases, it leads at the very least to favoritism. People tend to value others from their own group more than they do everyone else. Thus, in many cases individuals oppress certain groups during one life and afterward are sometimes born into the same groups they oppressed during the previous life. The problem is not the particular side or specific politics, but the oppression itself.

Unfortunately, just as with nationalism, we see that millions of people have died because of religious differences—all in the name of God. As stated before, in many instances the same consciousness has already died for both sides several times. More mature consciousnesses with a broader view understand this issue more deeply, and their thoughts and behavior reflect this understanding.

One of the ways in which religions often fail is precisely in their exclusivity and lack of universalism. There is even the radical phrase "If you are not with me, you are against me." Mature and evolved consciousnesses try to help anybody from any group, as long as the person wants to grow and evolve, independently of the group the person belongs to at this moment. Thus, because the helpers' criteria are not exclusive and narrow, we can understand how they do not follow any particular religion.[41] They are universalistic beings.

One thing to add to this discussion of religion is that because of the religious conditioning received since infancy, individuals tend to interpret everything from their particular ideology's point of view. Thus, in many cases they were helped by universalistic helpers throughout their lives and perhaps even received assistance that they would be inclined to interpret as "miraculous." Indeed, sometimes an event may be something beyond the individual's capability to comprehend. Yet it certainly does not mean that whoever helped them was someone from their religion—or even someone with religious ideas at all.

In some cases it may have been their nonsectarian helper who assisted them. Furthermore, in some instances some more *universalistic projectors (intraphysical consciousnesses)* who have already started to perform such assistantial tasks are also the ones behind such assistance. Since helpers focus on the well-being of all individuals independent of their ideology, helpers will assist anyone willing to grow. They know that with more development and evolution, everyone will understand better their own ideology, the influence it has on themselves, and the fact that such an ideology is not necessarily the better or only one.

It can be thus seen why universalistic and lucid assistance is a task performed by more mature consciousnesses who have already overcome their own initial conditionings and ideology. Again, they do not assist others because of an ideology or because any kind of influence, congregation, or book told them to. They do it because it is the correct, cosmoethical thing to do, and they deeply understand this. They individually and personally embrace assistance, and choose to perform it in a natural manner.[42]

It is important to realize that universalism does not mean "anything goes," "everything is accepted," or that there is a lack of discerning criteria.[43] Universalism goes against *pre*judging and discrimination of groups. However, more universalistic consciousnesses do in fact discern, dissect, and analyze everything to the smallest detail. Using their mentalsoma, they do this even so as to be able to choose what is best for them, for their own evolution and that of others.

With the concept of universalism at hand, we can better understand why blind guides and intruders defend their own personal interests during their intermissive periods. Their perspective is still anti-universalistic and narrow-minded (immature), so they manifest these qualities in their thoughts and behavior.

Ideal Assistance
Waldo Vieira (2007)[44]

Prior to Projection
On Tuesday, July 24, 1979, I went to bed at 8:05 PM. Shortly after, the extraphysical consciousness José Grosso began working with energy while coupled with me. I stayed semiconscious until 9:00 PM. I was alone in the bedroom with the door closed.

(continued) The helper, José Grosso, radiated energy through me, having me sit on the bed several times. Then the team of extraphysical consciousnesses attended to someone in front and to the right of my soma [penta practice[45]—see chapter 7].

The psychosoma is a condenser of cosmic energies (*psionics* in parapsychology). Emission of denser energy is used to assist psychotic post-mortems (earthbound spirits) as well as to reduce the density of the psychosoma while projected. With time, one becomes accustomed to living with both the dense soma and the subtle psychosoma.

During the semiconsciousness of the projective trance, I clearly felt an influx of energy concentrated on the right cerebral hemisphere. It involved pressure over my forehead, and after a while it remained on the right side of my forehead only. I fell asleep after 11:15 PM.

Extraphysical Period

I became lucid outside of the soma on an unfamiliar street in a neighborhood with regular and steep streets in the north zone of Rio de Janeiro. Something told me that it was shortly after midnight. I had a clear sensation of having been peacefully left on the street. I walked down one of the commercial avenues for quite a while, strolling among people and examining the street scenes—particularly in places with lights and small gatherings of people, like bars and nightclub entrances. I did not experience any attempt at interaction by the extraphysical pedestrians.

While passing a bar, I observed a conversation going on inside. Someone entered and bought some mint candy, which the cashier took out of a glass jar. I counted three intraphysical consciousnesses and two extraphysical consciousnesses inside the bar.

At the end of the main street in a small square with a few trees and benches, I came across an extraphysical consciousness who looked like a doctor [extraphysical helper]. His name came to mind: Calmene. Strong, athletic-looking, blondish, and appearing to be about forty-five years old, he was attending to some extraphysical consciousnesses needing assistance. That stretch of street seemed better lit than the others.

Upon exchanging mental messages with him, Calmene quickly explained to me that his routine work was helping the needy. At night, the specialized task becomes intense as extraphysical consciousnesses, especially sick ones, enter into contact with sleeping persons. Each assistant in that work takes care of a defined area of service.

The traffic, except on the main street, was light. Hardly any cars passed by at all. There were many cars parked in the square.

The doctor revealed plans to expand the assistance with the use of projected companions, creating a larger assistantial team. This special brigade would be used mainly for nighttime assistance services in a specific place in one of the poorly lit and deserted cross streets, where their services would be centralized.

The task did not appear to be simple. From 6:00 PM on—when the greatest human anguish begins—the assistantial team tries to diminish the depression, despair, sadness, longings, doubts, resentments, loneliness, and problems stemming from the unstructured relationships typical of big cities. Calmene told me that the least pleasant aspect is that some intraphysical as well as extraphysical consciousnesses refuse to be assisted. Sometimes they don't even want to be approached, rejecting the extraphysical assistants. Their assistance work—far more complex than it seemed—functioned by linking itself to a nucleus of police stations, emergency care units, hospitals, several temples, the Salvation Army, suicide prevention centers, Alcoholics Anonymous, and other physical crisis control groups.

I deduced that such services by *helpers* existed not only throughout the city but in other places as well, especially in larger metropolises.

Before saying goodbye, Calmene appeared to concentrate and, as an exercise in mental concentration, offered me the following short message regarding ideal assistance:

Every act of social assistance, no matter how small, signifies fraternity, is productive, and deserves praise. Any kind of human assistance is better than none. Nevertheless, *the ideal social assistance* has its own unmistakable universalistic characteristics:

- It is not official, since it is spontaneous.
- It is not a tax-deductible donation.
- It does not have a professional title.
- It has no secondary or political intentions.
- It does not back a personal image or cultivate myths.
- It does not encourage segregation of any kind.
- It is not restricted by prejudice.
- It does not expect gratitude nor require public understanding.

(continued)

- It does not announce the act of assistance, regardless of circumstances.
- It is the donation of one's self—simple, pure, and direct—without mediation, demands, or conditions. And everyone can practice it in silence.

On Earth, a planet with many countries, creatures, customs, religions, and interests, all inhabitants are naturally brothers and sisters. Happy are those who learn the universalistic principles: maximize fraternity, overcome taboos, and perform universalistic assistance while still in human life. In this way, they first receive the benefit of terrestrial liberation on the way to higher levels.

Could it be more logical? The message was clear, categorical, and unambiguous.

I expressed my thanks and said goodbye to the attentive doctor, who departed toward one of the cross streets. I walked through the lights and shadows of the main street, passing idle transients and lazy extraphysical consciousnesses, and then returned immediately to the soma.

Paragenetics

During the course of a physical life, we can observe (multidimensionally) that we are basically the product of *three* forces: (1) environmental influences, (2) genetics—our biological inheritance, and (3) paragenetics—our self-inheritance from previous existences.

Paragenetics (para = extraphysical + *genetics)*: our self-inheritance—tendencies, abilities, skills, experience, and other factors from our previous existences carried from life to life through the upper bodies, the psychosoma and the mentalsoma.[46]

If the strongest influences on a consciousness are the *environmental* influences, this consciousness then becomes a product of its current culture.[47] This means that during a life, the person will have values according to that specific culture. Therefore, if the culture dictates that people should be more of a specific religion or more detached from others, or more materialistic, or closer to their family, then most individuals will likely be so.

In these cases, the person becomes a "robot"—we name this condition *existential robotization*—or a "puppet" of the current popular ideas. Though it may seem as if the person is choosing ideas, more than anything the person was born into them and has been indoctrinated into them. Unfortunately, observations also show that *consciential evolution is not currently a big part of most intraphysical cultural values on Earth.*

Genetic influences are inherited through biological mechanisms. In other words, they are biological determinants that influence the way individuals behave. Sexual drives are a part of core biological impulses (maternity and paternity included). In many instances, genetic predispositions might dictate whether the person will have a tendency to be a good athlete, have a chronic disease, be more or less beautiful, and so forth.

If genetics are the strongest force driving the consciousness, then individuals may be more animalistic in their behaviors, acting more impulsive, instinctive (not to be confused with intuitive, which is more mentalsomatic), and therefore more intraphysical. It may be harder for these individuals to realize that they are *not* a female or a male, nor a physical body, but that *they are a consciousness that happens to temporarily have the body of a female or a male.*

Paragenetics is the inheritance from the consciousness—us—onto itself. In other words, it is the accumulation of experiences from previous existences that are brought into this life. Therefore, it is no coincidence that some people already at a young age start having OBEs, or are better suited to music, theater, or science, especially when no one else in their family shares their abilities. It can generally be said that any *well-developed* attribute that a child manifests at a very young age is the result of it having been developed in past lives. Usually, personal retrocognitive experiences can confirm this fact for us.[48]

In some instances, individuals are said to have been born with a specific capacity. This may be true, yet that capacity is not a "gift." It is a trait the person has already developed and earned in previous life experiences.

If paragenetics happen to be the strongest influence driving the manifestation of the consciousness, then the individual can carry over the lessons from one life to the next and avoid unnecessary repetition (self-mimicry) with greater success than others who might be more driven by environmental or genetic influences. These individuals will be more predisposed to become aware of what they really are: a consciousness in evolution.[49]

When this occurs, we can realize that we are not only the son or daughter of our parents. The body is born from these two other intraphysical consciousnesses, yet the individual consciousness itself is not born from any two individuals. Besides this, in previous lives perhaps one of our parents could have been our sister, and in another life our lover, and yet in another life our friend, and so on and so forth. We have already been in many different roles in many different lives. Therefore, the person with such a perspective is able to understand that the relationship with this person is much more than just simply a single parent-offspring relationship.

Individuals with stronger paragenetics are generally able to remain on track more easily with regard to their life task (see chapter 7). For these consciousnesses, their intraphysical life is more of a school where they can learn and develop their consciential attributes. Other physical endeavors, like earning money, social status, and social acceptance (although deserving of relative attention and effort according to the needs of physical life), become secondary. In other words, the references, values, and source of their decisions are not just from their current education (environment) or physical prowess (genetics) stemming from just this *one* single current life, but from the lessons and positive effects *of the accumulation of innumerable lives*. In this sense, when we understand ourselves even less as a human being and more as a consciousness, we demonstrate a higher level of consciential maturity.

Evolutionary Acceleration

As consciousnesses mature, they concern themselves more with evolving more rapidly, lucidly, and efficiently—assisting others in their endeavor to do so as well. They try to make their evolution more dynamic, as opposed to allowing it to stagnate. This is similar to a person in college who, upon understanding the value of education, does not want graduation to take several years longer than needed.

Neophilia

Neophilia is a fondness for new things and ideas. The opposite of neophilia is neophobia (fear of new things and ideas). By definition, *evolution entails change*. Thus, as consciousnesses mature, they inevitably desire to change and improve themselves. In general, more evolved consciousnesses present more neophilia in their holothosene.[50]

It is observed that the average consciousness tends to be conservative in its tastes, energies, habits, and attitudes. A simple example of this is the food people eat. Usually, most people like the traditional food of the region or culture in which they were raised. Yet this does not happen because that food *actually* tastes better than other foods, but merely because the person has become accustomed to eating it in their upbringing. Different individuals from different cultures tend to have the same conditioning with their traditional foods.

We can get an idea of the neophilia or neophobia of a person by observing whether they want to eat different foods and try different things. Though food is just a simple reference, this level of neophilia will carry over into other areas. An interesting realization is that, as consciousnesses evolve, they become more flexible, adaptable, and patient; yet when consciousnesses start to stagnate, they become more rigid, strict, inflexible, and impatient.

When thinking about our ideas and values, we can try to evaluate how old or new they are. A measure of our conservatism (stagnation) versus our progressiveness (evolution) can be determined by asking ourselves: From which century do the values I have or uphold come?[51] The older the idea, generally the more unrefined it is. In order to evolve (grow), our ideas and values need to be regularly renewed.

Anti-dispersion

When faced with a choice, more mature consciousnesses are able to select what is best for them and then follow through with it. They are able to better focus on the task at hand time and time again, regardless of the distractions around them. On the opposite end of the spectrum we find individuals who may start many projects, or even plan them out theoretically, but are not able to see them through to their conclusion. In many instances this also happens because the person tackles the task at hand only superficially.

The condition of having too much dispersion in one's holothosene (immaturity) leads individuals to become "butterfly seekers." When we see a butterfly in a field with many flowers, we notice that it flies from flower to flower, extracting some nectar from all of them without spending too much time with any one flower.

This apparently casual and fleeting behavior was the inspiration for the term "butterfly seeker." The butterfly seeker is anyone who looks for "alternative" information (many times pertaining to metaphysical ideas) from all kinds of sources and groups but remains superficial both in learning and experiencing, thus never implementing any significant change in their life.[52] Trying as always to be constructive, we always want to try to reduce our level of dispersion in our actions and energies—if there is any.

> **EXAMPLE / EXAMPLE**
>
> A pertinent illustration of dispersion is a person who has attended many classes about different New Age topics. Knowledge and experience is always positive; however, such individuals many times demonstrate that they did not absorb much from any of those classes. During an informal chat, they may even talk about those classes more like they would speak about a mediocre movie they watched last year. They can no longer remember even simple details of any of the topics.

Dispersion happens due to the superficial approach taken toward these classes—listening to the theory without really questioning, reasoning, discerning, or seeing if there is anything that could objectively help in their evolution. Also, it is clearly observed that many individuals regard consciential development with the same level of seriousness as they would a hobby. A very popular New Age or metaphysical magazine with articles and ads on such topics advertises the following: "One of the best ways to make new friends is to sign up for a class or group event. Polls show that 'meeting new people' was the single most popular reason given for attending classes."[53] The success of this line has been such that it has been running in their magazine for several years now (2010). This gives a clue as to what some people want. In other words, some individuals attend "spiritual classes" for social reasons.

It takes effort and focus to evolve with lucidity. It is easier to remain within the law of the least effort and just keep moving around in circles in the flow of all the different momentary fashions and trends as they appear and change.

It is more productive and efficient to evaluate and select what is best for us and then truly *dedicate* ourselves to it, evolving through the use of our mentalsoma more often and consistently. Otherwise, we become dispersed and lose our evolutionary opportunities.

There is a technique that can help us understand ourselves better: the technique of *three hours of waking physical immobility*. The effects of this technique can be many, including but not limited to understanding more in depth our holothosene and how we think; having OBEs; discovering which one of our bodies drives our manifestation more; having clairvoyant experiences; having recollections of past lives; developing focus, attention, and willpower; settling or calming ourselves emotionally; and developing mental, emotional, and energetic stability.

Here is the technique: Isolate yourself—completely alone—in a quiet room. Make sure you will be totally undisturbed. Select a blank wall with no or very minimal visual disturbances. Set an alarm clock (out of your sight) to alert you when three hours have gone by, and sit in a comfortable armchair facing this wall. With minimal light in the room (semidarkness), stare at the blank wall with your *eyes open* for three hours without moving your body—only the necessary relaxed breathing and minimum blinking. Try not to swallow and do not work with energy in this case. Do not give in to any desire to move until the alarm clock sounds.

If you (through your mentalsoma) want your physical body to stay completely still for three hours, will the body follow your command? Who controls your manifestations: your will (mentalsoma), your emotions (psychosoma), or your physical body impulses (soma)?[54]

Responsibility

The more a consciousness matures, the more the consciousness starts accepting and welcoming responsibilities.[55] As we grow, we realize that there are things we can do for others. However, thinking specifically about our own condition, a more mature perspective would help us realize that we are the only ones responsible for our own evolution.

Naturally, helpers will assist and guide us in our evolution, yet we are the ones who have to take the steps (actions). We can have the best information, the best instructors, the best helpers, and the best books, but nobody can actually grow for us, nobody can have an experience for us, and nobody can understand for us. The responsibility for our own growth and evolution is ours alone.

Many individuals still think that something or someone is going to come and save them. They do not realize that there is nothing to be saved from. We are in an evolutionary school, and it is just a matter of trying to take advantage of the opportunities. Less mature consciousnesses usually try to escape from the responsibilities that opportunities bring.

Evolutionary Criteria

As consciousnesses mature and start to better understand the concept of evolution, they start prioritizing it more. They start seeing life mainly as an activity that presents opportunities for us to evolve. Along these lines, they begin using evolutionary criteria when making decisions.

The use of evolutionary criteria in making decisions is not common for the majority of individuals. Yet we can always consider how to make any situation more evolutionary. At the same time, we can have more present in our mind the idea to look for ways to make any decision or action lead us to greater maturity.

All actions can be analyzed through this evolutionary lens. How do we spend our free time? Where does our money go? What are we most enthusiastic about? How much leisure time is enough for us to be productive and how much is too much? Which personal relationships deserve more time because they are evolutionary and which ones do not? To apply evolutionary criteria when making a decision is a sign of consciential maturity and evolutionary intelligence.

Helpers and mature consciousnesses realize that evolving is not a theoretical endeavor, but a practical one. It is in the manifestation of a person's energy, intentions, and actions where maturity is observed. Being too theoretical is counterproductive. In certain cases, individuals have so many theories in mind that basically anything is theoretically possible. Yet once we start having our own experiences, both intraphysical and extraphysical, all those theories collapse into one reality—and this one reality in many instances does not fit with any of the prior theories.

This condition is similar to the case of certain adolescents who do not understand why the world has to be the way it is, and why it could not be many other different ways. They are unable to realize, mainly because of their lack of experience, that it is not so much an issue of why it cannot be different (theoretical endeavor) but simply that the world *is already* presently structured in that way (reality). *In order to improve the world, we need to understand the current reality of how it is, and then **work in practice** to change that reality and make it better.*

Final Considerations

As we have more experiences, we realize that evolution is a relatively complex process. This is just a reflection of the fact that we are complex beings. As we mature and grow, our ideas also become more refined and complex.

As the consciousness matures, the evolutionary process becomes a welcomed one. We develop a sense of wanting to learn more and put more into practice. We feel a sense of accomplishment as we overcome challenges and grow.

In the next chapter, we will see in practice how many of these ideas work themselves into our daily life and life task (existential program). Thus, to end this chapter and try to place things in the proper perspective, we can paraphrase a quote from Dr. Waldo Vieira: *"If you think that trying to evolve with all this knowledge is difficult, try to evolve without it (with ignorance)."*[56]

Summary of Key Chapter Points

- Consciential maturity implies evolution and development of the consciousness, which is observed and studied with more ease extraphysically.

- Holomaturity is a synonym for consciential maturity, and it means the "whole" or "integral" maturity of the consciousness.

- Maturity of the consciousness when using the soma occurs when physical adulthood has been reached and when the consciousness understands its soma better and uses it in a healthy and productive manner.

- Maturity of the consciousness when using the energosoma is the condition in which the consciousness can perceive, understand, and control energy through its own will and at will (without any crutches). It also means being able to defend itself (de-intrusion) and process energies effectively.

- Maturity of the consciousness when using the psychosoma is the ability to recognize, understand, express, and deal well with emotions without allowing them to take control of our actions; in other words, emotional stability.

- Maturity of the consciousness when using the mentalsoma is expressed by the ability to understand and formulate ideas and thoughts and be able to put them into practice, and to make better decisions. It is also the condition of prioritizing the refined attributes of the mentalsoma due to the fact that this body is more permanent than the others.

- Evolutionary intelligence is both the understanding that physical life is a function of evolution and the ability to utilize—in practice—any resource we may have for our own evolution and that of others.

- The level of altruism, or assisting others, is a trait that shows the evolutionary level of the consciousness, since more evolved consciousnesses assist others more and consciousnesses who assist more tend to be more evolved. It implies having the capacity to help and the intention to assist, and being able to do so every time in a more sincere, selfless fashion.

- The consolation task, though assistantial and with faster effects, is more superficial and easier to perform than the clarification task and may lead to dependency.

- The clarification task requires the clarifier to possess some knowledge on the subject and the recipient to make an effort. The effects take longer; however, this type of assistance is more permanent and more effective in terms of evolution than consolation—thus more mature consciousnesses prefer clarification.

- Cosmoethics is the set of personal principles based on the individual's level of awareness and level of evolution. These principles hold true for the person wherever in the cosmos the consciousness is manifesting itself.

- The opposite of cosmoethics is self-corruption, which is when the consciousness *knows* what is the best thing to do but does not do it (incoherence).

- Universalism is the coherent (logical) behavior of the consciousness according to the broadest understanding of the universe. It is the philosophy of the more evolved consciousnesses and stands against prejudgments, discrimination, nationalism, racism, religiosity, and other kinds of dogma.

- Intraphysically, we are the product of three forces: (1) environmental influences, (2) genetics, and (3) *paragenetics*—our inheritance from previous existences. When paragenetics are stronger, we usually remain more in line with our reality of being a consciousness.

- More mature consciousnesses are neophilic, disperse themselves less, accept responsibility for their own evolution, and use evolutionary criteria in daily life to accelerate their evolution and that of others.

Chapter Notes

1. Minero, *Evolutionary*, 2006.

2. Minero, 1997.

3. Vieira, 1999, p. 56; Vieira, *What*, 1994, p. 16.

4. Minero, 2003, pp. 127–43.

5. Vieira, *700*, 1994, p. 707.

6. Vieira, 1999, p. 18.

7. Vieira, 2002, p. 797; and Almeida, 2005, p. 158.

8. Vieira, 2002, p. 368.

9. Vieira, *200*, 1997, p. 114.

10. Daou, 2005, pp. 22, 76.

11. Minero, *Evolutionary*, 2006; Razera, 1999, p. 38; and Razera, 2001, p. 149.

12. Vieira, *700*, 1994, pp. 500, 516, 524, 545, 578, 580, 677, 718; and Vieira, *Conscientiogram*, 1996, p. 144.

13. Daou, 2005, pp. 119–36.

14. Vieira, *Conscientiogram*, 1996, p. 144; and Vieira, *Homo Sapiens Pacificus*, 2007, p. 551.

15. Vieira, *Conscientiology*, 1997, p. 174.

16. Vieira, *Conscientiogram*, 1996, pp. 232–33; Vieira, *700*, 1994, p. 629; and also see Takimoto and Almeida, 2002, and Worrall, 1989, for a good idea of assistantial holothosenes.

17. Minero, *Evolutionary*, 2006.

18. Vieira, *Conscientiogram*, 1996, p. 93.

19. Vieira, *700*, 1994, pp. 410–11.

20. Vieira, *Conscientiogram*, 1996, p. 183; and Vieira, *700*, 1994, p. 455.

21. Vieira, 2002, p. 352; and Vieira, *Homo Sapiens Pacificus*, p. 179.

22. Alegretti, 2001.

23. Vieira, *700*, 1994, p. 465; and Minero, *Lucidocracy*, 2002, pp. 60–62.

24. Minero, 1997.

25. Alegretti, 2001; and Vieira, 1999, p. 49.

26. Alegretti, 2001.

27. Rocha, 1999, p. 103.

28. Vieira, 2000, pp. 270–71.

29. Vieira, 2002, p. 355.

30. Alegretti, 2001.

31. Rampa, 1995, pp. 134–35.

32. Balona, 2004, p. 61.

33. Alegretti, 2004, p. 143.

34. Minero, 1999.

35. Arakaki, 2005, p. 230.

36. Ibid., pp. 31–58.

37. Arakaki, 2005, pp. 90–95; and Minero, *Globalization*, 2006, p. 302.

38. Arakaki, 2005, pp. 105–18; and Guerra, 2001, p. 94.

39. Arakaki, 2005, pp. 211–15.

40. Vieira, *700*, 1994, p. 136.

41. Ibid.

42. Almeida, 2005, p. 122.

43. Arakaki, 2005, p. 194.

44. Vieira, *Projections*, 2007, p. 29.

45. See chapter 7 for an explanation on the penta practice.

46. Vieira, 1999, pp. 32–33.

47. Vicenzi, 2005, pp. 27–62.

48. Alegretti, 2004, p. 141.

49. Ibid., p. 143.

50. Vieira, *Homo Sapiens Pacificus*, 2007, p. 999.

51. Minero, *Evolutionary*, 2006.

52. Vicenzi, 2005, p. 64.

53. See *Open Exchange*, 2007–2010.

54. Bonassi, 1999, p. 255; and Azambuya, 2003, pp. 217–26.

55. Minero, *Evolutionary*, 2006.

56. Vieira, 1999, p. 11.

Planning a Life

With time, while having lucid projections, some of the most important and practical pieces of information projectors come across are the ones that pertain to the meaning of their physical life. Intraphysical consciousnesses evolve through many lives, and many have specific preplanned life tasks that should be executed during their physical lives. They prepare for these endeavors before being born. In this chapter we will discuss techniques that can be used to get information about our individual life task, as well as other relevant ideas in detail, thus giving the reader an overall view of the evolutionary process by means of units called physical lives.

Existential Seriation

Intraphysical consciousnesses are going through a series of existences during which they learn, evolve, and gain experience.[1] Using an analogy from previous chapters, the consciousness is like a child learning through successive school days[2]—the equivalent of physical lives. This concept of existential seriation has received the popular name of reincarnation, or successive lifetimes. As with the phenomenon of lucid projection, the idea of reincarnation has existed for many centuries, and countless cultures and groups have made reference to it.

Through extraphysical observation, the reality of existential seriation can be directly observed. As a result of this, the issue becomes one of trying to understand the reason that consciousnesses find themselves in these series of existences. In other words, in certain cases the following questions are asked: Why do we take on a physical body at all? Why is it that consciousnesses cannot evolve solely in the extraphysical dimensions? What are the advantages of the physical dimension over the extraphysical dimensions? In order to try to answer these questions, let us refer to the response of Wagner Alegretti:[3]

> We cannot say that we understand all of the reasons [for existential seriation] completely, yet we can already trace some initial ideas:
>
> Perhaps the main reason [for the seriation] is that the intraphysical dimension allows consciousnesses of very different evolutionary levels, when inside the body, to coexist in the same environment and to interrelate, as a means of catalyzing their maturation. Otherwise, in the extraphysical state, these consciousnesses would be dispersed throughout several different consciential dimensions that would allow, at maximum, short mutual visits. If a more lucid extraphysical consciousness goes to a denser dimension, it needs to be atten-

tive so as not to let itself be absorbed by the holothosenic pressure of that extra-physical dimension. This means that the somatic rebirth acts in a democratic way, propitiating a larger interaction and imposing the same basic "game rules" for everybody. Without this possibility, the less mature and lucid extraphysical consciousnesses would not have the possibility to coexist with healthier and more balanced consciousnesses, and this would decrease the possibilities and incentives for growth.

Another reason for the seriation is the fact that it places the consciousness on "rails." On the one hand, the somatic rebirth restricts the consciousness from going and coming and the freedom of its manifestation. On the other hand, for the same reasons, it specifies and directs in a more rigid and efficient way certain experiences, tasks, conditions, and opportunities. The old comparison with a school is inevitable here. What gets lost in freedom is won in efficiency and learning effectiveness.

The inertia of physical matter and of this biological body allows the consciousness to think before accomplishing something; to have a destructive impulse and to moderate it before acting; to have a strong emotion without losing the structure of its vehicle of manifestation; or even, to feel something towards somebody and hide these same feelings. In the extraphysical state, to generate a certain thosene is to act: everything is fast and public.

The loss of memory, natural for the absolute majority of intraphysical consciousnesses, represents a new chance or opportunity for the improvement of certain groupkarmic relationships, because it allows us to re-meet consciousnesses and to face situations again, without strong emotions or traumas that hinder the perfecting of energetic links. Due to the reduced consciential maturity in humanity, the complete recollection of the past would impair, for example, the overcoming of enmities and passions.

It is observed that intraphysical lives are units of development that allow the consciousness to gain experience. As the experience accumulates, the consciousness forms better points of reference and matures. The physical dimension provides this richness of experience in one single condition.

There are two basic types of consciousnesses in relation to existential seriation: the ones who are aware of it and working toward consciential evolution, and the ones who have not started to prioritize it and are, in most cases, as of yet unaware of it. By being aware, the first group can be involved in planning their own physical lives and apply their efforts more in line with the evolutionary mechanism (seriation) in which they find themselves, so as to have successful and productive evolutionary lives. They are already able to see the connection that one life has to the next, similar to links in a chain. For the second group, most of them are not aware of the seriation since they are unable to derive conclusions from this sequence; for them, a physical life is a series of isolated experiences with less connected meaning.

Existential Program

Success in any endeavor, big or small, is more likely when the endeavor is planned. A physical life, which is a complex project of several decades for most consciousnesses and which will affect many other consciousnesses, is likewise organized and planned for in advance. The most common synonyms for the term *existential program* are "life mission" or "life task." This planning takes place during the intermissive period of the consciousness, and its main objective is to help the consciousness evolve.

The *existential program* is the plan, the agenda, for organizing time during the intraphysical life of the consciousness; life task.[4]

When passing through the first deactivation and not the second one, the consciousness is and remains in a confused state most of the time. From this condition, the individual is unable to become aware of the process of existential seriation. Therefore, such a consciousness is directed through the process of existential seriation, for its own benefit, by helpers and other more lucid consciousnesses.[5] This process is similar to children in kindergarten who are taken to school by their parents without the children being able to appreciate the magnitude and benefit of the educational system.

The process of developing an existential program for the next physical life is much more complex for consciousnesses that pass through the second deactivation. Once the extraphysical consciousness discards the remnants of its energosoma, it is able to distance itself from the recently terminated physical existence. This condition allows the extraphysical consciousness greater awareness over its multidimensional existence. The consciousness is able to access its holomemory more directly, and is also able to remember (to different degrees) its previous lives and previous intermissive periods—including the last one.[6]

Upon remembering the last intermissive period, the consciousness is also able to recall its existential program for the just recently terminated physical existence. Naturally, the consciousness will compare the actual physical actions performed and their results with the stated program. Moreover, from this comparison, the consciousness will try to infer what the next steps should be in its evolution.

Since the existential program of one consciousness will affect the lives and existential programs of others, the actual planning of the next physical life is performed in groups. This planning effort is orchestrated by helpers plus the immediate group of consciousnesses who will undergo rebirth together. Individuals contribute more or less to the planning of their own existential program depending on their level of lucidity, awareness, and understanding of evolution.[7] The need to plan such efforts in a group arises due to the principle that *what one consciousness becomes naturally affects (limits or expands) what other consciousnesses can be.*

As an example, in a family of three siblings, whoever decides to be the oldest automatically decides that the other two cannot be the oldest brother or sister, thus limiting their options. This single initial element, for example, will play a big role in their interrelationships for the rest of their lives. Because of this, the decisions are made as a group in order to arrive at the best provisions that will offer the best evolutionary opportunities for all.

At the same time, with this example, this decision will expand other opportunities for all involved as well; for example, one of them will get to be the middle sibling and the other the youngest sibling, both roles providing for specific opportunities they would not have as the oldest sibling. When one door closes, another always opens. Thus, it is important to determine which doors are the ideal for the evolution of each individual.

The group that "sits down" to plan the existential program is not necessarily the blood-line family that will be born together. In most cases, the existential program entails important projects that will be carried out by consciousnesses who are not relatives. In these cases, it is these consciousnesses who will be there to plan the details beforehand. It is usually the consciousnesses who will work or evolve together that will be at this "meeting"—in other words, the evolutionary group.[8]

The consciousness that oversees the entire process is the *evolutiologist*. An evolutiologist is a highly evolved helper and a specialist in consciential evolution.[9] These consciousnesses are the helpers of the helpers and the administrators of the existential programs of the entire evolutionary group. Helpers may assist dozens, hundreds, or thousands of consciousnesses, while evolutiologists are helpers of hundreds of thousands and maybe even millions of consciousnesses. They are the ones that know in detail the evolutionary history of every single consciousness of the group, and can therefore recommend certain tasks and experiences that will accelerate the evolution of these consciousnesses.

Evolutiologists are the ones with the necessary lucidity to organize all the interconnectivity and intertwining of existential programs between all consciousnesses in the group. Likewise, it is the evolutiologist who knows what other evolutionary groups are trying to accomplish and how the existential projects of those groups will relate, help, fit, and interweave with the plans of this group.

With the help of these participants—the helpers, the evolutiologist, the respective evolutionary group, and us—the existential programs are designed and customized for each consciousness.[10] In order to evolve, consciousnesses will have opportunities during the upcoming life, through different projects, to work on their attributes and improve them. Because different consciousnesses have different levels of maturity and evolution, the existential programs are planned according to their own evolutionary level and for their specific condition. Thus, existential programs are completely personalized for each consciousness.[11]

Nothing is programmed for individual consciousnesses that cannot be accomplished by them. A programmed task beyond the capacity of an individual at that moment in their evolutionary history would be counterproductive (anti-cosmoethical), and therefore, it does not exist. Likewise, a life task that is too easy for a consciousness and would not take full advantage of physical time and opportunities, and would therefore be a waste of consciential resources (anti-cosmoethical), naturally does not exist either.

An *existential maxiprogram* is the life purpose that is larger in scope of tasks and corresponds to a consciousness that is more developed and evolved.[12] These plans usually involve assistantial tasks that reach a larger number of individuals and are also commonly more related to multidimensionality. An *existential miniprogram* is a smaller program in scope. Usually these programs entail more self-evolution and are more physical in nature,[13] benefiting perhaps us and our own very immediate evolutionary group.

All programs, whether mini or maxi, are equally challenging for consciousnesses because they involve expanding the limits of the *individual*. Notice that although these programs are not impossible to complete, they present a certain level of difficulty, since *truly expanding our capacities always requires effort.* Certain programmed tasks are so complex and broad in scope that they can take an individual several physical lives to complete.[14]

The personal attributes and overall capacities of the individual to be developed are the evolutionary criteria that enter into the planning of the existential program. Yet beyond this and depending on the multi-existential history of the individual, different conditions might determine what the priority for their next life is. In some instances, consciousnesses are part of a larger group trying to accomplish a specific task that may take several lives for the group to complete. In this case, the the group's activity takes priority over the individual's task. This is called the *activity* criterion.[15]

In other cases, individuals are trying to conclude an existential program that was designed to be executed over four lives, for example, but started only one or two lives ago. Or they did not complete the existential program from their previous life and need to finish learning some skills before moving on to "new" tasks. In both cases, it is the criteria of *complementarity* that may weigh more on the planning of their existential program. In addition to these criteria and many others, an element that usually is a big part of the existential program of most consciousnesses is *karma*.

Holokarma

Karma is the law of action and reaction, or cause and effect. In other words, any action (thought, word, deed) we perform has a consequence; whether this consequence is evolutionarily positive or negative will depend on the initial intention and action. The consequence, depending on the action, may take years or sometimes lives to occur, while in other cases it may be almost immediate.

Karma can be divided into three groups in order to understand it better:[16]

1. *Egokarma* is the law of cause and effect related to the consciousness itself; it is the effect of a consciousness's own decisions and actions upon itself. For

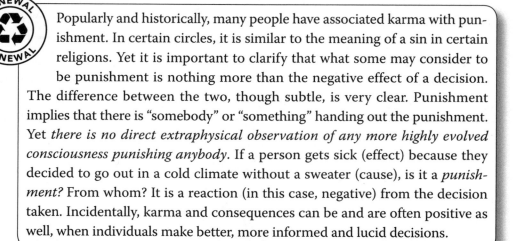

Popularly and historically, many people have associated karma with punishment. In certain circles, it is similar to the meaning of a sin in certain religions. Yet it is important to clarify that what some may consider to be punishment is nothing more than the negative effect of a decision. The difference between the two, though subtle, is very clear. Punishment implies that there is "somebody" or "something" handing out the punishment. Yet *there is no direct extraphysical observation of any more highly evolved consciousness punishing anybody.* If a person gets sick (effect) because they decided to go out in a cold climate without a sweater (cause), is it a *punishment?* From whom? It is a reaction (in this case, negative) from the decision taken. Incidentally, karma and consequences can be and are often positive as well, when individuals make better, more informed and lucid decisions.

example, a consciousness that spends a certain amount of time training its vibrational state will derive positive consequences from this. A consciousness that spends too much time in superfluous activities throughout its entire life and delays its evolution will have to learn some of the lessons that were meant for this life during the next life. The first and main repercussions of these actions will be for the consciousness itself.

2. *Groupkarma* refers to the law of cause and effect between the consciousness and the rest of its evolutionary group; i.e., relatives, colleagues, friends, helpers, blind guides, intruders, and others. The groupkarma of an individual can be quite large. It involves all consciousnesses with whom the individual has ever exchanged energy directly, with all the lives of the consciousness taken into account. The number of consciousnesses within the groupkarma can reach into the hundreds of thousands. The evolutiologist is the overseer of the groupkarma.

3. *Polykarma* refers to the interactions between the consciousness and the rest of humanity and extraphysical consciousnesses with whom the individual does not have direct energetic contact.

These categories of karma can be thought of as bank accounts, where the actions of the consciousness are transactions within these accounts. If the action is positive (evolutionarily productive), it is the equivalent of a deposit into this account. If the action is negative (evolutionarily unproductive), it is the equivalent of a debit. For example, individuals who apply their time and energy to their own evolutionary development will have a good balance in their egokarmic account. If individuals are good parents, they are placing a deposit in their groupkarmic account. In the opposite scenarios, the individuals would be making withdrawals or debits instead of deposits.

All consciousnesses have their egokarmic and groupkarmic accounts open and active. Basically, they are processing transactions in both accounts with every thosene manifested. However, most individuals have not opened their polykarmic account.

In order to affect the polykarmic account—the rest of humanity—individuals need to make decisions or take actions that will have repercussions beyond their family and immediate group. What activities have such a reach? An example of this is a doctor who develops a vaccine for an illness, and its application will affect consciousnesses in countries and continents to which the doctor may never travel. Other examples include an author who writes a book that is translated into several languages and is distributed across the globe, or the president of an influential country whose decisions have an effect on people in the far corners of the globe. As with the other karmic accounts, the quality of the action will dictate whether it is a credit or debit in the polykarmic account.

Each one of the accounts has a specific balance depending on the actions of the individual. Some individuals may have a positive balance in one account and a negative one in another. For example, certain individuals may be very capable on their own and have developed many individual skills (egokarma), yet their relationships with others are poorly developed (groupkarma). Within conscientiology, the "total balance" of all three accounts receives the name of *holokarma*.[17]

As was already stated, karma acts by itself, without the need for any regulating agent. With karma, there is no punishing or rewarding entity involved. Karma is intrinsic to the consciousness in the same way that gravity or electromagnetism is intrinsic to material objects. It seems to be a condition from which consciousnesses cannot escape and is an unavoidable and present condition in the reality in which we as consciousnesses exist. Therefore, in order to understand how this mechanism works in practice, let us explain—using a passage from a CDP course on existential programs and seriation that I developed—first the more extreme condition of *groupkarmic interprison* (being a prisoner within the elements of the groupkarma):

A consciousness in one of its lives decides to become involved with a more radical and negative group, such as a mafia, a group of terrorists, an assasination group, a radical and violent religious group, or any other group with destructive, anti-cosmoethical tendencies. This consciousness, as it spends time with its new group, starts to create close energetic links with the members of this group. They bond among themselves and become a group. As with any group, this physical group has its extraphysical companions that have affinities with them as well. In this case, these are blind guides and intruders that share the same ideas of the group overall and help them in their unethical objectives. The group is composed of both extraphysical and intraphysical consciousnesses, who exchange much energy.

This consciousness can stay with this group for several years or several lives. The greater the amount of time spent with the group, the greater the affinity that is created among them and the stronger the energetic links. Eventually, the time will come when the consciousness is going to want to leave this group. This can occur because the consciousness starts doubting whether the objectives of the group are actually as absolute and correct as the group believes them to be, or it can be because the consciousness sees another group or set of ideas that makes more sense, and starts refining its own perspectives (maturity), and so forth. However, the moment the consciousness tries to leave the group, it will find out that it is not so easy. The group will not want to let the consciousness leave, or rather, they will try to prevent it from leaving. What will the rest of this closed group—which is absolute and trying to convert/convince others about their ideas—think about this individual, who is one of their own yet now disagrees and is trying to leave them? They will think that this consciousness is a traitor. Furthermore, they will not want to lose their companion. Being that they are consciousnesses with less lucidity (intruders, or blind guides at best), they will feel betrayed and will create great pressure to stop this from happening (intrusion). Since they have a *strong energetic connection* with the individual, the door to him is open for them. All the connected intraphysical and extraphysical blind guides and intruders will go after the individual. As a result of having created strong energetic links (karmic) with them, the individual will be unable to physically and extraphysically distance him/herself from them, even in certain cases over several lifetimes.

As a consequence, this individual who no longer wants to be part of the group will go from being one of their own to now being one more of their victims. This consciousness will find itself having less freedom, in a condition of *group-karmic interprison*. Because of the nature of the group, the pressure they apply can be merciless in making the individual stay close to them, and they will do what they can to deprive the consciousness of its free will, trying to reverse the condition.

The individual will spend some time under the influence of his ex-friends and on the receiving end. In order for the consciousness to cut these links with those consciousnesses, and to regain its karmic and overall freedom, the consciousness will have to change the element that is binding them—any residual affinity in ideas, emotions, energy, or, in other words, the holothosene. Yet, consciousnesses do not change their holothosene, or their way of thinking, that quickly. Therefore, as a general rule, the more time the person spent with the group, the more time it will take to disconnect from them. We can think, as a general rule, that if the consciousness spent ten years with them, it will take about ten years to fully disconnect from them; if it was five lives, it will take about five lives to fully disconnect from them, and so forth.

Depending on the level of lucidity of the consciousness and the actions taken, the time frame may be much less or much more. It is during this period in which the individual is on the receiving end that outsiders will judge the condition as punishment for previous actions—even though it is not. An efficient and productive activity that can help individuals accelerate the condition of changing their holothosene is unbiased and lucid assistance. This is because this type of assistance is contrary to the holothosenes of most radical, negative, absolutistic groups.[18]

Karma acts as a function of an individual's decisions and reactions. The previous example relates to the condition of any extremist group. A similar situation occurs,[19] though to a *lesser degree*, with most individuals with regard to friends, colleagues, and, in many instances, family—especially when the family wants to control and direct the life of the individual.

In terms of groupkarma, we can analyze how different the relationships for individuals will be if, in a past life, the person was a nurse versus a soldier. Generally, nurses have many individuals who are grateful toward them, while the soldier may have created many enemies. If they both now happen to be businessmen, for example, as the former nurse finds his former patients, these individuals in general will have the tendency to want to go the extra mile to do business with the former nurse. The energetic and karmic links are clean and based on greater trust. The case for the former soldier, as he encounters his former victims, will be the opposite—even if he has the best product.

To understand the karmic concerns of the evolutiologist and helpers for the rebirth candidate, the following questions can be asked: What is my history with the rest of my group? Have I done something to any of them for which they still want some sort of payback? Who are the individuals who are trying to take my free will away from me and leave me with less karmic freedom? On the other hand, from which individuals do I still want some sort of payback? Which individuals do I want to apologize to me? To whom should I apologize still? Which of these and many other scenarios still exist within each one of our karmic realities?

Many of these types of karmic conditions still bind people from life to life. Because of these conditions, individuals preparing to undergo rebirth, before being fully free to evolve and grow, need to resolve some of these issues. Otherwise, some lesser evolved relations from the past will become a negative influence on the individual. Some of the main issues that may anchor individuals in their next life will be determined by how many of these types of situations are still *pending* and have not been reconciled.[20]

The healthy and mature way to deal with pending karmic issues is to identify them, face them, and proactively think of a cosmoethical solution for them. This cosmoethical solution will imply different actions for different situations.[21] In many instances, if individuals do not proactively look to settle these pending karmic issues, the situations will have a way of appearing in our lives at inopportune moments. This can create unfortunate situations that tend to lead to delays in our evolutionary progress.

For this reason, the evolutiologist—who has a more complete vision of overall evolutionary efficiency—may recommend to the individual in certain cases to spend one whole life settling pending karmic issues so that the person is able to evolve with greater freedom in the following life. Otherwise, the person may be evolutionarily "crippled" during their trajectory for several lifetimes, taking greater evolutionary efficiency away from the person. As mentioned previously, the time that is required to solve karmic issues varies from case to case, and depends on how "deeply" the person was involved in different situations. For some people, an entire life may not be needed to settle the karmic issues. For others, a full ten years may be needed, while in other cases ten lives may be required.

On the other hand, individuals can have strong karmic links with their helpers and more evolved consciousnesses. Since these more developed consciousnesses do not interfere with the free will of the consciousness, these relationships promote greater freedom, growth, and evolution. After all the holokarmic details have been incorporated into the existential program, certain extraphysical preparatory activities will be recommended to the consciousness. Several of these activities take the form of *intermissive courses*.

Intermissive Courses

During the intermissive period, certain courses are recommended for an individual consciousness—mainly by the evolutiologist—that will aid in the preparation for the upcoming life's existential program. The objective of these courses is to increase the probability that the consciousness will be successful in its physical endeavors and in accomplishing its existential program. They also help to prevent the consciousness from being "completely sedated by genetics or swallowed by environmental influences."[22]

Intermissive courses are educational courses that prepare consciousnesses to accomplish their existential program.[23]

Intermissive courses are similar in a sense to university classes, with students and instructors, study and research groups. They are offered by veteran helpers who are specialists in certain areas. The curriculum of available intermissive courses is quite extensive. They range from more phenomenological courses, such as projectability, existential seriation (the process of having a series of lives), paranormal phenomena, resomatics (the study of rebirth) and desomatics (the study of death), retrocognitions, and paraperceptions, to courses that deal more with the understanding of the consciousness and its evolution (conscientiology), including assistance to others, mature application of free will, neophilia, holomaturity, cosmoethics, universalism, evolution, holokarma, and deconditioning.

The courses the consciousness attends are determined by the specific existential program. For consciousnesses that have just recently started to pass through the second deactivation (a basic requirement for attending intermissive courses[24]), one of the first courses they attend is on existential seriation. The reason for this is that once consciousnesses are more aware extraphysically, they need to understand the rebirth/deactivation process in which they are embedded so that they can decide to apply their effort in agreement with this process and therefore accelerate their evolution.

In a lucid projection, a projector can have an OBE to an intermissive course and attend a class. We may not be able to attend the entire "term"—because we will have to return to the physical body—but we can "drop in" on some classes as a listener—or auditor.

During these courses, some groups of extraphysical students take occasional "field trips." These are educational trips that allow students to observe a process, phenomenon, or aspect of evolution as it occurs in the universe that will help them to better understand their studies.[25] There are field trips to other planets, to different dimensions, and even to the physical dimension to observe intraphysical consciousnesses in their attempts at leaving the body, among other things. In many instances these students are part of the team of consciousnesses who work with helpers in trying to assist individuals in their projections.

The reason that extraphysical consciousness are interested in observing the physical dimension is because they—though very lucid at this moment—will undergo rebirth yet again and will also be restricted by matter and the physical body, and this will cause them to forget some or most of the details of their intermissive experiences. As a consequence of this realization, many of them want to study and understand the strategies that current intraphysical consciousnesses are using to reconnect with their native extraphysical reality, mainly through lucid projections, classes, studies, and books on extraphysical reality (similar to what you are doing right now). There is an example of an OBE to an intermissive course later in this chapter.

During this preparatory period before rebirth, there are rehearsals of important physical events—similar to a theater rehearsal—that will be played out afterward in the intraphysical dimension. This strategy is performed for important, critical physical events that will have consequences for millions of intraphysical consciousnesses (i.e., meetings on disarmament between presidents, environmental summits, and others). These rehearsals are performed so there is a greater probability that during the "live show" nobody will "forget their lines," since so much is at stake and so many are to be affected by a particular decision.

Finally, after all the preparation, the consciousness has to undergo rebirth. The entire intermissive period can last from hours to centuries, depending on each specific case. It is estimated that most individuals presently spend, on average, the same amount of time in each intermissive period as they do in each physical life[26]—around sixty to eighty physical chronological Earth years.

Living

The consciousness is born and starts living its life according to its existential program. Even though individuals do not make many decisions while they are children, the condition they are in (family, country, culture) is not random, but is, more than likely, part of what they and their helpers decided on.

Life, as a general rule, can be divided into two parts with regard to the existential program: the first part is called the *preparatory phase*, and second part is the *executive phase*.[27] The consciousness is born into a condition that will allow the development of necessary skills to accomplish its existential program. Many intraphysical preparatory activities are designed more to help individuals *recall the necessary skills* for their life task than to actually learn new abilities.

Regarding karma, individuals are placed in a position in which they will have the opportunity to resolve karmic issues. Even though that is the intention, in many cases instead of resolving those issues, consciousnesses revert to old patterns of behavior and end up repeating the fights and arguments of previous lives. *Self-mimicry* is the name given to the unnecessary, unproductive repetition of the same type of human experiences and patterns from previous physical lives.[28] In many instances, individuals may have a retrocognition of several lives ago, and realize that back then they were more or less in the same situation, arguing and fighting with the same consciousnesses they are fighting with now, and being influenced by the same dogmas[29]—an experience that gives support to the fact that it takes dozens of lives to evolve considerably.

Existential Program Detours

Many consciousnesses make a detour from their intended existential program.[30] Self-mimicry is just one of the myriad ways in which this can occur.[31] It is important to study these detours so as to become aware of these situations and be better prepared to avoid them. An existential detour is a deviation from the preplanned existential evolutionary objective. Individuals can end up participating in activities that are not necessarily harmful to others or to themselves; however, they are not evolutionary activities. In this sense, detours are not necessarily negative, but they are a waste of energy and consciential resources.

As a result of making life decisions without evolutionary criteria in mind, many individuals opt to pursue non-evolutionary endeavors. In many instances, the person does not have the necessary life experience to discern what is best or most evolutionarily productive. This is the case, for example, with many teenage mothers and fathers. The ideal is to make life decisions based on evolutionary criteria, yet in many cases these decisions are impulsive and/or based on some momentary goal. The existential program is based on consciential evolution, so if the person uses other criteria when making decisions, chances are this may lead to existential detours.

In many cases, individuals enter into groups that are more evolutionarily restrictive; or have children, in many cases, not because they wanted to but because their spouse or family wanted them to—or perhaps by accident. Sometimes they pursue a specific career because they are more concerned about making money than developing themselves.[32] Likewise, trying to get away with applying the least amount of effort is counterproductive. In order for a consciousness to develop, the person needs to push their limits, and for this, significant effort and energy need to be applied.

Emotional issues are more difficult for individuals to overcome, and are what most often cause consciousnesses to make a detour. Choosing a life partner is commonly done based on emotional or purely aesthetic or sexual criteria (less stable and less mature) rather than for evolutionary reasons. *Passion* is an emotion that decreases the lucidity of the consciousness.

Ideally the consciousness will learn from experiencing existential detours, yet these detours do not *necessarily* have to occur. They are not a requirement for evolution, just as suffering is not a requirement for growth. Most individuals can look back on their lives and see activities, relationships, or endeavors that would have been better avoided and that were unnecessary. In many cases, individuals change certain behaviors only after they have hit rock bottom. Yet there is no need to reach such extremes. The consciousness, when more lucid, can decide to change direction before reaching such a saturation point.

In general, people do not know or even have an idea of what their existential program is, and this usually results in them not completing it. However, the most fundamental reason that individuals do not accomplish their existential program is not because of a lack of knowledge but because most people never *fully assume* (responsibility) that they even have an existential program to begin with.

Many individuals have heard of the idea of a life task (or mission). Some understand it well theoretically, though their actions are not in agreement with their theoretical understanding. In certain cases, individuals are already too settled in a relatively comfortable physical condition—in terms of money, career, and relationships—and have no interest in changing. Many may even think that the idea of an existential program is interesting, yet they do not actually do much about it.

The problems related to the existential program can be thought of in two ways. First, our life is a temporary stay in the physical dimension whose main objective is the evolution of the consciousness. Individuals will not carry any strictly physical achievement into the extraphysical dimension, or into the next life, for that matter. Regardless of what physical positions they held, how many titles they earned, how much money they had, or how many awards they won, if an individual did not evolve *conscientially*, then that life will be considered an evolutionary failure and the person will have to make up any unfinished work in the next life (see the section on extraphysical melancholy later in this chapter).

Second, since the existential program is designed to help individuals evolve, and it was planned by the individuals themselves while in a more lucid condition, along with helpers and an evolutiologist, would it not make sense to try to achieve it? People who truly *fully understand* the overall condition will apply their will to accomplish it; otherwise, they still do not actually "get it."

Some individuals justify not accomplishing their existential program by saying that they did not know what it was. Yet consciousnesses who begin by *assuming* they have one *actively look for it*, and eventually begin to arrive at and understand their pre-planned tasks. Therefore, the way to find out what the existential program entails is to begin looking for it. In most cases, the search to find the elements of the existential program is also part of the existential program itself.

SELF-RESEARCH
SELF-RESEARCH

Do you think that you have an existential program? If the answer is yes, then what have you done in practice to try to look for it and accomplish it? Think about the relative importance you have given to this. If this is the main goal of physical life, then how much energy have you applied in this endeavor? We can see here how physical commitments (survival, bills, and others) are sometimes like a steamroller that does not allow us to focus on more evolutionary endeavors. Also, in certain instances, individuals spend more energy, enthusiasm, resources (money), and time on activities that are less relevant. If we choose to renew our objectives and place our efforts in line with our existential program, then we'll gain evolutionary efficiency.

Existential Program Techniques

Notice that if we do not assume we have an existential program, then the following techniques will not be useful at all. Yet the person who "gets it" will try to use them. These techniques can aid individuals in recalling their existential program in order to accomplish it. Here is a description of the four more common techniques.

1. **Strong and weak traits formula.**[33] Unavoidably, the existential program deals with the evolution of our attributes. Furthermore, as a strategy, we should rely on our strong traits to help us develop and overcome our weak traits. In order to do this, we need to know with greater accuracy what the balance of our personal traits is. As an exercise to help you accomplish this, pick an hour of a day in which you are more relaxed and calm and have a clear mind—maybe on a Sunday. Lock yourself in a room with a desk and work with energy as if you are going to do a projective technique.

   Take a sheet of paper and divide it into two columns with the following headers: "Strong Traits" and "Weak Traits." Proceed to list and classify all traits that apply to you. Search within your memory for instances in life in which your reactions may have been positive or not. After making the most complete list possible, label it "Version 1" and store it in a safe place. This exercise should take at least thirty minutes.

   During the following week, you will naturally keep this list in mind. As you come across situations in daily life, you will notice several traits about yourself—

both positive and negative—that are missing from your list. After a week has gone by, return to the list and do a revision, creating "Version 2" and saving it again. Repeat this procedure every week to create "Version 3," "Version 4," and so on.

After completing version 4, you will have a list that fairly accurately represents the condition of your traits, as the list will have naturally matured. Interestingly enough, but quite logically, when you compare version 4 with version 1, you may realize that they are very different. This implies that who you thought you were in the first week is just a small reflection of who you actually are; and after week 4 the list will represent you more accurately and objectively.

Furthermore, it would be ideal if you could give a similar blank sheet with two columns labeled "Strong Traits" and Weak Traits" to other individuals who know you, for them to evaluate you as well. It is recommended to hand out these lists to individuals with whom you get along and to individuals with whom you do not. Individuals with whom you get along are many times somewhat biased—they do not want to say anything bad about you—and in some cases their lists may be less valuable. Yet individuals with whom you do not get along that well will tend to be more straightforward in their assessments.

Afterward, you can compare these lists with your version 4 (at least) or later. If all the other lists have a trait (whether weak or strong) that you do not have on your list, then you should add it—maybe with a question mark next to it, to observe it in the following days.

Sincerity is of the utmost importance with this technique—as with all consciential and personal endeavors. Having the strong-traits column full with only a few items in the weak-traits column may reflect insincerity and could be a sign of immaturity and vanity. However, having many weak traits and only a few strong ones may be a sign of escapism. The person may be trying to escape the responsibility that comes with having certain developed characteristics.[34] Neither of these two conditions is ideal, and they show a certain level of immaturity and self-corruption.

Certainly, more accurate knowledge of our traits will give us a lot of information about our existential program.

2. **Reciprocation formula.**[35] The idea in this technique is to evaluate the preparatory phase of our life. The skills, conditions, and experiences we underwent in our early years and during our adolescence were not by coincidence. These experiences were part of what we planned in order to develop the skills for the execution phase of the

existential program. It is especially important to pay attention to activities or skills developed that were rare for the condition or place in which we lived. Such rare skills or activities might include, for example, learning Japanese while being born in Latin America, or going to a school that develops a particular trait or skill—while our other friends or siblings went to a different type of school.

Pay attention to the games you liked to play as a child. Evaluate the impressions your parents made on you as you were growing up, especially those examples that were more unique or specific to them. Likewise, while you were a five-year-old, for example, try to remember whom you wanted to be when you grew up. Try to remove from this everything that pertains to influences from existential robotization, like a professional athlete, or an actress, or other professions that were more appealing because of social popularity. Upon removing these, you will arrive at a less contaminated memory of what you wanted to be. Notice that at this age, your intermissive period and intermissive courses were still fresh.

Pay close attention also to the hardships and relatively negative experiences that you lived through as you were growing up. They also have shaped you into what you are right now. Pay special attention to those experiences that left you with greater resiliency, a broader perspective, and more patience, organization, and discipline, among other positive qualities.

After this analysis, you can ask yourself: What effect have these skills had on my life? How have these skills contributed to my life? *Which skills have not contributed to my life as of yet?* The idea is not to pay back what was received but to apply it evolutionarily; what has been the reciprocation level in this context of the individual's skills for the existential program.

3. **Lucid projection.** The lucid projection can help in two ways. First, when lucidly projected, the person may be able to obtain information on their existential program from more developed consciousnesses, namely helpers and evolutiologists (even though it is more rare and difficult to be able to project to evolutiologists). They both can give many helpful indications.

However, the projector should not expect a helper or an evolutiologist to directly disclose the existential program in detail. The reason for this is because they do not want to turn the projector into a passive follower. They understand the importance of us being more self-sufficient and independent and want us to make our own decisions. However, these types of experiences are some of the most useful, because those consciousnesses will be helpful and informative and will especially give us information on perspectives that are new to us so as to assist us in accomplishing our existential program.

The second helpful part of this technique is to have a lucid projection to our *extraphysical origin,* or *hometown,* where we were during our intermissive period. Every consciousness has a specific extraphysical dimension where it spent the previous intermissive periods—our extraphysical home. Projecting to these locations has an effect similar to listening to an old song on the radio, since a lot of memories from that period are remembered.

While we are at our extraphysical origin, we will probably start remembering the plans, preparations, and concerns we had—regarding the upcoming life tasks—during the intermissive period. Thus, it will help us to effectively remember the major outlines of the existential program. This same type of effect may occur if the consciousness projects to an intermissive course.

4. **Technique of one more year of life.**[36] In life, we tend to have a routine that we settle into after a while. Certain elements of this routine may take up a significant amount of our time. Problems may arise when some of these elements do not have much significance for the existential program. Thus, we can question any element of our routine.

This technique can help us to determine what is important (priority) and what is not. Realistically imagine the following:

We wake up in the morning and, after feeling internal discomfort, decide to go to the hospital. The doctor, after completing many tests and consulting with several colleagues, tells us at the end of the day that we have a rare, incurable disease that is fatal. There is no known cure for this disease, and estimates are that a cure will not be found in this lifetime. The doctor also mentions that with medication the disease will not produce any pain. We will more than likely pass away, while sleeping, *one year* from now, and unfortunately there is nothing anyone can do about it.

(continued) We leave the clinic, and after the initial shock wears off, we realize that we have certain decisions to make now. How should this last year of our life be lived? Maybe there are activities that we have been involved in up to now that we knew were not ideal but were temporary until we found something else. Now there is no time to wait for something else to show up—it is time to look for it, to make it happen. We can question anything and everything about our life to try to plan this last year. Everything, everybody, and any aspect of our life is open to scrutiny and analysis. We realize that changing anything in life is up to us. For example:

- Sometimes individuals spend a lot of time in evolutionarily insignificant activities, like watching too much TV (leisure) or following old traditions. Therefore, will we choose to spend four hours a day (an average of two months of the next year) watching TV during our last year of life?

- In certain cases individuals have been working at a job they disliked from day one, yet they are already settled into it. If this is the case for us, will we continue doing something we do not like during this last year of life? There is a price that comes with making any change in life. Are we willing to put in the required effort to make a change for the better?

- Two people may be involved in a relationship in which the feelings that existed between them at the beginning went away a long time ago, or they happen to realize that maybe this relationship is not evolutionary for either of them. Yet they both are still with one another because it is what is expected or simply because it is comfortable. If this is the case for us, will we stay with this person for this last year?

- Certain other relationships may be in disarray. Thinking in karmic terms, and trying to solve issues now rather than wait for another (or another, or another ...) life, how many individuals do we need to contact so as to apologize to them? On the other hand, how many individuals do we need to forgive, even if they have not apologized to us?[37] People can stay in the condition of *Tom and Jerry* (the cat and mouse cartoon), with one doing something to the other in this life and the other returning the action in the other life, for many lifetimes. At some point, it is up to one of them to grow up and put a stop to it.

- Individuals may spend most of their week working to make money, to pay for material things that in essence are not that important for the evolution of the consciousness. Will you spend this last year working sixty hours a week?

Some individuals consider themselves "more spiritual" and they go to certain lectures from time to time and/or buy certain items that seem to help in different aspects. Yet now that there is less time, will we keep on going at this more leisurely pace? For certain individuals, it is almost as if they are "entertained" (butterfly seekers) by these endeavors; they do it more as a hobby (immaturity) than out of a real desire to grow internally. Usually, *"low-impact"* evolution is very superficial and does not yield productive results. In practice, how much time, effort, and dedication have you placed on these endeavors? How much will you place on them in this last year?

The basic questions that we want to ask ourselves are the following: What is it that we *really* want? What is *really* important in life? What is really a *priority?* The main things that consciousnesses take from one life to the next are their experiences and the lessons and knowledge gained from them.

Any and all of these techniques will provide a lot of information to individuals regarding their existential program.

Evolutionary Duo

One of the best strategies for remaining on course with and accomplishing the existential program is the forming of an evolutionary duo: two individuals who have consciential evolution as an objective.

An *evolutionary duo* is the union of two mature, lucid, intraphysical consciousnesses who have *affinities* for one another and who positively interact, having as an objective the planned potentialization of their evolutionary performances through a productive, integrated, constant, and multifaceted life together.[38]

The evolutionary duo is a lucid relationship between two individuals who want to prioritize the achievement of their existential programs. The partners share common goals and interests that are cosmoethical (lucid, sincere) and help each other develop and overcome their weak traits. They help each other with energetic work, de-intrusions, projectability, and the achievement of their *multidimensional self-awareness*. In this sense, one person can leave the body one night and help the other to leave the body, then they can switch roles the following night.

Also, as a result of the lucid condition between them, they mutually satisfy their somatic sexual desires and their psychosomatic need for affection. This condition is important because individuals who have their sexual and emotional needs fulfilled have a more efficient existential, energetic, and projective performance.[39] Many individuals planned to form an evolutionary duo in their existential program.

The condition of an evolutionary duo implies lucid love and a lack of possessiveness. Love is also the sincere respect shown toward the evolutionary level of any other consciousness. Individuals in an evolutionary duo prioritize consciential gestations (i.e., clarification task, written works, evolutionary projects) over biological gestations. Their interest is in consciential evolution through assistance to themselves and others.

Penta

Upon continuing our evolution during the course of our life, we can reach a stage whereby our understanding of assistance takes center stage. Thus, as we grow older, another activity that can help in accelerating our evolution is becoming a *professional* of multidimensional assistance by performing *penta*. Penta stands for **P**ersonal **E**nergetic **Ta**sk and is performed mainly by stable individuals in the second half of their life. In many instances, people prepare themselves for years so as to be ready to perform penta. This task is characterized mainly by the daily donation of energies at a prescheduled time.[40] In simple terms, the penta practitioner dedicates approximately one hour a day to send out energies to consciousnesses in need, mainly extraphysical consciousnesses.

Penta is performed through teamwork between the penta practitioner, who is (intraphysically speaking) alone in the room, and the extraphysical helpers.[41] The helpers who participate in this process are usually the helpers of the consciousnesses who are being assisted and the helpers of the penta practitioner. The penta practitioner and the main helper connecting to this practitioner develop a very close and intimate link. Even though the range of assistantial effects that penta provides is very broad, it mainly helps with de-intrusion.[42]

Such activity works precisely because of a good combination of lucidity and the availability of denser physical bioenergies for assistance. In other words, extraphysical helpers have the awareness of and information on the specific type of aid extraphysical consciousnesses need. The penta practitioner, on the other hand, has available the denser energies associated with the intraphysical body and the energosoma, which are necessary to provide assistance for disturbed (and dense) extraphysical consciousnesses. The penta practitioner is the one who basically "initiates the show." The extraphysical helpers are the ones who direct the flow, type, intensity, and content of the energies (thosenes) being transmitted by the penta practice. Likewise, they are the ones who decide to whom the assistance is directed.

Penta is a serious and effective way to assist other consciousnesses in their evolutionary process. As such, there are many requirements for someone to become a penta practitioner, since the person must have a reasonable knowledge of how bioenergy works, what multidimensional factors are involved, what the obligations of the penta practitioner are, and the evolutionary implications of starting such a practice. As basic requirements, in terms of energy, the person should already be able to install the vibrational state with relative proficiency, working with energy at will and not using any psychophysical crutches. Individuals should already have a minimum amount of universalism, meaning they have already overcome any type of religious, mystical, or traditionalistic philosophies, groups, absolute truths, and preconceived ideas regarding race, among others.

These individuals should also have a more stable and settled life in terms of health, finances, family, relationships, and so forth.[43] Likewise, the penta practitioners should already have a good level of evolutionary self-organization.[44] These conditions are reached by the interested individuals before starting penta so as to minimize possible obstacles (both intraphysical and extraphysical) that may work to undermine individuals once they have begun doing penta. *Likewise, penta is strongly not recommended to people who want to start because they are curious or have some other personal agenda or interest at hand.*

The responsibility of becoming a penta practitioner can be appreciated once we understand all the factors involved. The person who is interested in this type of multidimensional assistance must be prepared for it and be fully aware of all its implications, since a whole extraphysical mechanism is ignited once one decides to become a penta practitioner. Many extraphysical consciousnesses become involved in contributing to this assistantial task. Since many consciousnesses take part in this process, the penta practitioner must have a satisfactory level of holomaturity, including cosmoethics. Once someone makes the conscious decision to practice penta, they understand that *it will be performed every single day for the rest of the physical life*.[45]

Penta is the conscious and intentional desire to help others through the *organized and regulated* donation of energy. It is usually the case that once people start their penta sessions, though it is a responsibility, they actually look forward to their time performing penta. This occurs because of the level of connectivity and involvement with helpers, as well as the manifold expansion of the experiences of the practitioner. The practitioner also understands that penta will take priority over any other social commitment on any day. The fact that the practitioner makes such a commitment already shows the level of maturity and understanding and of how much the person prioritizes assistance.

In the beginning, penta practitioners are bound by the schedule and intraphysical conditions of their penta sessions.[46] With time and experience, the process does not depend so much on the place and time of penta, but rather on the practitioners themselves. The constant donation of energies helps them in the mastery of their energosoma, increasing energy potential and efficacy. In turn, this makes the penta practitioner more self-sufficient and stronger in terms of energetic self-defense.

It is interesting to add that the penta practice is not a replacement for our nontransferable, interpersonal karmic obligations (groupkarma). In other words, in some instances people use the remote donation of energies (which is not penta) in order to resolve interpersonal conflicts, sending positive energies with the best of intentions to those they are in disagreement with. As beneficial as the donation of positive energies may be, it is not enough to resolve several types of karmic issues with others. In certain cases, this is done in order to *escape* from having to deal with the other person face to face, since even though this may be very efficient and healthy, sometimes it can also be less comfortable. In many cases, in order to resolve serious personal disagreements, a healthy face-to-face conversation coupled with understanding and respect may be required. Notice that the penta practitioner becomes energetically stronger and does not shy away from a healthy, constructive discussion.

Penta must also not be mistaken for being just a simple donation of energies—even if this donation is done with the best of intentions and with an assistantial objective. What differentiates and potentializes penta is the disciplined, day-to-day "professionalism" and practice—without exception. Likewise, the commitment of the practitioners with their helpers is key, being that it is their *mentalsomatic approach and understanding* that will couple them more deeply with helpers.

Describing penta in detail goes beyond the scope of this book. For more information, please refer to other sources like the *Penta Manual* book.[47] Likewise, for a better understanding of greater levels of evolution that can be reached by the cosmoethical execution of penta, please refer to the CDP program from IAC. Furthermore, it is strongly recommended for individuals not to start penta impulsively, and to look for more information and understand well the practice and all the requirements before starting. Visit LearnOBEs.com for information on classes and more resources.

Helping with Awareness
Luis Minero
August, 18, 2007, Los Angeles, California

I was relaxing at home at night, watching TV before my penta session. I looked over to my penta room and saw the materialization of the energy of an extraphysical consciousness and knew that it was related to the upcoming penta, and that there was probably more assistance than usual to be done tonight. I decided not to wait any longer, and prepared myself for penta. The practice itself was more intense than usual. After it ended, I fell asleep and lost consciousness.

(continued) I regained awareness extraphysically and was inside a dark place, which looked like a narrow cave. There were other consciousnesses there, but I could not tell how many. I could not recognize anybody from the energy. I started to look for a place to get out of the cave, until I saw an opening. It seemed as if all the consciousnesses were waiting for me to lead them out.

I told them to follow me, that I had found an exit. I exited the cave, and realized that I was in the ruins of a city. Something had happened, and it seemed as if this disaster had occurred just recently. The roofs of all the houses were gone, and really only about half of the walls remained, and they were also broken.

There was a lot of smoke in the distance. I looked back and realized that none of the consciousnesses who were inside the cave with me had come out. One of my helpers was there, and he told me that we needed to bring those individuals out, and we needed to energize them. I got the first one and brought him to where the helper was, and he energized him. The extraphysical consciousness was disoriented and confused.

I kept on bringing them out, but there was something not quite right with the energy. It seemed as if the process was going to take more than what was initially expected. I understood that I not only had to bring them out but also needed to put more of my dense physical energy into the assistance. Since the energization had not been enough for the first two or three consciousnesses, we needed to reenergize them once more.

These consciousnesses were completely disoriented and unaware of their condition. I got the first one again and laid him on top of a rock, next to a broken wall. We started energizing all of these consciousnesses again. I kept bringing more people and understood that there were more extraphysical consciousnesses in the cave.

As we energized one of them, I focused on his face, eyes, and energy, and noticed that he was completely unaware of where he was. Though he was not passed out, he was still in shock because of whatever had happened there.

As I started to focus more of my dense energy on these tasks, I noticed I was starting to lose my awareness. I let it happen, knowing that my part from now on was going to be the donation of dense energy, and that the helpers would take care of the rest.

When I later woke up physically, I remembered what had happened, and thought about what could have happened in that place. I remembered that there had been a monster earthquake in Peru, magnitude 8.0, about three days earlier. It is hard to be certain of where I had actually been.

Yet as I thought about it, I realized the connections I have with that scenario. I have experienced many earthquakes in my life. I know well about buildings collapsing and people getting trapped inside and passing away. Also, though I'm not specifically from South America, I have a very strong association with the Hispanics of that region, being myself Hispanic.

Bringing these consciousnesses to be assisted one by one reminded me of an advanced course of assistance we organize at the International Academy of Consciousness (IAC).[48] One of the descriptions we give of this course is that it is a type of "group penta."

These consciousnesses had probably passed away during the earthquake—which happens in an instant in cases of collapsing buildings—and that is why they were completely disoriented and in shock. I realized also that some of the intense sensations from penta before the projection were already due to helpers bringing some extraphysical consciousnesses related to this event for assistance.

Existential Recycling and Inversion

As we start to better understand our existential program, we realize in many instances that we need to change certain attitudes and behaviors in order to develop more efficiently and to accomplish our program. As previously mentioned, individuals can take existential detours for many reasons. Once we have taken such a detour, we need to rectify it so as to return to our intended plan. This rectification is cosmoethical and is called *existential recycling*.

Existential recycling is the positive renovation of values and perspectives performed by the individual as the level of awareness expands so as to develop and evolve more efficiently; it is the rectification of certain commitments acquired in life that were not part of the individual's existential program.[49]

The beginning of existential recycling is in many instances the moment of true sincerity (cosmoethics) in which we "face ourselves in the mirror" and admit to ourselves that we have made certain mistakes and could have done better. Helpers can aid in this realization. The reason why and means through which people reach this moment are many.

In certain cases, the decision to recycle oneself can arise due to an internal dissatisfaction a person has with their own life (see the section on intraphysical melancholy later in this chapter). At other times, it can come after the person reaches a critical moment or experiences a major event, such as a car accident, a death in the family, the loss of a job, the breakup of a relationship, the "nothing seems to be working" feeling, constant intrusion, a saturation point (hitting rock bottom), and others. Many of these situations actually occur because as individuals go off on tangents with regard to their planned existential trajectory, they become involved with other activities, intraphysical and extraphysical consciousnesses (for example, blind guides), and energies that were not ideal for their existential program.

Helpers take advantage of these critical moments to try to make individuals more aware of other options and to help them to recycle themselves. It is observed that while things are going well intraphysically—even though these activities may not have much to do with the life task—individuals tend to *get too comfortable* and do not want to change. In this last case, even though everything is "going well," the person often also feels frustrated. To evolve, individuals need to keep refining themselves through constant positive change, in a constant state of recycling.

Existential recycling mainly implies healthy *internal* changes in evolutionary values and perspectives. In certain cases these internal changes will naturally trigger greater or lesser *external* changes.[50]

In order to undergo a cosmoethical existential recycling, individuals need to have energy. They will need it in order to face the *counterflow* that any change brings about (see chapter 2). The world is already used to us being a certain way, though people commonly do not see us as who we really are. As a result, when we change ourselves to better represent our own level of being, non-lucid extraphysical consciousnesses, relatives, colleagues, and others will often complain—in some cases more, in other cases less. We need to stand energetically firm and be evolutionarily courageous[51] so as to not to yield to the more generally anti-evolutionary holothosenic pressure of the world.

Existential inversion is another evolutionary strategy and is the condition that individuals can opt for when they have not taken a detour from their existential program—usually when they are still young.

> *Existential inversion* is the technical execution of physical life according to the existential program without any existential detours. Existential inverters often act according to values that are the opposite of those held by most of intraphysical society.[52]

The existential inverter, a rare condition, is a person who keeps their evolution and existential program as the basis for their major decisions. These are individuals who have not acquired any commitments to any institution, activity, or person that were not contemplated in their existential program. This shows that these individuals tend to better withstand social pressures (avoiding existential robotization) and possess greater holomaturity.

Existential inverters generally present characteristics such as self-learning, valuation of mentalsomatic activities, altruism, efficient communicability, and a good degree of self-organization and psychism, as well as beyond-average cosmoethics and universalism.[53] Existential inverters revert, or "invert," most ordinary and common popular values, as they usually act in ways that go against the common flow of society. Most societies follow nationalistic ideas and religions and value the lifestyle of working to make money, marrying, and having children. It is not a common practice in most societies to question their own values, and thus many societies have difficulty seeing beyond their own narrow parameters. Naturally, inverters have to worry about many typical activities (working to survive and so forth), yet they are also working toward achieving their existential program, and see all of those activities as a function of it.[54] Thus, their holothosene is different and in many cases the opposite (inverse) of the overall intention of most societies.[55]

Normally, it is seen that people who value and perform assistantial work tend to be older in age when they do it. The inverter reverses this condition and decides not to wait until later in life to assist others. The inverter starts trying to assist others from an early age (inversion). They will constantly refine themselves during their life—undergoing countless and constant renewals.

If you cannot opt for the condition of existential inversion because you have already needed to undergo a consciential recycling, or have already rectified some of your values in this life (or still need to rectify some values), then a good technique to evolve more efficiently and be able to opt for inversion in your next life is the following.

Looking back on your life, you will see many decisions that could have been made more lucidly. Some decisions may have been made impulsively, in some cases with little experience and few criteria; in other cases, the decisions made were blatant self-corruptions (where you knew better but did not do better). Thus, make a list of all the activities, relationships, and decisions that you *would not like to repeat* in your next life. Write down what would have been the better and more evolutionarily productive choice. Try to do this with as much detail as possible.

This exercise will help you plan your next life. You will be training yourself to understand consciential issues and evolutionary decisions while in the physical body and through the physical brain. Thus, in the next life you will be aware of these issues earlier because of this training. The idea is to remember these issues while in the body in the next life and not just during the intermissive period.

Visit to a Training Center for Inverters Awaiting Rebirth
Laura Sánchez (2004)[56]
September 19, 2003, Barcelona, Spain

During the period in which this projection took place, I had been questioning myself regarding the executive phase of my existential program; I found myself thinking about how good it would feel to access information from my intermissive course. On that particular night, I went to bed physically tired, falling asleep almost immediately. I cannot remember having worked with my energy before falling asleep.

I recovered lucidity in the extraphysical dimension and discovered I was by my partner's side. I felt that I was in a big city, albeit one considerably different from those we know in the intraphysical dimension. The city appeared flat, with no buildings in view. It seemed we were quite some distance from planet Earth. A diaphanous white luminosity fascinated me. A multitude of future inverters were studying at wide, white tables. My partner and I were on a kind of well-tended lawn, suspended in air above though fairly close to the ground, our legs crossed. We chatted peacefully as though the place was familiar to us. The trip did not feel like a unique visit, but more like a return to a well-known location. The atmosphere was of intense and serious study by these thousands of future inverters for their next existential programs.

The candidates for existential inversion displayed young psychosomas, appearing as teenagers. They sat at tables on an esplanade adjacent to the lawn where we sat cross-legged. Study was conducted in silence, in an introspective environment, without chatter among themselves. From time to time those studying would consult with extraphysical consciousnesses who appeared to be directing the work. These extraphysical consciousnesses did nothing to interfere but rather seemed to be present simply in case they could be of assistance to the inverters, which apparently was unnecessary most of the time.

The scene was interrupted abruptly by events that captured my complete attention; a group of extraphysical consciousnesses, appearing as children ranging in age from six to fifteen, ran out of what seemed to be a depression or hollow, holding their arms in the air as if in despair and asking for help. They were not in the same environment, and it seemed that I was experiencing some sort of clairvoyance. At that moment, my partner spoke: "Are you seeing these images? They are for you," he said. These phrases were transmitted telepathically, and I realized we both had a good level of lucidity during this experience.

(continued) I could not understand what was happening; the children were inside a sort of hollow or depression while the surrounding environment was clearly positive, mentalsomatic, and tranquil. Then the children began walking, no longer seeming desperate. I saw no helpers, but my intuition told me the children had been joined by some caretaker-helpers. I realized I was no longer making these observations through clairvoyance, but rather that these children had joined us in the same environment. The children walked in formation, tidy and neatly dressed, carrying food in their hands, which appeared to be morphothosenes, created for them by the caretaker-helpers. The children observed the tables where the inverters were working, but they seemed unable to see or perceive their presence or the place where they actually were. I realized the children were being assisted by the surrounding environment and the presence of the group of helpers. It was then that the basis for the whole situation suddenly became apparent.

The children were youngsters who had recently died due to a detour in their existential program, a detour sufficiently serious that other consciousnesses may have been endangered.

Following their death, the children were moved to an environment where the example of the students of inversion, in serious preparation themselves, gave the children the opportunity to begin their own preparations for their new existential programs. It seemed that the majority could not even perceive or see the location where we were gathered because of their lack of lucidity.

The helpers had encapsulated the children in the hollow, periodically taking them for walks until eventually they would "awaken" and begin the preparation for their existential programs. In this case, having them in this kind of "enclosure" was the lesser of two evils; until such time as each could awaken to the dimension they inhabited, they required patient nursing and care. Over there, time was no longer time, but an opportunity for reaction and change.

At the same moment, I acquired a deeper understanding of the importance of our existential programs. The work of the extraphysical helpers was to present us with renewed opportunities to study this theme, and to help ensure by all possible means that our existential programs will be carried out successfully.

I could also understand how an inverter, despite his or her high-level intermissive course and the guidance of an evolutionary orienter (evolutiologist), was nevertheless far from guaranteed existential completism, or even a lucid death with direct access to a new intermissive course.

As I grasped all this information, recognizing that I was projected with lucidity, I understood that the time had come for me to depart. I held my partner by the hand and we left, flying away from that environment.

My flight was slower than that of my partner; I found myself alone. A girl appeared ahead of me, lying on her back and flying at great speed. I decided to fly in the same position, which sped up my flight, although I was afraid of bumping into someone, as my eyesight was restricted. There was plenty of traffic. Many consciousnesses were flying toward a specific place, and this did not surprise me, as it felt as if I had already flown there many times along this "extraphysical highway."

My speed increased and I decided to return to the physical body, trying my best to feel re-coincidence with the soma and looking at my partner lying on the bed. At that instant I felt very happy about the level of lucidity I was experiencing.

I traveled down through very narrow, dark tunnels at high speed. This did not seem to be the sort of tunnel effect common to a near-death experience; I was coming down vertically, something I interpreted as a return to the physical dimension.

To my surprise, I found myself not in the physical body but in an environment that looked unfamiliar to me at first glance. A very lucid retrocognition helped me understand that, in spite of all the information gained from our intermissive course, we often continue in much the same fashion, doing the same things we have done in past lives—an unnecessary self-mimicry.

I returned to the body with lucidity and, upon awakening, remembered the entirety of these events. My partner had no recollection—but for me there was no doubt. This projective experience afforded me the opportunity to reflect on many consciential issues, especially the importance of the existential program, the intermissive course, and all the work, patience, and care the helpers show us.

End Result

As the life of a consciousness advances, two results are possible: either the consciousness is satisfied with the execution of its existential program or it is not. This condition is subjective, yet for the individual person, it is usually very clear. And as the consciousness passes through the second deactivation, it will become even clearer and more obvious what the end result of that life was.

Intraphysical and Extraphysical Melancholy

While still an intraphysical consciousness, we may feel an inner sensation of dissatisfaction that may indicate to us how the execution and direction of this physical life is going. This sensation is called *intraphysical melancholy,* which is the condition where the person feels unsatisfied with themselves and their life due to poor execution of their existential program.[57] Certain cases of mid-life crises are a result of an intraphysical melancholy, a lack of meaning that the individual feels in life.

In some cases, individuals find themselves in a good physical situation: they have a good family, a decent job, financial stability, and friends. Though everything on the surface seems to be fine, they still feel emptiness, a void inside, and they cannot quite identify why. In many cases they feel this emptiness because they have detoured from the path of their existential program. Commonly, they have done everything that society has asked of them (existential robotization), yet they have not executed the commitments they have to themselves—in the first place—and also to their evolutionary group and their helpers.

Depending on the person's age, they may still have a lot of time to accomplish most or at least part of those commitments. In society, when people reach sixty or seventy years of age, they usually have to retire. The person often is seen as an unproductive being by the established social system. Yet these individuals may live another ten, twenty, or more years in this physical life, which is ample time to solve karmic issues and accomplish many other tasks. This depends on the individual.

If people are conditioned by the physical idea that they are too old and should not or cannot do much more, then they will certainly not produce much more. The physical body certainly ages, but the consciousness does not—there is never retirement of the consciousness.[58] Therefore, acting old is a state of mind. Intraphysical melancholy can work as an evolutionary catalyst, promoting existential recycling.[59]

In certain senior citizens, the condition of intraphysical melancholy can be clearly seen—especially in specific cases of people in their seventies or older. It is seen in people who complain about everything and are perpetually dissatisfied. They remember episodes from their life with obvious disappointment and tell (sometimes the same) sad stories repeatedly. The energy emanating from such a person is clearly negative and manifests a strong sense of failure.

When the individual passes through the first deactivation, the condition of disappointment, depending on its strength, can hinder the person from passing through the second deactivation. Unfortunately for the extraphysical consciousness in this condition, when it regains some lucidity, it will be able to see clearly the unproductive failure of the just-terminated human life. This is the condition of *extraphysical melancholy*,[60] which is worse than intraphysical melancholy because now there really are no more opportunities for the execution of the existential program for that life.

As previously mentioned, no one punishes anyone extraphysically. The consciousness in this situation is not feeling this because it is afraid of some sort of reprimand from someone. The condition is more personal and internal, which makes it worse. The extraphysical consciousness realizes and understands on its own that it simply did not do what it was meant to do. It realizes that many times when opportunities were there during the life, when doors were open and the right people appeared at the right time, it simply did not take advantage of them. The consciousness may have accomplished only 20 percent of its existential program.

In many instances, individuals realize that they did not do anything harmful to others during their life; however, the life that just ended was something they had already repeated the previous two lives, for example. Thus, there was little evolutionary gain. During the physical life, individuals can justify their behavior with many rationalizations and ideas, fooling everybody in the physical world; but extraphysically, where everybody knows everyone else's thosenes, this condition of melancholy is inescapable. The extraphysical consciousness feels and knows that it is solely responsible for its own evolution.

When encountering its old evolutionary friends—helpers, evolutiologist, and other extraphysical consciousnesses—the consciousness has obvious strong feelings of embarrassment and failure. It knows that its failure has in some fashion already affected the existential programs of others in the evolutionary group who were counting on its contributions in some way. Unfortunately, a high percentage of consciousnesses fail at accomplishing their existential program.[61] One of the chief intentions of understanding the consciousness better (conscientiology), of studying extraphysical reality and raising awareness, is to help consciousnesses avoid this negative condition of melancholy.

Intraphysical and Extraphysical Euphoria

On the other hand, there is the condition of intraphysical consciousnesses who are accomplishing their existential program. These individuals manifest an obvious *intraphysical euphoria.* These people smile more, are more patient, and are less concerned with small, unimportant details.

This condition can also be more clearly observed in senior citizens (especially those over seventy years of age). Individuals in this condition include the happy grandfather or grandmother who is "all smiles," with much patience and satisfaction with themselves and life in general. This condition is further enhanced once we reach the condition of *existential completism,*[62] which occurs when we accomplish our existential program—whether a maxiprogram or miniprogram—through effort, dedication, perseverance, and so forth.

In the case of an existential miniprogram, individuals may not be fully conscious of the fact that they have completed it, though they will manifest sensations of inner satisfaction. Examples of individuals completing miniprograms are many and may include eminent surgeons who have assisted many others through their skills; parents who raised all their children well and settled many groupkarmic issues; writers who have published books that have had positive effects on the lives of others; and individuals who do charity work and have already achieved all the goals they set out to accomplish.[63]

After reaching the condition of existential completism and passing through the first and second deactivations, we will feel *extraphysical euphoria.*[64] The following paragraph, taken from a CDP course, gives an example of this sensation.

Imagine that during physical life, we receive a task that is extremely hard and important and its due date is in one month. We realize that it will not be easy to complete. Yet there is no one else to pass it on to, and it is up to us to do it. We resolve to dive in and try to do our best. We start applying ourselves the best we can; some nights go by without much sleep. At the halfway point, it seems we will not finish the task. We realize that the due date is getting closer, and with concern we try to redouble our efforts. Finally, on the last day, and on time, we finish it; we present it and everything is fine. How do we feel after this? Relieved … happy … euphoric … confident … This is the sensation of accomplishing a task of one month. Life is around eighty years of twelve months each. Therefore, to get an idea of extraphysical euphoria, multiply the sensation felt after accomplishing that difficult task of one month by 960—literally almost a thousand times greater.[65]

The best condition is when we are aware of the entire mechanism of the existential program throughout our life and understand it fully. We realize that we are doing a *self-relay* with our intraphysical lives, in which the accomplishments of one life are passed on to the next—the same way runners in a relay race pass on a baton.[66]

Existential Moratorium

A moratorium is an extension of time. An *existential moratorium* is an extension of the lifetime of an individual.[67] This occurs because it is advantageous in certain cases for some people to live longer—days, months, or years. The moratorium can occur for two reasons. First, it can occur because we are *not* accomplishing our existential program (condition of evolutionary deficit), and it is important for us to accomplish at least a specific aspect of it in this life. This condition is called *existential mini-moratorium*.[68] Second, it can occur because we have already reached the condition of existential completism, and we can take advantage of the current conditions to evolve even further than what was planned (condition of surplus). This condition is called *existential maxi-moratorium*.[69]

The mini-moratorium occurs only in certain situations for some individuals; in other words, not everybody who is off course regarding their existential program receives one. This can be due to karmic conditions. In certain instances individuals may be surrounded by several others with whom they have karmic issues. The other people in the group are accomplishing their existential programs, and in the next life more than likely this group will move on to something else and will be geographically spread out. The same set of individuals will not undergo rebirth together. In this case, if the person in question does not solve his or her karmic issues now, then the individual may have to spend several more lives with more things pending, sort of "following" each member of the group (which has now dispersed) in order to solve something that currently may be solved in only a few years' time.

In other cases, a group of consciousnesses have been working to achieve something and they are accomplishing it. Yet one of the consciousnesses in the group has not kept up with the pace of the rest of the group. For this reason, in the next life, the group will move on to something else, but the slower-moving individual will not be able to. This consciousness will have to join a different group that is starting to deal with the task the first group is finishing. This would unequivocally represent a definite setback for the individual, and at the same time the person will have to spend some time (lives) with the other group until they can accomplish the task. This condition of mini-moratorium is very similar to when a child has to repeat a school year as a result of failing grades. In this case as well, it would be best if before the "final exam," before life ends, individuals can have some extra time to "study" so as to continue with their group.

The evolutiologist is the consciousness that decides whether the case merits an existential moratorium of either type. Certain cases of near-death experiences are utilized by helpers and evolutiologists as a means of shaking individuals out of their existential malady. It has been observed that after most near-death experiences, people return with greater lucidity, intensity, and effort. The evolutiologist is the consciousness that more clearly understands how critical it is for individuals to accomplish certain tasks in their current life. The intention is to try to make people rethink their actions and the course of their life.

The second type, the maxi-moratorium, occurs when the condition of the individual by the end of his or her life is such that said person and others can profit even further from a longer stay. This second type is usually given by the evolutiologist during an OBE, as the helpers and evolutiologist congratulate the projector. In many cases, the option of accepting the moratorium is the individual's own choice to make: the person can choose to pass through the deactivations (deaths) now or to spend some more time as an intraphysical consciousness.

There are advantages and disadvantages to both positions. On one hand, when consciousnesses choose to pass through the deactivations, they guarantee their existential completism (since, for example, in some instances there may be a small possibility of rehashing a karmic wound if they come back). Also, individuals in this situation will have the opportunity to take new intermissive courses and generally prepare themselves better for the tasks to come (next life). On the other hand, if they decide to stay, they can execute additional tasks now without having to pass through the intraphysical restriction of birth again before doing so. In many instances, individuals are still at a relatively good level of health and economic stability and may still have ten or more years ahead, which can be very productive.

Existential moratoriums can last from a few months to a few decades; in some rare cases individuals may receive a second, third, or even more moratoriums. In addition, in some instances of moratoriums, there is an energetic and physiological regeneration performed by helpers so as to allow the body (and the energosoma) of the person to complete the task.[70] In these cases the helpers infuse energy into the physical body of the person to help them live longer.

Critical Life

Just as a child attending school has some days that are more critical—when there is a test, for example—consciousnesses also have physical lives that are more critical. If children do well or not on a test day, this will have (positive or negative) repercussions that will be felt beyond that day, and the same is true of physical lives.[71] It can be observed that for most individuals, this current life is more critical. There are two main things that account for this: the level and quantity of information available and the demographic explosion.

As a result of the *level of information* available in this day and age, individuals usually have easy access to information that can profoundly help them to complete their existential program.[72] In past centuries, this was not the case. During a life in the eleventh century, when resources were scarce, learning to read was still extremely rare. Therefore, if a priest in the next town, who was going to teach us to read, died in the plague, then we might have gone an entire life without this skill. The problem is that in some instances that priest was the only available person capable of teaching us how to read. As a result of such a misfortune, we would have finished our life with some gaps in our existential program. However, in an instance like this, it would not have been our fault and there would not have been anything we could have done about it.

However, nowadays the information has accumulated to such a degree that individuals usually know where to get the skills and/or information to accomplish what they want. Consequently, this condition brings us greater responsibility, since fewer excuses (self-corruptions) can be made if existential completion is not achieved.

The *demographic explosion* is such that individuals today can interact with as many people in one week as they did in an entire lifetime in the Middle Ages.[73] Because of this, the karmic accounts have "more transactions." The person can affect many more consciousnesses either positively or negatively on a daily basis, not to mention after an entire lifetime.

Therefore, this life for most individuals is the equivalent of a dozen or more lives in the Middle Ages and earlier. The person can accomplish much more and affect many more consciousnesses. If the intraphysical consciousness has a good or bad performance, then this effect is multiplied and amplified.

Finishing the Cycle

Finally, after undergoing the first and second deactivations and becoming an extra-physical consciousness again, more lucid individuals are back concerning themselves with planning their next existence. The consciousness remains in these cycles of existential seriation until it has evolved enough to undergo the *third deactivation* for the first and last time, and becomes a free consciousness. This process certainly takes many, many lives. Yet it can be accelerated or delayed by the consciousness itself, depending on how much its evolution is prioritized.

Let us propose an idea that deserves more research. Helpers, evolutiologists, and more evolved consciousnesses usually project energies of calmness, control, and serenity; and there is a satisfaction, confidence, and unshakable innate happiness to them. Could it be that this holothosene they emanate is the result of them having reached the condition of existential completism (intraphysical and extraphysical euphoria) time and time again?

Conclusions

Based on all the observations and evidence accumulated thus far, it is clear that we as consciousnesses are not able to simply stop evolving. All evidence points to the fact that consciousnesses cannot be destroyed and do not stop their evolution. Consciential evolution takes place inherently with the accumulation of knowledge derived from experiences inside and outside the physical body; and these experiences compel us to make better decisions, to learn and grow all the time. The consciousness continues with the cycle of rebirths and deactivations until they have completed this cycle in its totality and fulfilled their full evolutionary potential—as in the case of the free consciousnesses.

As was mentioned previously, the best evolutionary strategy is to be practical in terms of our existential program. When observing helpers and more evolved consciousnesses, we are able to recognize that they focus on the task at hand. In our case, this would be our existential program, this current life in a multidimensional perspective and reality. They give very little priority to speculations and philosophical endeavors.

Now, at the end of this introductory volume, we realize that visiting extraphysical realities and learning from more evolved consciousnesses is within the grasp of any self-motivated and interested individual. Along the same line of reasoning, evolution is an endeavor that depends strictly on us. As our experiences increase, we realize that all of those realities help us grow. They exist even if we do not fully understand them, and as we personally discover them, they continually challenge us to dig deeper into the nature of the consciousness itself, as we continue to evolve and help others evolve as well. The best of energy to all of you in your evolutionary endeavors.

Summary of Key Chapter Points

- Existential seriation is the series of physical lives, or the process of successive lives, with consciential evolution as its goal.

- The existential program is the life task, the organizational plan for time during the intraphysical life of the consciousness; it is life's main objective.

- Individuals plan their existential program during intermissive periods when they are more lucid, together with helpers and the evolutiologist.

- Existential programs are unique and personalized and take into account everything about the consciousness: their strong and weak traits, their evolutionary group's objective, their performance in previous lives, and their holokarma.

- Karma is the law of action and reaction, of cause and effect, and can be divided into three groups: (1) egokarma, pertaining individually to the person; (2) groupkarma, pertaining to the relations with other consciousnesses; and (3) polykarma, pertaining to the interactions with the rest of humanity and extraphysical consciousnesses.

- Intermissive courses are preliminary educational courses that prepare the consciousness for accomplishing its existential program. These courses have as a prerequisite the second deactivation, and as projectors, we can attend these courses during our physical lives.

- Many individuals take a detour from their existential program because they make decisions without taking into account evolutionary criteria—which are the basis of their existential program.

- To find out information about our existential program, we can use certain techniques; for example, the strong and weak traits formula, the personal reciprocation formula, the lucid projection, and the technique of one more year of life.

- Forming an evolutionary duo can help to catalyze our evolution.

- Penta (**P**ersonal **En**ergetic **Ta**sk) is an assistantial practice that requires discipline and the prioritization of assistance.

- Existential recycling is the renovation of values and priorities according to consciential evolution and the existential program of the individual.

- Existential inversion is the technical execution of physical life according to the existential program without any existential detours, and usually goes in general counterflow with society as a whole.

- Existential melancholy is the internal dissatisfaction individuals manifest when not accomplishing their existential program. It can be intraphysical and/or extraphysical (after biological death).

- Existential euphoria is the joyous condition individuals manifest when reaching the condition of existential completism. It can be intraphysical (nearing the end of life) and/or extraphysical (after biological death).

- An existential moratorium is an extension of a lifetime given to a person (1) because of evolutionary deficiency reasons (mini-moratorium) or (2) because of an evolutionary surplus (maxi-moratorium).

- The current life is a critical life for most people because of the greater amount of information accumulated in modern times and because of the high number of karmic and personal interactions.

Chapter Notes

1. Kardec, 1976, p. 117; Vieira, *700*, 1994, p. 596.
2. Stack, 1988, p. 29.
3. Alegretti, 2004, pp. 67–68.
4. Vieira, *700*, 1994, p. 612.
5. Alegretti, 2004, pp. 74–75.
6. Ibid., p. 69.
7. Ibid., p. 74.
8. Vieira, 1999, p. 13.
9. Vieira, *700*, 1994, p. 678.
10. Alegretti, 2004, p. 74.
11. Vieira, *Existential*, 1997, pp. 20–21.
12. Ibid., pp. 14–16.
13. Ibid., pp. 17–19.

14. Vieira, *Existential*, 1997, p. 126; and Vieira, 2002, p. 919.
15. Vieira, *700*, 1994, p. 600.
16. Ibid., p. 624.
17. Vieira, 2002, p. 384.
18. Minero, 1996.
19. Gross, 2001, pp. 102–7.
20. Vieira, *700*, 1994, p. 129; Balona, 2004, p. 81.
21. Loche, 2001, p. 17.
22. Alegretti, 2004, p. 77.
23. Vieira, *700*, 1994, pp. 603–4.
24. Ibid., p. 609.
25. Vieira, 1999, pp. 15, 109.
26. Vieira, *700*, 1994, p. 600.
27. Ibid., pp. 286, 619.
28. Ibid., p. 617.
29. Ferraz, 2003, pp. 197–216.
30. Vieira, *700*, 1994, p. 609.
31. Guzzi, 1998, pp. 16–24.
32. Ibid., p. 19.
33. Vieira, *Existential*, 1997, pp. 29–30.
34. Vicenzi, 2005, pp. 119–22.
35. Vieira, *Existential*, 1997, pp. 31–32.
36. Vieira, *700*, 1994, p. 607.
37. Balona, 2004, pp. 209–26.
38. Vieira, *Evolutionary*, 1997, p. 11.
39. Trivellato and Alegretti, 2003, p. 295.
40. Vieira, *Penta*, 1996, p. 11.
41. Ibid., p. 21.
42. Ibid., pp. 18–19.
43. Ibid., p. 54.
44. Ibid., p. 24.
45. Ibid., pp. 23, 70.
46. Ibid., p. 25.
47. See *Penta Manual* by Dr. Waldo Vieira, 1996.
48. The name of the course is "CDP-Advanced 2: Assistantial Energetic Field."
49. Vieira, *700*, 1994, p. 682.
50. Guzzi 1998, pp. 42–46.

51. Vicenzi, 2005, p. 141.
52. Vieira, *700*, 1994, p. 690.
53. Couto, 2002, pp. 286–87.
54. Almeida, 2005, p. 40.
55. Arakaki, 2005, pp. 169–70.
56. Sanchez, 2004, p. 181.
57. Vieira, *700*, 1994, p. 614.
58. Vieira, 1999, p. 88.
59. Vieira, *700*, 1994, p. 685.
60. Guzzi, 1998, pp. 42–46.
61. Vieira, *700*, 1994, p. 609.
62. Ibid., p. 610.
63. Ibid., p. 703.
64. Ibid., p. 614.
65. Minero, 1996.
66. Alegretti, 2004, p. 87.
67. Vieira, *700*, 1994, p. 611.
68. Vieira, *Existential*, 1998, p. 129.
69. Ibid., pp. 130–32.
70. Vieira, *700*, 1994, p. 611.
71. Alegretti, 2004, pp. 88–89.
72. Ibid., p. 182.
73. Ibid.

Glossary

The following is a list of the more technical words used in this book. For the official list of all conscientiology terms, please visit LearnOBEs.com.

assistantiality. Helping or assisting others.

auric coupling. Fusion of energosomas, greater exchange of energy between two parties; energetic coupling.

blind guide. Extraphysical consciousness who may have good intentions but has a low level of lucidity and disturbs more than helps.

body. A vehicle of manifestation of the consciousness.

consciential energy (CE). Energy that has information of the consciousness and therefore has already been processed by a consciousness.

consciential paradigm. Paradigm founded on the principle of the existence of the consciousness, as well as matter and energy.

conscientiology. Science that studies the consciousness and all of its manifestations inside and outside the body.

consciousness, the. Essence or intelligent principle behind all beings, beyond matter and energy; the soul or spirit.

cosmoethics (*cosmo* + *ethics*). Set of personal principles according to the individual's own level of awareness and level of evolution. These principles hold true for the consciousness, regardless of where in the cosmos the consciousness is manifesting.

desoma (*de*activation + *soma*). The deactivation of a soma, the passing away of a body, or the process we call death.

energosoma. Energetic or energy body that surrounds the physical body and gives the physical body its vitality; holochakra.

evolutionary duo. The union of two mature, lucid, intraphysical consciousnesses who have affinities for one another and who positively interact, having as an objective the planned potentialization of their evolutionary performances through a productive, integrated, constant, and multifaceted life together.

evolutionary intelligence. The understanding that physical life is a function of evolution, as well as the ability to utilize and apply any resource we may have for the consciential evolution of ourselves and others.

existential inversion. The technical execution of life according to the existential program; the integral investment in evolution without any existential detours.

existential program. The evolutionary organizing plan or agenda of time and activities of the consciousness during the intraphysical life; life tasks.

existential recycling. The positive renovation of values and perspectives performed by the individual as the level of awareness expands in order to develop and evolve more efficiently; the rectification of certain commitments acquired in life that were not part of the individual's existential program.

exteriorization. The transmission, externalization, or outbound broadcasting of energy.

golden cord. The connection between the psychosoma and the mentalsoma. The golden cord, much like the mentalsoma, is not seen, yet its connecting effects are felt.

helper. Evolved positive consciousness with increased awareness and unbiased, refined evolutionary criteria who wants to help us evolve.

holokarma (*holo* = whole, integral, total + *karma*). Set of three karmic accounts: egokarma, groupkarma, and polykarma.

holomaturity (*holo* = whole, integral, total + *maturity*). Condition of integral maturity within the consciousness—biological, psychological, intellectual, holosomatic, intraconsciential, and multidimensional.

holosoma (*holo* = whole, integral, total + *soma*). Set of the vehicles of manifestation of the consciousness: soma, energosoma, psychosoma, and mentalsoma.

holothosene (*holo* = whole, integral, total + *thosene*). The collection of thosenes, or energetic information, associated with something specific (e.g., object, place, person, idea, word, etc.).

immanent energy (IE). Energy inherent in nature, unprocessed and without perceivable information.

intermissive courses. Extraphysical educational courses that prepare consciousnesses to accomplish their existential program.

intruder. Extraphysical consciousness with a low level of evolution, who lacks awareness, is needy, and/or has ill intentions toward others.

mentalsoma. Intellectual body with no shape or form; used by the consciousness to manifest in the mental dimensions.

morphothosenes (*morpho* = form + *thosenes*). Extraphysical forms, elements, and realities created through or with thosenes; thosenes that acquire a shape.

near-death experience (NDE). Occurs when an individual is forced outside his or her body by critical human circumstances.

out-of-body experience (OBE). The phenomenon whereby individuals project (separate) themselves from their physical body, manifesting in dimensions beyond the physical one using other subtler bodies, or vehicles of manifestation.

paragenetics (*para* = extraphysical + *genetics*). Inheritance from previous existences of tendencies, abilities, skills, experience, and others, carried from life to life through the upper bodies, the psychosoma and the mentalsoma.

penta. Penta stands for **Pe**rsonal **En**ergetic **Ta**sk and is performed mainly by stable individuals in the second half of life. This task is characterized mainly by the daily donation of energies at a prescheduled time. The penta practitioner dedicates approximately one hour a day to send out energies to consciousnesses in need, mainly extraphysical consciousnesses.

projectiology. The science that studies the projections of the consciousness (OBEs, astral travel), bioenergy, and related phenomena.

psychosoma. Extraphysical body identical in shape to the soma; used by the consciousness for manifesting during out-of-body experiences in the extraphysical dimensions; emotional body or astral body.

silver cord. The silver cord is responsible for keeping us connected to the soma while projected. It transfers information and energy from the soma to the psychosoma and vice versa.

soma (Greek for *body*). A soma, or body, is a vehicle of manifestation of the consciousness; physical body.

sympathetic assimilation. The condition reached when the amount of energetic information being exchanged between two people is increased; it is an intensification of the auric coupling.

thosene (*tho*ughts + *s*entiments + *ene*rgy). A unit of manifestation of the consciousness; consciential energy.

universalism. The coherent (logical) behavior of the consciousness according to the broadest understanding of the universe; anti-dogmatism.

VELO (Voluntary Energetic Longitudinal Oscillation). Movement of the energies inside the body continuously from head to feet, then from feet to head. Upon acceleration of this movement, it leads to the vibrational state (VS).

Bibliography

Alegretti, Wagner. *Cosmoethics.* Intensive course. Miami, FL, USA: International Institute of Projectiology and Conscientiology, 2001.

———. *Extraphysical Environment and Paratechnology.* Short intensive course. Los Angeles, CA, USA: International Academy of Consciousness, 2008.

———. *Retrocognitions: An Investigation into Memories of Past Lives and the Periods between Lives.* 1st ed. Miami, FL, USA: International Academy of Consciousness, 2004.

———. *Theorice of Bioenergies* [Span.: *Teáticas de las Bioenergías*]. Extracurricular course. Miami, FL, USA: International Institute of Projectiology and Conscientiology, 1996.

Almeida, Julio. *Qualifications of the Consciousness* [Port.: *Qualificações da Consciência*]. 1st ed. Foz de Iguaçu, PR, Brazil: Associaçao Internacional Editares, 2005.

Aparicio, Marisela. "Bioenergetic Self-Experimentation." *Journal of Conscientiology* 4, no. 13 (July 2001): 49.

Arakaki, Kátia. *International Travels: The Conscientiology Nomadism* [Port.: *Viagens Internacionais: O Nomadismo da Conscienciologia*]. 1st ed. Foz de Iguaçu, PR; Brazil: Associaçao Internacional Editares, 2005.

Atwater, P. M. H. *The Complete Idiot's Guide to Near-Death Experiences.* Indianapolis, IN, USA: Alpha Books, 2000.

———. "What the Near-Death Experience Reveals about Consciousness." *Journal of Conscientiology* 4, no. 15S (May 2002): 83.

Azambuya, Martin. "Physical Immobility Waking State Laboratory Experiment." *Journal of Conscientiology* 5, no. 19 (January 2003): 217.

Balona, Malu. *Self-healing through Reconciliation* [Span.: *Autocura a través de la Reconciliación*]. 1st ed. Lisbon, Portugal: International Academy of Consciousness, 2004.

Bonassi, João. "Three Hours of Physical Immobility: A Self-Experiment." *Journal of Conscientiology* 1, no. 3 (January 1999): 255.

Bonin, Werner F. *Dictionary of Parapsychology 1 (A–I)* [Span.: *Diccionario de Parapsicología, 1 (A–I)*]. Madrid, Spain: Alianza Editorial, 1983.

———. *Dictionary of Parapsychology 2 (J–Z)* [Span.: *Diccionario de Parapsicología, 2 (J–Z)*]. Madrid, Spain: Alianza Editorial, 1983.

Bruce, Robert. *Astral Dynamics: A New Approach to Out-of-Body Experiences.* Charlottesville, VA, USA: Hampton Roads Publishing, 1999.

Buhlman, William. *Adventures Beyond the Body: How to Experience Out-of-Body Travel.* 1st ed. New York, NY, USA: HarperOne, 1996.

———. *The Secret of the Soul: Using Out-of-Body Experiences to Understand Our True Nature.* 1st ed. New York, NY, USA: HarperOne, 2001.

Castaneda, Carlos. *The Art of Dreaming.* New York, NY, USA: HarperCollins, 1994.

Corte, Ivo, and Julio Royer. "Volcanology and Extraphysical Reurbanization." *Journal of Conscientiology* 1, no. 2 (October 1998): 99.

Couto, Cirleine. "Conscious Projection and Lucid Dreams." *Journal of Conscientiology* 6, no. 23 (January 2004): 251.

———. "Eurípedes Barsanulfo: Possibly An Existential Inverter." *Journal of Conscientiology* 4, no. 16 (April 2002): 271.

Crookall, Robert. *Case-Book of Astral Projection 545–746.* Secaucus, NJ, USA: Citadel Press, 1980.

———. *Out of the Body Experiences.* Secaucus, NJ, USA: Citadel Press, 1992.

Cubarenco, Ivone. "An Experiment in the CHSC Laboratory of Thosenology." *Journal of Conscientiology* 4, no. 15 (January 2002): 191.

Daou, Dulce. "Capitalist Civilization and Consciential Evolution." *Journal of Conscientiology* 4, no. 15S (May 2002): 97.

———. *Self-consciousness and Multidimensionality* [Port.: *Autoconsciência e Multidimensionalidade*]. 1st ed. Foz do Iguaçu, PR; Brazil: Editares, 2005.

Denning, Melita, and Osborne Phillips. *The Llewellyn Practical Guide to Astral Projection.* 2nd ed. St. Paul, MN, USA: Llewellyn Publications, 1992.

Dries, Silda. *Theory and Practice of the Out-of-Body Experience* [Port.: *Teoria e Práctica da Experiencia fora do Corpo*]. 1st ed. Foz do Iguaçu, PR, Brazil: Editares, 2006.

Farina, Bernardo. "Continuous Conscious Projection Provoked by Vibrational State." *Journal of Conscientiology* 4, no. 14 (October 2001): 127.

Felsky, Camila. "My First Lucid Projection." *Journal of Conscientiology* 3, no. 9 (July 2000): 55.

Fernandes, Luísa Cristina. *Thanatophobia* [Span.: *Tanatofobia*]. *Journal of Conscientiology* 1, no. 2 (October 1998): 129.

Ferraz, Marcelli. "Religious Self-Mimicry: A Study." *Journal of Conscientiology* 5, no. 19 (January 2003): 197.

Fox, Oliver. *Astral Projection: A Record of Out-of-Body Experiences.* 4th ed. Secaucus, NJ, USA: Citadel Press, 1962.

Freire, Augusto, Lourdes Pinheiro, and Eliane Wojslaw. "Criteria for Creating and Evaluating Neologisms." *Journal of Conscientiology* 9, no. 33 (July 2006): 27.

Green, J. Timothy. "The Varieties of Ecstatic Experience: A Preliminary Report from a Personal Journey." *Journal of Conscientiology* 4, no. 15S (May 2002): 131.

Gross, Júlio. "Consciential Imprisonment." *Journal of Conscientiology* 4, no. 14 (October 2001): 99.

Guerra, Teresa Pimentel. "Ethics, Cosmoethics and Universalism" [Span.: "Ética, Cosmoética y Universalismo"]. *Journal of Conscientiology* 4, no. 14 (October 2001): 89.

Guidini, Angélica. "My First Out-of-Body Experience as an Adult." *Journal of Conscientiology* 3, no. 10 (October 2000): 151.

Gutierrez, Alfredo. "Understanding the Fear of Out-of-Body Projection." *Journal of Conscientiology* 2, no. 5 (July 1999): 53.

Guzzi, Flavia. *No Option but to Change* [Port.: *Mudar ou Mudar*]. 1st ed. Rio de Janeiro, RJ, Brazil: International Institute of Projectiology and Conscientiology, 1998.

Haymann, Maximiliano Torres. "Joint Flight" [Span.: "Volitación Conjunta"]. *Journal of Conscientiology* 5, no. 19 (January 2003): 227.

Kardec, Allan. *The Book of Spirits* [Span.: *El Libro de los Espíritus*]. Caracas, Venezuela: Mensaje Fraternal, 1976.

Kircher, Pamela M. "Near-Death Experiences: On the Journey toward Understanding." *Journal of Conscientiology* 4, no. 15S (May 2002): 9.

Krippner, Stanley. "Extraordinary Dreams: A Cross-Cultural Study." *Journal of Conscientiology* 4, no. 15S (May 2002): 67.

LaBerge, Stephen, and Howard Rheingold. *Exploring the World of Lucid Dreaming.* New York, NY, USA: Random House; 1992.

Lima, Thaís. "The Dualism of Descartes and the Conscientiology Science" [Span.: "El Dualismo Cartesiano y la Ciencia Concienciología"]. *Journal of Conscientiology* 1, no. 3 (January 1999): 229.

Loche, Laênio. "Healthy Conviviality and Karmic Dynamics." *Journal of Conscientiology* 4, no. 13 (July 2001): 13.

Lutfi, Luci. *I Came Back to Tell* [Port.: *Voltei para Contar*]. 1st ed. Foz de Iguaçu, PR, Brazil: Associaçao Internacional Editares, 2006.

Machado, Daniel, and Denise Paro. "An Approach to the Theorice of Consciousness' Self-Research." *Journal of Conscientiology* 4, no. 15 (January 2002): 163.

Martin, Anthony. *The Theory & Practice of Astral Projection.* 3rd ed. Wellingborough, Northamptonshire, UK: The Aquarian Press, 1980.

Medeiros, Rodrigo, and Patricia Sousa. "Image Target Research Project: A Methodology to Support Research on Remote Perception Phenomena." *Journal of Conscientiology* 4, no. 15S (May 2002): 111.

Meira, Silvana. "Assisted Lucid Projection." *Journal of Conscientiology* 8, no. 31 (January 2006): 249.

Minero, Luis. "Correspondence." *Journal of Conscientiology* 5, no. 17 (July 2002): 63.

———. "Evolutionary Intelligence." Intensive course. Madrid, Spain: International Academy of Consciousness, 2006.

———. "Existential Program and Seriation Class." Consciousness Development Program, Module 4, Class 1. Miami, FL, USA: International Institute of Projectiology and Conscientiology, 1996.

———. "Globalization and Conscientiological Expansion through Languages." *Revista Conscientia* 10, no. 4 (2006): 302.

———. "Intuition: The Basic Sense of Perception." Intensive course. Miami, FL, USA: International Institute of Projectiology and Conscientiology, 2002.

———. "Lucidocracy." *Journal of Conscientiology* 4, no. 15S (May 2002): 47.

———. "Qualitative Experience and Quantitative Experience." *Journal of Conscientiology* 6, no. 22 (October 2003): 127.

———. "Universalism: Evolution without Limits." Intensive course, Los Angeles, CA, USA: International Institute of Projectiology and Conscientiology, 1999.

———. "You and Your Level of Assistantiality." Intensive course. Miami, FL, USA: International Institute of Projectiology and Conscientiology, 1997.

Mitchell, Janet Lee. *Out-of-Body Experiences: A Handbook.* New York, NY, USA: Ballantine Books, 1990.

Monroe, Robert Allan. *Far Journeys.* New York, NY, USA: Doubleday, 1985.

———. *Journeys Out of the Body.* New York, NY, USA: Doubleday, 1977.

Montenegro, Rodrigo Santa Rosa. "Evolutionary Inertia." *Journal of Conscientiology* 3, no. 10 (October 2000): 91.

Muldoon, Sylvan, and Hereward Carrington. *The Projection of the Astral Body.* York Beach, Maine, USA" Samuel Weiser, Inc., 1992.

Musskopf, Tony. "Consciential Paradigm: Leading Theory of Conscientiology." *Journal of Conscientiology* 1, no. 1 (July 1998): 53.

Nascimento, Marco Aurelio. "Mentalsomatic Parasurgery and Thosenic Restructuring." *Journal of Conscientiology* 8, no. 29 (July 2005): 31.

———. "Thosenic Self-Analysis." *Journal of Conscientiology* 6, no. 23 (January 2004): 231.

Oderich, Cecília. "Projection with Assisted Takeoff" [Span.: "Proyección con Despegue Asistido"]. *Journal of Conscientiology* 3, no. 12 (April 2001): 357.

Open Exchange. Quarterly magazine. Berkeley, CA, USA: 2007–2010.

Ouspensky, P. D. (Peter Demianovich). *Psicologá de la Posible Evolución del Hombre* [Span.: *Psychology of the Possible Evolution of Man*]. Mexico: Queipo Hnos. Editores, 1980.

Peterson, Robert. *Out of Body Experiences: How to Have Them and What to Expect.* Charlottesville, VA, USA: Hampton Roads Publishing, 1997.

Plato. *Plato in Twelve Volumes: The Republic.* Cambridge, MA, USA: Harvard University Press, 1921–1925.

Presse, Paulo. "Assistencialidad." *Journal of Conscientiology* 6, no. 22 (October 2003): 155.

Rampa, Lobsang. *You Forever* [Span.: *Usted y la Eternidad*]. Buenos Aires, Argentina: Editorial Troquel, 1995.

Razera, Graça. "Attention Deficit and Hyperactivity Disorder—AD(H)D: A Critical Approach." *Journal of Conscientiology* 2, no. 5 (July 1999): 3.

———. Effective Hyperactivity [Port.: *Hiperatividade Eficaz*]. 1st ed. Rio de Janeiro, RJ, Brazil: International Institute of Projectiology and Conscientiology, 2001.

Rocha, Adriana de Lacerda. "A Legal Outlook on Cosmoethics." *Journal of Conscientiology* 2, no. 6 (October 1999): 101.

Rogo, D. Scott. *Leaving the Body: A Complete Guide to Astral Projection.* New York, NY, USA: Prentice Hall, 1986.

Sanchez, Laura. "Visit to a Training Center for Inverters Awaiting Rebirth" [Span.: "Visita a un Centro de Preparación de Inversores para la Resoma"]. *Journal of Conscientiology* 7, no. 26 (October 2004): 181.

Sarasvati, Sivananda. *Exercises for Concentration and Meditation* [Ger.: *Übungen zu Konzentration und Meditation*]. Berlin, Germany: Goldmann Verlag, 1959.

Stack, Rick. *Out-of-Body Adventures.* Chicago, IL, USA: Contemporary Books, 1988.

Swedenborg, Emanuel. *The Spiritual Diary.* New York, NY, USA: Swedenborg Foundation, 1971.

Takimoto, Nário, and Roberto Almeida. "Conscientiotherapy: A Clinical Experience of Integral Assistance for the Consciousness." *Journal of Conscientiology* 4, no. 15S (May 2002): 21.

Taylor, Albert. *Soul Traveler: A Guide to Out-of-Body Experiences and the Wonders Beyond.* New York, NY, USA: Dutton, 1998.

Thiago, Gloria. *Living in Multiple Dimensions* [Span.: *Viviendo en Múltiples Dimensiones*]. 1st ed. Rio de Janeiro, RJ, Brazil: International Institute of Projectiology and Conscientiology, 1999.

Tornieri, Sandra. "The Effect of Tobacco in Multidimensionality" [Span.: "El Efecto del Tabaco en la Multidimensionalidad"]. *Journal of Conscientiology* 1, no. 1 (July 1998): 43.

Trivellato, Nanci. "Chakras: Subtle Organs." Extracurricular course. Miami, FL, USA: International Institute of Projectiology and Conscientiology, 1997.

———. "Measurable Attributes of the Vibrational State Technique." *Journal of Conscientiology* 11, no. 42 (October 2008): 165.

Trivellato, Nanci, and Luisa Fernandes. "Chamber Optimized to Support Out-of-Body Experiences." *Journal of Conscientiology* 5, no. 17 (July 2002): 3.

Trivellato, Nanci, and Wagner Alegretti. "Dynamics of the Evolutionary Duo." *Journal of Conscientiology* 5, no. 20 (April 2003): 287.

———. "Public Opinion Research about Projection of Consciousness through the Internet." In *Annals of the 1st International Forum on Consciousness Research and 2nd International Congress on Projectiology.* Rio de Janeiro, RJ, Brazil: International Institute of Projectiology and Conscientiology, 1999.

———. "Quantitative and Qualitative Analysis of Experimental Research Project into Out-of-Body Experience." *Journal of Conscientiology* 4, no. 15S (May 2002): 153.

Vicenzi, Luciano. *Courage to Evolve* [Port.: *Coragem para Evoluir*]. 2nd ed. Foz de Iguaçu, PR, Brazil: Asociaçao Internacional Editares, 2005.

———. *Multiexistential Ecology* [Span.: *Mesologia Multiexistencial*]. *Journal of Conscientiology* 1, no. 4 (April 1999): 337.

Vieira, Waldo. "Concealment (Cosmoethics)." *Journal of Conscientiology* 2, no. 8 (April 2000): 267.

————. *Conscientiogram: Technique for the Integral Evaluation of the Consciousness* [Port.: *Conscienciograma: Técnica de Avaliação da Consciência Integral*]. 1st ed. Rio de Janeiro, RJ, Brazil: International Institute of Projectiology and Conscientiology, 1996.

————. *Conscientiology Themes* [Port.: *Temas da Conscienciologia*]. 1st ed. Rio de Janeiro, RJ, Brazil: International Institute of Projectiology and Conscientiology, 1997.

————. *Evolutionary Duo Manual* [Port.: *Manual da Dupla Evolutiva*]. 1st ed. Rio de Janeiro, RJ, Brazil: International Institute of Projectiology and Conscientiology, 1997.

————. *Existential Program Manual.* 1st ed. Rio de Janeiro, RJ, Brazil: International Institute of Projectiology and Conscientiology, 1997.

————. *Homo Sapiens Pacificus.* Foz de Iguaçu, PR; Brazil: CEAEC Editora & Editares, 2007.

————. *Homo Sapiens Reurbanisatus.* Foz de Iguaçu, PR, Brazil: Asociação Internacional do Centro de Altos Estudios Da Conscienciologia (CEAEC), 2003.

————. *Our Evolution.* 1st ed. Rio de Janeiro, RJ, Brazil: International Institute of Projectiology and Conscientiology, 1999.

————. *Penta Manual: Personal Energetic Task.* 1st ed. Rio de Janeiro, RJ, Brazil: International Institute of Projectiology and Conscientiology, 1996.

————. *Projectiology: A Panorama of Experiences of the Consciousness Outside the Human Body.* 1st ed. Rio de Janeiro, RJ, Brazil: International Institute of Projectiology and Conscientiology, 2002.

————. *Projections of the Consciousness: A Diary of Out-of-Body Experiences.* 3rd ed. New York, NY, USA: International Academy of Consciousness, 2007.

————. *700 Conscientiology Experiments* [Port.: *700 Experimentos da Conscienciologia*]. 1st ed. Rio de Janeiro, RJ, Brazil: International Institute of Projectiology and Conscientiology, 1994.

————. *200 Theorice of Conscientiology* [Port.: *200 Teáticas da Conscienciologia*]. 1st ed. Rio de Janeiro, RJ, Brazil: International Institute of Projectiology and Conscientiology, 1997.

————. *What Conscientiology Is* [Port.: *O Que é a Conscienciologia*]. 1st ed. Rio de Janeiro, RJ, Brazil: International Institute of Projectiology and Conscientiology, 1994.

Vugman, Ney Vernon. "The Weak Will Syndrome." *Journal of Conscientiology* 2, no. 6 (October 1999): 93.

Worrall, Ambrose and Olga. *The Gift of Healing: A Personal Story of Spiritual Therapy.* Marble Hill, GA, USA: Ariel Press, 1989.

International Academy of Consciousness (IAC)

The International Academy of Consciousness (IAC) is a nonprofit, multicultural, and universalistic organization dedicated to research and education in conscientiology and its subdisciplines. The objective of the IAC is to catalyze evolution through clarifying the multidimensional nature of the consciousness and all the implications arising from that fact. The IAC stimulates expanded awareness through the dissemination of pragmatic information, employing logic, discernment, and the highest principles of cosmoethics. The work of the IAC is founded on updated scientific precepts and aims to further human knowledge based on the consciential paradigm. Information offered by the IAC is the result of decades of investigation and represents a consensus from numerous personal experiences, and it is grounded in historical and ongoing investigations.

The IAC was founded in October 2000 with the aim of establishing Europe's first conscientiological research campus. In May 2002, the scope of the organization expanded when all of the International Institute of Projectiology and Conscientiology (IIPC) offices outside of Brazil were transferred to the IAC, including its research, educational programs, human resources, and scientific publications. The IAC thus inherited the experience and accomplishments of the IIPC team, which had worked internationally since 1994.

Since its formation, the IAC has hosted a number of large events at its research campus in Portugal, including the First Symposium on Conscientiological Research in October 2005, the Global Symposium on Existential Inversion in November 2006, and the Second Symposium on Conscientiological Research in October 2008, as well as the VI Consciential Health Meeting in October 2010. It has also performed several large research experiments, and its instructors have developed 92 original courses on themes within conscientiology (as of June 2012). The IAC's courses emphasize the practical experience of multidimensionality and parapsychism, with the following three being salient examples: (1) The Projective Field; (2) The Praxis: Ectoplasm and Clairvoyance, a three-day immersion course for inducing lucid out-of-body experiences, clairvoyance, and materialization experiences; and (3) Goal: Intrusionlessness, a one-year course that focuses on developing parapsychism and freedom from intrusion.

Staffed by 118 volunteers, including 56 instructors, the IAC has a permanent presence in 13 cities in 9 countries across 4 continents (as of June 2012). It has organized and presented events in 61 cities within 19 countries: Australia, Brazil, Canada, Cyprus, Finland, France, Germany, Holland, Italy, Japan, Mexico, New Zealand, Portugal, Romania, Spain, Switzerland, the United Kingdom, the United States, and Venezuela.

Beyond educational activities, IAC's original objective of founding a research and education campus is being pursued, with ongoing construction occurring on approximately 62 acres of wooded land in Évoramente, Portugal. Among the installations is the world's first Projectarium—a specialized laboratory for inducing out-of-body experiences. Please refer to the IAC Research Campus section (which follows) for more information.

The IAC also publishes books and periodicals based on the consciential paradigm. It publishes the *Journal of Conscientiology*, the official vehicle for the presentation and scientific debate of conscientiology. The *Journal* is distributed to individuals and organizations in 35 countries. The IAC has also published 13 books, and has another 37 in production (including translations) in 7 languages (as of June 2012).

The following contact information can be found at LearnOBEs.com.

IAC Main Offices

IAC Research Campus
Campus@iacworld.org
Phone: +351 268 959 148
Phone: +351 918 797 924
Fax: +351 268 950 053
Herdade da Marmeleira
EN 18, km. 236—Cx. Postal 06

Evoramonte, Estremoz 7100-500
Portugal

Portugal, Lisbon
Lisbon@iacworld.org
+351 (21) 386 80 08
Fax: +351 (21) 386 80 33
Avenida Ressano Garcia
Nº 39, 5º andar Direito
Lisbon 1070-234
Portugal

Spain, Barcelona
Barcelona@iacworld.org
Tel/Fax: +34 (93) 232-8008
Calle Ausias Marc
49, 5º despacho 30
Barcelona 08010
Spain

Spain, Madrid
Madrid@iacworld.org
Phone/Fax: +34 (91) 591-2587
Calle Jacometrezo
nº 15—5º G (Metro Sto. Domingo)
Madrid 28013
Spain

United Kingdom, London
London@iacworld.org
Phone/Fax: +44 (0) 20 7631 5083
60 Tottenham Court Road
London W1T 2EW
United Kingdom

USA, Los Angeles
California@iacworld.org
Phone: +1 (310) 482-0000
Fax: +1 (310) 482-0001
Toll Free: +1 (877) IAC-4OBE (422-4623)
3961 Sepulveda Blvd, Suite 207
Culver City, CA 90230-4600
USA

USA, Miami
Florida@iacworld.org
Phone: +1 (305) 668-4668
Fax: +1 (305) 668-4690
7800 SW 57th Ave., Suite 207D
Miami, FL 33143
USA

USA, New York
NewYork@iacworld.org
Phone: +1 (212) 867-0807
Fax: +1 (877) HAVE-OBE (428-3623)
Toll Free: +1 (800) 778-3778
55 West 21st Street, Suite 601
New York, NY 10010
USA

IAC Associate Offices

Australia, Sydney
Sydney@iacworld.org
+61 (02) 9966 4283
Unit E6.04/599 Pacific Hwy
St. Leonards
Sydney, NSW 2065
Australia

Brazil, Iguaçu Falls
Brazil@iacworld.org
+55 (45) 8404-5923

Cyprus, Nicosia
Cyprus@iacworld.org
You can also contact our London office:
+44 (0) 20 7631-5083

Finland, Helsinki
Suomi@iacworld.org
+358 (0) 922 433 550
+358 (0) 400 761 939
You can also contact the London office:
+44 (0) 20 7631-5083

Germany, Frankfurt
Germany@iacworld.org
+49 7802 706370

Italy, Bergamo
Bergamo@iacworld.org

Italy, Milan
Milano@iacworld.org

Mexico, Mexico City
Mexico@iacworld.org
Phone: +52 (55) 5171-9369
Phone: +52 (55) 8421-6016
Fax: +52 (55) 5004-4445

Netherlands, Zutphen
Netherlands@iacworld.org
+31 (0)6 41 22 79 29

You can also contact the London office:
+44 (0) 20 7631-5083

New Zealand, Auckland
NewZealand@iacworld.org

Portugal, Porto
Porto@iacworld.org
Tel.: +351 226 064 025
      +351 918 797 926
Fax.: +351 226 064 025
Rua Júlio Dinis, nº 880, 5º Frente
Porto 4050-322
Portugal

Romania, Bucharest
Romania@iacworld.org
You can also contact the London office:
+44 (0) 20 7631-5083

Spain, Sevilla
Sevilla@iacworld.org
+34 (91) 591-2587

Sweden, Stockholm
Sweden@iacworld.org
You can also contact the London office:
+44 (0) 20 7631-5083

USA, Austin (TX)
Austin@iacworld.org
(305) 668-4668

USA, Boston (MA)

Boston@iacworld.org
(800) 778-3778
(212) 867-0867

USA, Gainesville (FL)

Florida@iacworld.org
(305) 668-4668

USA, Houston (TX)

Houston@iacworld.org
(305) 668-4668

USA, Phoenix (AZ)

Arizona@iacworld.org
(877) IAC-4OBE (422-4623)
(310) 482-0000

USA, Portland (OR)

Oregon@iacworld.org
(877) IAC-4OBE (422-4623)
(310) 482-0000

USA, San Francisco Bay Area (CA)

California@iacworld.org
(877) IAC-4OBE (422-4623)
(310) 482-0000

IAC Research Campus

Alentejo, Portugal

The IAC Research Campus is located on a greenfield site of approximately sixty-two acres (250,000 m²) near the village of Évoramonte, in the bucolic Alentejo region of Portugal. The center is dedicated to conducting research and providing individuals with opportunities for producing parapsychic experiences and expanding their self-awareness. In essence, it comprises an environment dedicated to scientific debate and investigation into the manifestation of the consciousness, as well as the overarching theme of evolution.

The complex features a number of laboratories, each designed and constructed to provide an optimized environment for personal experimentation and research on a particular theme. Among the full set of laboratories planned are the following: cosmoconsciousness, energetic self-control, energosomatology, holokarma, intermissive course, intraconsciential recycling, macrosoma, multidimensional self-awareness, neo-thosenes and original ideas, paratechnology, retrocognitions, universalism, vibrational state, waking physical immobility, and the Projectarium (see upcoming section on Projectarium for more details).

In its final form the complex will include the following:

- Consciential laboratories: providing specialized and optimal environments for self-experimentation on specific themes
- Multipurpose auditorium: for conferences, debates, group practical courses, research meetings, and exhibitions

- Library and holo-archive: comprising a multimedia library, special collections, archives and objects related to consciousness research, online computer terminals, and research room
- Administrative center
- Lodge: providing accommodations for visitors and researchers
- Restaurant: serving campus-based visitors and researchers
- Support building: business center, café, and reading center; it will also provide Internet-enabled laptop stations plus a lounge area for networking and meetings
- Campus house: long-term accommodation for the head resident researcher or faculty

Nature

The campus is located in a protected, peaceful countryside filled with native plants, small wild animals, and many bird species, providing exceptionally reinvigorating immanent energies.

The property features some three hundred mature cork and scarlet oak trees, which will remain intact as construction takes place in the glades between them. As most of these trees are well over a hundred years old, they cloak the campus with natural, exceptionally calming bioenergies that promote relaxation, serenity, and personal balance. This characteristic of the immanent energies of the campus has proven to facilitate the manifestation of parapsychic phenomena and the expansion of the mentalsoma.

Ongoing efforts will be made to contribute to the already prolific verdant site and indigenous animal life. As an example, an initiative called Sponsor a Tree has been established to help raise funds to protect the trees from fungi and other diseases. (More information is available on the IAC website at http://iacworld.org.)

Consistent with the aim of creating an environment in natural harmony, the IAC has also implemented Project Oasis, whose main objective is environmental sustainability. This will be achieved through the development and care of natural vegetation, the preservation of biodiversity, the management and use of natural resources such as water, and sewerage treatment. The development and construction plans are based on the most up-to-date techniques and approaches for making the campus complex an example of environmental sustainability in the region.

Architectural Design

The buildings at the IAC Research Campus have been devised and constructed for holding advanced educational events related to conscientiology, and thus include tailored architectural characteristics and a specialized energetic field. The sturdy construction techniques take into consideration the bioclimatic architecture strategies used in the region, and provide for healthy conditions and thermally comfortable spaces, with efficient use of electric energy.

The laboratories and main buildings feature organic, spherical, and semi-spherical architectural designs that have proven ideal for activities involving energies and multidimensional phenomena. They also provide an inspiring, mentally expansive environment that is in keeping with the natural environment.

Acknowledging the pre-existence of the local flora and respecting the existing lay of the land, an aesthetically pleasing spiral layout for the laboratories was conceived and developed, with the Projectarium centrally positioned.

Self-Experimentation and Consciential Laboratories

The term self-experimentation refers to experiments or self-research carried out by individuals seeking a more complete understanding of themselves and an expansion of their parapsychic experiences. This kind of self-experimentation engages the individual as both the subject of study and the researcher, observing and analyzing the experience.

In projectiology and conscientiology, experience is considered more valuable than theoretical ideas alone. Firsthand experience is self-convincing and eliminates conditioning and brainwashing. These scientific fields place emphasis on theorice, which is the indivisible association of theory and practice.

The reasoning behind this approach is described by the consciential paradigm, a leading-edge perspective on existence that places consciousness at the center and suggests a need for investigation beyond the material world and the purely objective explorations of traditional mechanistic science.

To foster such individual experiences, a number of optimized consciential laboratories are being constructed. Physically, the laboratories are designed to provide optimized comfort and control of light, temperature, and sound. In addition, the laboratories provide a specialized extraphysical (nonphysical) environment through the installation of an energetic-informational field specific to the theme of each laboratory.

This specialized arrangement of the physical, extraphysical, and energetic elements creates a multidimensional chamber, providing opportunities for deep self-research, expansion of consciousness, and increased multidimensional self-awareness. Consciential laboratories may facilitate parapsychic experiences even for individuals with no history of such experiences. The self-experimentation laboratories are open to those who have taken IAC's core curricular course at its educational centers, or any course at the IAC Research Campus.

Projectarium

Among the existing laboratories at the IAC Research Campus is the Projectarium, a remarkable spherical building with a diameter of 29.55 feet (9 meters) and a hollow internal space. The Projectarium is the first construction of its type in the world, and includes a number of characteristics known to facilitate out-of-body experiences (OBEs, conscious projections).

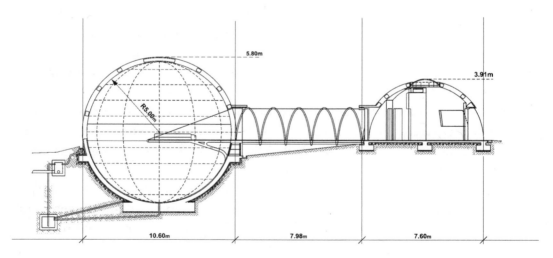

Projectarium

The Projectarium aims to harmonize architectural, psychological, energetic, and nonphysical elements to reduce environmental stimuli and enhance opportunities for interaction between the physical and nonphysical dimensions. The self-experimenter lies with their head in the center of the sphere, on a suspended platform (surrounded by a safety net), giving them the sense of being in a void. The main structure of the Projectarium will be connected to a semi-spherical support building, which will comprise a reception area, monitoring room, and preparation area.

The OBE is an evolutionarily valuable and life-changing experience that provides a unique opportunity to develop multidimensional awareness and holomaturity. Few psychic phenomena raise more questions concerning consciousness and the mind-body relationship. Given that the OBE can be willfully induced, it is the ideal phenomenon for studying and understanding realities beyond the purely physical.

In addition to being an important vehicle for self-research, the Projectarium also aims to be the focal point for a multiplicity of other investigations, conducted under the IAC's high code of ethics. Such investigations will be conducted by researchers from the IAC and diverse affiliated organizations, with the objective of enhancing humanity's understanding of this unique phenomenon.

IAC Research Campus

Herdade da Marmeleira
EN 18, km. 236—Cx. Postal 06
7100-500 Evoramonte—Estremoz; Portugal
E-mail: campus@iacworld.org
Phone: +351 268 959 148
Phone: +351 918 797 924
Fax: +351 268 950 053
Coordinates: Latitude: N 38 47' 46", Longitude: W 07 41' 10"

Conscienciocentric Organizations (COs)

Addresses

AIEC—Associação Internacional para Expansão da Conscienciologia
(International Association for Expansion of Conscientiology)

www.worldaiec.org

APEX—Associação Internacional da Programação Existencial
(International Association of Existential Program)

www.apexinternacional.org

ARACÊ—Associação Internacional para Evolução da Consciência
(Aracê—International Association for Consciousness Evolution)

www.arace.com.br

ASSINVÉXIS—Associação Internacional para a Inversão Existencial
(International Association for Existential Inversion)

www.assinvexis.org

CEAEC—Associação Internacional do Centro de Altos Estudos da Conscienciologia
(International Association of the Center for Higher Studies of Conscientiology)

www.ceaec.org

*COMUNICONS—Associação Internacional de Comunicação
Conscienciológica*
*(Comunicons—International Association of Conscientiological
Communication)*
www.comunicons.org

*CONSCIUS—Associação Internacional de Conscienciometria
Interassistencial*
*(Conscius—International Association of Interassistantial
Conscientiometry)*
http://www.conscius.org.br

EDITARES—Associação Internacional Editares
(International Association Editares)
www.editares.org

*EVOLUCIN—Associação Internacional de Conscienciologia para
Infância*
(International Association of Conscientiology for Youth—Evolucin)

IAC—International Academy of Consciousness
www.iacworld.org

IIPC—Instituto Internacional de Projeciologia e Conscienciologia
(International Institute of Projectiology and Conscientiology)
www.iipc.org.br

*INTERCAMPI—Associação do Campus Internacional de Pesquisa da
Conscienciologia*
*(Intercampi—Association of the International Research Campus of
Conscientiology)*
intercampi.org

OIC—Organização Internacional de Consciencioterapia
(International Organization of Conscientiotherapy)
www.oic.org.br

UNICIN—União das Instituições Conscienciocêntricas Internacionais
(Union of the International Conscientiocentric Institutions)
www.unicin.org

Index

To Write to the Author

If you wish to contact the author or would like more information about this book, please write to the author in care of Llewellyn Worldwide Ltd. and we will forward your request. Both the author and publisher appreciate hearing from you and learning of your enjoyment of this book and how it has helped you. Llewellyn Worldwide Ltd. cannot guarantee that every letter written to the author can be answered, but all will be forwarded. Please write to:

Luis Minero
℅ Llewellyn Worldwide
2143 Wooddale Drive
Woodbury, MN 55125-2989

Please enclose a self-addressed stamped envelope for reply,
or $1.00 to cover costs. If outside the U.S.A., enclose
an international postal reply coupon.

Many of Llewellyn's authors have websites with additional information and resources. For more information, please visit our website at http://www.llewellyn. com.

ASTRAL
PROJECTION
FOR
PSYCHIC
EMPOWERMENT

The Out-of-Body Experience,
Astral Powers, and their
Practical Application

CARL LLEWELLYN WESCHCKE
JOE H. SLATE, PH.D.

Astral Projection for Psychic Empowerment

The Out-of-Body Experience, Astral Powers, and their Practical Application

CARL LLEWELLYN WESCHCKE AND JOE H. SLATE, PH.D.

Astral projection is far more than an out-of-body experience. It is a doorway to new dimensions—and opportunities to grow spiritually, increase your love potential, develop psychic skills, and change reality. More than in-depth theory, this innovative and comprehensive guide introduces the huge benefits and applications of astral projection. Learn to induce an out-of-body experience, safely visit astral realms, explore past lives, practice astral sex, communicate with astral guides and entities, create powerful thought forms, and much more. Fascinating case studies reveal astral projection's undeniable therapeutic value in overcoming fears and healing. The empowering seven-day developmental program will help you grow in more ways than you can ever imagine.

978-0-7387-3029-5, 528 pp., 7 x 10   **$24.95**

To order, call 1-877-NEW-WRLD
Prices subject to change without notice
Order at Llewellyn.com 24 hours a day, 7 days a week!

LIFE
BETWEEN
LIVES

HYPNOTHERAPY
FOR SPIRITUAL REGRESSION

MICHAEL NEWTON
Ph.D.

Life Between Lives

Hypnotherapy for Spiritual Regression

MICHAEL NEWTON, PH.D.

A famed hypnotherapist's groundbreaking methods of accessing the spiritual realms.

Dr. Michael Newton is world-famous for his spiritual regression techniques that take subjects back to their time in the spirit world. His two best-selling books of client case studies have left thousands of readers eager to discover their own afterlife adventures, their soul companions, their guides, and their purpose in this lifetime.

Now, for the first time in print, Dr. Newton reveals his step-by-step methods. His experiential approach to the spiritual realms sheds light on the age-old questions of who we are, where we came from, and why we are here.

978-0-7387-0465-4, 240 pp., 6 x 9   **$15.95**